TINDER BOX

TINDER BOX

THE IROQUOIS THEATRE DISASTER 1903

Anthony P. Hatch

ACADEMY CHICAGO PUBLISHERS

Published in 2003 by
Academy Chicago Publishers
An imprint of Chicago Review Press Incorporated
814 North Franklin Street
Chicago, Illinois 60610

© 2003 by Anthony P. Hatch
ISBN 978-0-89733-609-3

Printed in the United States of America

Library of Congress Cataloging-in-Publication Data on file with the publisher

Dedicated to Lenore

To the memory of my parents
Archibald Lewis Hatch and Pearl Berkman Hatch

To Gerald Miller and George Syverson, CBS News,
Killed in Cambodia, 1970

And to America's firefighters, police and emergency service
personnel, heroes all

❧

"We learn from history that we learn nothing from history"
GEORGE BERNARD SHAW

CONTENTS

FOREWORD

ON FEBRUARY 13, 1875, the *Chicago Times* stunned its readers by predicting a terrible theatre disaster waiting to happen. In a city that only four years earlier had been devastated by what was called "The Great Chicago Fire," the *Times*, in lurid detail, described a tragedy in an "absolutely fireproof" theatre filled to overcapacity one winter's day with women and children who were watching a musical comedy.

In this fictionalized account, audience members jammed the exits in a mad rush to escape while the show's leading comedian rushed on stage just as the fire safety curtain burst into flames. Hundreds were horribly burned, crushed to death or asphyxiated and the *Times* warned that safety provisions were generally so lax that the make-believe story could "at any time become a reality."

Twenty-eight years later, on one winter day, the nightmare prediction came true in almost every ghastly detail.

Now nearly forgotten, the horror of the Iroquois Theatre remains to this day the worst catastrophe in the history of the American stage.

INTRODUCTION

THE IDEA FOR THIS BOOK began before the advent of color television, the personal computer, the fax machine or the internet. I developed a childhood interest in the disaster when I read a book called *Lest We Forget,* a compilation of press stories of the fire, some of them contradictory, published in 1904 as a means of raising money for the victims' families.

When I read the late Walter Lord's *A Night to Remember,* in 1955, I was struck by the similarities between the Iroquois tragedy and the *Titanic* disaster, which Lord so brilliantly documented:

A magnificent ship said to be "unsinkable," and an equally magnificent theatre advertised as "absolutely fireproof."

A luxurious new vessel on its maiden voyage, and a luxurious new playhouse, open only a matter of weeks, presenting its dedicatory performance.

The incredible human miscalculations. Not enough lifeboats on the ship, and virtually no firefighting equipment in the theatre.

A vessel possessing the new wireless technology that proved useless because the nearest ship did not receive its signals, and a theatre boasting every modern convenience but lacking any means to communicate by telephone or alarm with a fire station one block away.

A ship rushing through a dark sea on orders from its owners who ignored warnings of danger; a theatre opened hastily by its owners who ignored warnings that it was dangerously incomplete.

The hubris and greed displayed by the owners of the ship and the owners of the theatre.

The terrible and inexcusable loss of life of passengers on the *Titanic* and of the audience in the Iroquois Theatre. Many passengers on the ship locked behind gates, the theatregoers trapped behind locked and bolted gates and doors.

The worldwide disbelief, horror and outrage when the news of each disaster became known and the reforms each catastrophe brought about.

I have drawn heavily from accounts in the 1904 book and have done original research in contemporary newspapers and magazines published in Chicago, New York, London and other cities, and in accounts published later.

My research began in 1961 in Chicago when I interviewed former Fire Commissioner William Corrigan, who had fought the fire and who gave me a detailed description of everything from piles of snow in the street that day to the rescue attempts inside the burning theatre.

A few months later, while on assignment for CBS News, I had an opportunity to make repeated visits to the Chicago Historical Society to examine its materials on the disaster, including its extensive collection of photographs. More importantly, while I was in the city, I was able to record a lengthy interview with Charles Collins, who had covered the story as a young newspaper reporter. In response to public solicitations here and in England, I received letters from many people including an

AP reporter who was there, as well as a former Northwestern University student who had helped in the rescues.

Though I had accumulated much research material, a career path that led to the Middle East, then to New York City and eventually to Los Angeles and Santa Fe, prevented me from completing the story until now, three decades later.

All the accounts in this book are based on original newspaper and magazine reports, on interviews and correspondence from the 1960s, and on conversations over the past three years with social historians, theatre specialists, librarians, lawyers, doctors, forensic experts, fire department historians and distant relatives of victims who had knowledge of the disaster. There are no fictionalized characters or quotations in these pages. Despite having spent most of his adult life as a writer, Charles Collins died without apparently leaving any memoir, diary or journal describing highlights of his career. I interviewed him at length in 1962, and after he died two years later I filled in some information on his early years from various sources.

Contemporary newspaper accounts of the tragedy were, in some cases, contradictory or even mistaken, and, owing to the poor quality of microfilm reproduction, often almost impossible to read, even with a magnifying glass. Perhaps the most difficult fact to pin down was the actual number of victims. The official list as tabulated by the coroner's office, for instance, is missing the names of some victims mentioned in the Chicago papers. This is probably because of great initial confusion at the scene, and, too, because some victims were removed by families who failed to notify authorities.

News photography of the time was still in its infancy, dependent on bulky cameras, glass plate negatives, magnesium flash powder, which could sometimes injure cameramen, and the need for the subject usually to stand absolutely still, to avoid blurring of the image. This would explain why most of the pho-tographs of the theatre's interior after the fire have more defini-tion and detail than those shot in the street at the time of the fire, and would explain also why some Chicago newspapers quickly dispatched courtroom sketch artists to capture "visu-als" that photographers were unable to record.

A search around the country via the internet and through personal phone calls turned up little in the way of publicity shots of the *Mr. Bluebeard* production as it appeared on stage, either in New York or Chicago. That seems to me to be remark-able, given the fact that extensive production shots were taken of other shows that same year. The photo of the "Pale Moon-light " double octet is reprinted here, along with others like the "Pony Ballet" chorus, from sheet music published at the time. My thanks to Scott Stephen of Santa Fe for his deft digital engi-neering to restore many of the visuals to their original state or even to enhance them.

If there are errors or omissions in this account, I alone am responsible for them.

Anthony P. Hatch
Santa Fe, New Mexico
December, 2002

{1}

OPENING NIGHT

"[A] glorious place of amusement . . ."
—*Amy Leslie, Arts Critic,* CHICAGO DAILY TRIBUNE

THE IROQUOIS THEATRE GLOWED like a luminous jewel between the darkened commercial buildings on Chicago's busy Randolph Street. Charles Collins, a new general assignment reporter who had just turned twenty, had never seen anything like it. The theatre's grand opening was being called "the event of Chicago's century," and purely by chance the *Record-Herald*, the city's leading morning paper, had assigned Collins to cover it.

It was the evening of Monday, November 23, 1903, when the century seemed as young and optimistic as the tall, slim, neatly dressed reporter. "It was a fairly lush time," wrote one columnist years later. "We had come trumpeting out of the Spanish American War with the buck-toothed image of Teddy Roosevelt and we hadn't yet gone down the drain in the financial panic of 1907."

After many postponements, the Iroquois was ready: a glittery million-dollar showplace that proud city boosters declared was without doubt the best theatre in the Midwest and that would rival, if not exceed, anything seen along New York's Great

I

White Way or in prominent European capitals. Chicago, America's second city now that it had surpassed Philadelphia in population, was described as "on the make for the almighty dollar." Chicagoans would not settle for being second best in anything.

Interest and excitement about the opening had gathered momentum during the fall, with newspaper ads proclaiming, "No resident of Chicago imbued with the proper amount of local pride can afford to miss the dedicatory performance of the best theatre on Earth. Chicago Always Leads. Biggest, Brightest and Best in every other way, it now has the theatre to correspond."

Bundled against the biting cold, Charles Collins watched helmeted police officers in heavy woolen blue coats direct traffic as expensive—$1,200—horse-drawn Studebaker Broughams and Oldsmobile Landaus, private omnibuses or "opera buses," hansom cabs, rockaways and even an occasional chauffeur-driven automobile pulled to the curb to discharge the city's Brahmins. Along with other shivering journalists, Collins eyed the crowd of elegant men and women emerging from the vehicles in top hats, tuxedos, furs, muffs and the latest Paris fashions, who quickly crossed the pavement under a striped awning to walk through highly polished glass-and-mahogany doors into one of the most imposing playhouses ever built in America. The audience had come out on this cold November night not only to see and be seen in the newest showplace in the nation but to be entertained by a spectacle from London's Drury Lane Theatre, featuring a favorite son of Chicago, Eddie Foy, one of the leading comedians of the time, who headed a cast of hundreds.

John G. Shedd—who in three years would head the Marshall Field department store and would later endow the city's excellent aquarium—strode in, accompanied by his wife and daughter. Entering too was one of the city's biggest advertisers,

Alexander Revell, the marketing genius who attracted hoards of customers to his furniture mart each day because of the fully furnished cottage he had set up on its fifth floor. Already occupying an upper box were the Plamondon brothers, George and Charles, owners of a large machinery plant. Charles, the firm's president and an official of the Chicago Board of Education, maintained a residence overlooking Lake Michigan and a country home in Wheaton called Green Gables. R. Hall McCormick of the McCormick Reaper family was there, along with Mr. and Mrs. Edward Leicht, who had given a dinner party before leaving for the theatre. Mrs. Leicht wore a pink etamine gown, a white satin-and-lace coat and a frilled hat of pink chiffon.

Days earlier, many of these Chicago moguls had participated in a highly publicized auction where box seats for the opening night had gone for as much as $225 — nearly ten times Charles Collins's salary of twenty-five dollars a week. Tonight Collins was working as an unpaid theatre critic, substituting for the *Record-Herald*'s noted drama critic James O'Donnell Bennett, who was attending the premiere of *Ulysses*, which Bennett considered more worthwhile than *Mr. Bluebeard*, even though that British import was billed as a musical comedy "extravaganza."

Collins was well qualified to function as a critic: he had graduated from the University of Chicago the previous June with a degree in philosophy. His classmates described him as a "strong, silent man, difficult to approach socially," with a "slightly sardonic, wry sense of humor." From the time he entered the university, he knew he would become a journalist, and immediately after graduation he had joined the *Record-Herald*, one of the two newspapers he had served as a campus correspondent, regularly phoning in sports scores and other items. He represented a new trend: "for the first time in history, college graduates [were working] on newspapers . . . bringing a new literary flair to a world once considered beneath the dignity of the educated elite."

His deeper love, however, was for the theatre and virtually all forms of popular entertainment, and he harbored a secret desire to become a full-time theatre critic. "Charlie knows his theatre," said a friend. "He inwardly revels at the Stratford-on-Avon Shakespearians, the D'Oyly Carte Gilbert and Sullivanians. . . . barring revivals, he never sees a play twice." The opportunity to cover the opening performance in the Iroquois was a plum assignment.

Collins, like most reporters, spent much of the day on his feet. There was no overtime pay, and it was quite common to get one day off every two weeks. Rumor had it that one fortunate newsman had scraped together enough money for a down payment on a "wheel," as bicycles were called, to get from one assignment to another, but Collins's modest salary did not permit that luxury. As a new hand at the paper, he was probably sent to cover minor events, like "neighborhood pet shows, high school debating society finals, or conventions of the National Association of Paper Clip Manufacturers." On occasion, he might land a more important assignment.

To Chicago city officials, burdened with continuing revelations of corruption, accusations of immorality and what must have seemed like endless labor strikes, the debut of the lavish theatre not only offered a brief respite from their mundane problems but was also a symbol of hope for the new millennium. The opulent playhouse was located in the heart of the city's great commercial Loop, so named for the two-track Union Elevated trains, 1,600 of them a day, which twisted and ground above the downtown district like some giant species of screeching snake. By day, the area was choked with horse-drawn vehicular traffic, sidewalks crowded with visitors to the new "high rise" office buildings and to Marshall Field's, Mandel Brothers, Carson, Pirie, Scott and other fabulous retail emporia, and filled with the never-ending political hustle at the ugly, ponderous, block-long City Hall and County Building. At night, the area was so thick with theatres, hotels, restaurants and wine rooms — as cabarets were then called — that it was becoming known as the "Rialto of the Midwest."

Collins, along with the rest of the local press corps, was overwhelmed by the physical splendor of the theatre. The *Record-Herald's* arch rival, the *Chicago Tribune*, would lose itself in superlatives, describing it as "a virtual temple of beauty — a place where the noblest and highest in dramatic art could find a worthy home." *Tribune* typesetters had already blocked out the next day's theatre page headline:

BEAUTY OF IROQUOIS
ONE OF THE SPLENDID THEATRES OF THE
WORLD OPENS WITH "MR. BLUEBEARD"
EDDIE FOY IS WELCOMED

Under that headline, Amy Leslie, the *Tribune's* respected arts critic, wrote breathlessly, "No theatre anywhere is handsomer than the Iroquois, a noble monument to dramatic art. Except L'Opera in Paris no theatre I ever saw is so resplendently spirited in its architecture . . . it is perhaps as glorious a place of amusement as Chicago shall care to demand."

And the wonder of it all, as the *Chicago Journal* correctly noted, was that "the marvels . . . had been wrought in the short space of six months." On opening night a group of friends entering the building exclaimed to one of the theatre's owners, "You must have had Aladdin's lamp to accomplish all this!"

ABSOLUTELY FIREPROOF

"If this thing starts going they will lynch you."
—*Captain Patrick Jennings, Engine Company 13*

THE THEATRE'S DEBUT HAD generated national interest for months. On its front page the previous May, the *New York Times* had reported, "Buildings in Dearborn and Randolph Streets, occupying the proposed site of the Iroquois Theatre are being razed for the new playhouse, which it is expected will be completed by October 12 when 'Mr. Bluebeard' will be given its Chicago opening."

When the cornerstone was laid on July 28, the *San Francisco Chronicle* carried a drawing of the Iroquois' main entrance below the headline, "Chicago to Have a Palatial Theatre." Its owners were officially listed as Will J. Davis and Harry Powers of Chicago and their partners, Klaw and Erlanger of New York and Nixon and Zimmerman of Philadelphia. "It will be a Syndicate House," noted the *Chronicle*, referring to the New York-based Theatrical Trust, which then controlled most of America's major theatres.

Only steps away from where the broad cobblestone arteries of Dearborn and Randolph streets intersected, and the new elec-

tric trolleys topped with pentagrams clutched a web of spark-
ing overhead wires, the Iroquois formed a great L extending
from Randolph to a narrow alley and, in the rear, west to Dearborn. The stage occupied the toe of the L. The building's dimensions were impressive: its frontage covered sixty-one feet
along Randolph, and extended ninety-one feet north to a lot
fronting 110 feet on Dearborn. The main entrance on Randolph
opened into a huge vestibule, foyer, grand promenade and staircase, all of it at a sharp right angle to the auditorium and stage.
Parallel to the six-story edifice and across a narrow eighteen-
foot cobblestone alley, were Northwestern University's schools
of law, dentistry, pharmacology and chemistry, in a building
that had been the Tremont House hotel. On the alley side of the
theatre were the scenery doors and fire escapes, and at the back
of the theatre was a small stage door adjoining an empty lot.

Sandwiched between the dark stone Delaware office building on the corner and John Thompson's street-level restaurant,
the Iroquois protruded boldly into Randolph Street—a baroque
palace in a block of nondescript four-story structures: stores,
offices, a small hotel and a bowling alley. Built of steel, brick
and concrete, materials considered impervious to fire, the theatre and its furnishings represented an investment of $1.1 mil-
lion, an astronomical sum at a time when twelve dollars a week
was considered a reasonable salary and a Chicago workingman's
family existed on an average yearly income of $827.

It seemed to Collins that no expense had been spared in
building and outfitting the Iroquois. Its impressive French-style
façade was polished granite and Bedford stone; huge twin Corin-
thian columns, each weighing thirty-two tons, bracketed an
entrance with ten glass doors. Atop the columns were pilasters
ornamented with the epic figures of Comedy and Tragedy, and
the whole edifice was crowned with a broken pediment and a

large carved stone bust of the theatre's namesake Indian, an idea said to have originated with the theatre's co-owner and manager, Will Davis, who owned a large collection of Americana.

The interior was not only elegant but the epitome of modern technology. Two thousand Edison Mazda bulbs blazed above and around the grand entry foyer and around a 6,300-foot auditorium where seats were arranged so that everyone in the audience, whether in boxes, balcony or gallery, had an unbroken view of a stage sixty feet wide by 110 feet deep. The stage floor had been designed to be much lower than standard to permit people in the front rows a view from the footlights to the rear wall. The auditorium was second in size only to that of the cavernous Chicago Municipal Auditorium.

The ceiling towered fifty-three feet over the entrance hall, supported by ten columns of pavanazzo marble bracketing a grand promenade, its design a blend of elements adapted from both the U.S. Library of Congress and L'Opera Comique in Paris. Ornate chandeliers and illuminated globes in the Beaux Arts style lighted graceful arched staircases bordered with filigree wrought-iron balustrades ascending to the box seats and upper tiers.

Apart from walls of gleaming mirrors, the rich Indian red of the painted wall panels and the dull gold of the arched ceiling, what space remained had been covered with seemingly endless yards of red and green plush velvet drapery. The seats in the auditorium were also covered with plush velvet and stuffed with hemp, as were the settees arranged around the promenade and the landings. Virtually nothing had been overlooked.

High above the auditorium, the theatre's ornate dome was circled by a frieze illustrating the history of the Chicago stage, from the relatively primitive Rice Theatre to the ultra-modern Iroquois.

Backstage, out of the audience's sight, the opulence ended, but there were still many points of interest that stagehands were eager to point out. There were no fewer than thirty-eight brick-walled dressing rooms rising from the basement on different tiers, and capable of housing as many as four hundred performers—a practical accommodation at a time when big musical productions often had casts of three hundred or more, including very young children.

A large electric elevator could whisk the actors silently and speedily from their dressing rooms to the stage and the stagehands to the very top of the scenery loft. Eleven miles of two-inch greased Manila rope were needed to support the Iroquois' main drop curtains and the approximately 280 heavily painted *Bluebeard* scenery flats suspended from wooden battens high above the stage. Virtually all interior and stage lighting was controlled from a large central switchboard just offstage, its electric cables sheathed in heavy metal conduits.

On opening night, the theatre's *wunderkind* architect, handsome twenty-nine-year-old Benjamin H. Marshall, scion of one of Chicago's oldest families, sat with his parents and friends in a two-hundred-dollar box seat, listening to Will Davis deliver a rousing second-act curtain speech interrupted by cheers and bursts of applause. Davis, gesturing toward the embarrassed young architect, assured the audience that it was no Aladdin's lamp that had caused the building to be completed in five months, but Ben Marshall, the George Fuller Construction Company and other enterprising Chicago firms and workers. With barely concealed contempt for the Eastern theatre establishment, Davis said that the Iroquois was the creation of Western talent, abilities and enthusiasm, that Western appreciation and encouragement were all that were desired, and "they were good enough for any man."

For the opening night audience, Davis and his partner Powers had produced a thirty-page souvenir brochure with a red, gold-embossed cover, containing pictures of Benjamin Marshall, Davis, Powers and their partners, along with sketches of the theatre's entrance, lobby, promenade, magnificent twin staircases, and many other lesser features including the smoking room, a clubby cave in the basement where men could retire between the acts to enjoy cigars and cigarettes while the ladies gossiped in the powder rooms.

Charles Collins received one of these brochures; it said in effect that the Iroquois Theatre was a magnificent creation, worthy in every respect of Chicago's self-image as a modern metropolis and the sophisticated center of that other America that existed beyond the lights of Broadway and the Hudson River. "The American public now, more than ever before, demand elegance of environment for their amusements, as well as provisions for comfort and security," the brochure stated in the florid language of the time. It noted the "unstinted financial outlay with a determination to secure the best as befitting such an important and artistic adventure," praised the "ripe experience" of the co-owners, Davis and Powers, and called the theatre's builder, "the George A. Fuller Company . . . second to none in handling enterprises of magnitude, and in carrying them to completion in spite of all obstacles that the uncertain temper of the times may impose." The booklet was heavily illustrated, including photographs of the theatre's New York minority shareowners and *Bluebeard* impresarios, the notorious, powerful Klaw and Erlanger.

For his part, Marshall had not been modest about describing his creation. He had studied architecture in Paris, had previously designed Powers' Illinois Theatre, and readily acknowledged that Chicago, still trying to forget the inferno that had nearly wiped out the city thirty-two years earlier, placed a great premium on safety. In public statements, Marshall emphasized that he had carefully studied every theatre disaster in history to avoid errors in the design of his new building. In the unlikely event that an emergency should arise, he said, the Iroquois could be emptied within five minutes if all thirty exits were used. That message was further reinforced in the upper right-hand corner of the front page of each playbill handed to theatre patrons. In bold black type, it reassured the public that the Iroquois was "Absolutely Fireproof."

The claim might have been substantially altered, challenged or completely eliminated had anyone taken notice of a scathing report that had appeared in an obscure Chicago trade journal months earlier. Apparently no one had paid any attention to an investigative piece in the August number of *Fireproof Magazine*. Its editor, William Clendennin, had made an inspection of the theatre while it was still under construction, and had noted "[t]he absence of an intake, or stage draft shaft; the exposed reinforcement of the concrete [proscenium] arch [above the stage]; the presence of wood trim on everything and the inadequate provision of exits."

There were other indications of trouble ahead. In a November 2 report to Mayor Carter Harrison, Jr., and the city council, the building commissioner said that of virtually all the city's theatres, only the Municipal Auditorium met all safety code requirements. The structural conditions of the Iroquois were not included in the survey because construction and fitting out of the interior was still under way and the expectation was that the theatre's management would complete all necessary changes and additions before the doors opened. For a metropolis growing as fast as Chicago, the building department was woefully undermanned, consisting of nineteen inspectors, one fire escape inspector, eleven elevator inspectors, one ironworker and three clerks, one of whom was responsible for issuing all permits. The aldermen took the report under advisement, but to spare theatre owners substantial added expenses, turned the survey back to the mayor, requesting a special committee to study the problem. The press paid little attention to what was in effect a tabling of the issue.

Most disturbing of all was the result of a tour by an officer of the Chicago Fire Department that was not made public. In addition to having no ambulances, the department had no formal fire prevention bureau—one would not be established until 1911. The closest thing to a preventative-measures unit was a small group called the Bureau of Explosives, but that too had neither the time nor the manpower to make inspections throughout the city. That job was apparently the responsibility of local battalion chiefs and their direct reports.

Days before the official opening, the Iroquois was visited by Patrick Jennings, the respected captain of Engine Company 13, housed in a three-story building less than a city block from the theatre. Because the Iroquois was in his jurisdiction, "Paddy" Jennings, as he was affectionately called by his men, made a routine inspection accompanied by a department retiree named William Sallers, who had been hired as the Iroquois house fireman, and who was required to be on hand for each performance.

Jennings was appalled at what was missing.

By 1903, telephones were no longer a novelty in Chicago, but the Iroquois had no backstage phone. In the auditorium, Jennings saw no exit signs, and some of the exits were concealed by thick drapery. But it was the absence of backstage "appliances," as they were then called, that he found the most outrageous. There was no fire alarm system. No sprinkler system. Standpipes had not been connected. There were no backstage fire buckets or pike poles and the number of fire hoses was totally inadequate. The only fire-fighting equipment in America's newest theatre were six thin, two-foot-long metal canisters containing a popular dry chemical product called "Kilfyre." The white powder inside each narrow two-inch tube, according to label instructions, was to be forcibly thrown in a fan-like arc at the base of flames. The word *"Forcibly"* was emphasized, as were the words, *"Never Sprinkle."* The instructions also included the information that Kilfyre, retailing for three dollars a tube, could be used to control common household chimney blazes.

Jennings demanded to know the reason for this obvious lack of equipment. Sallers replied that he feared for his job if he raised objections and besides, the theatre's management had been well aware of the problem for some time. Somewhat apologetically, Sallers confirmed that all he had on hand were the six canisters of Kilfyre.

The infuriated Jennings was blunt. "If this thing starts going," he told Sallers, "they will lynch you."

Jennings reported his findings to his superior, First Battalion Chief Jack Hannon, whose offices occupied the third floor of Engine 13's station house. Jennings told his boss, "If a fire ever starts on that stage it will be frightful."

"What can we do about it?" Hannon was said to have answered. The theatre owners, he said, "have a fireman there and they know all about it." In the Chicago civil service of the time, bucking a superior officer amounted to political suicide, to the instant termination of a career. The discussion was over.

For Charles Collins, safety was not an issue. Overwhelmed by the Iroquois' luxurious appointments, he didn't notice any safety violations. But he did see something that struck him as disquieting. At the Randolph Street entrance, the monumental arch-

way with its sculptural decorations looked, except for minor
details, almost exactly like a monument erected in Paris to com-
memorate the deaths of one hundred and fifty people who had
lost their lives in a horrible flash fire in the city's 1897 Charity
Bazaar. It was never recognized as such, Collins would later
recall, and was only mentioned in shoptalk among architects
who had studied in the French capital. But the resemblance, he
thought, was "a sinister omen."

{3}

A NEW YEAR'S SURPRISE

"It is the new theatre which is the talk of the town."
— *Walter Hill, Correspondent,* NEW YORK CLIPPER

AFTER THE SHOW ON opening night, co-owners Davis and Powers held an informal reception, to the accompaniment of popping champagne corks, in the Iroquois' resplendent lobby. Collins had a review to turn in and as he left the theatre he noted crowds of people, usually anxious to get home, lingering in the lobby to compliment the owners at length on their stunning accomplishment. "They were congratulated by many people upon the handsome theatre, which begins its career in their control . . . they, [and many members of the cast] received floral tributes [from] all parts of the country . . . enough to fill out three or four . . . greenhouses."

The *Chicago Journal* observed: "Without a doubt the audience that separated and went its many ways . . . had less thought for the performance which had just been given than at any time in the history of a Chicago theatre. It was the theatre that all wished to see, not the Drury Lane spectacle [presented by] Klaw and Erlanger."

Walter K. Hill, Midwest correspondent for the theatrical trade paper the *New York Clipper* (forerunner of *Variety*), came to the same conclusion. The excitement was not about *Bluebeard*'s songs and skits, its remarkable aerial ballet, Foy's comic routines or even the beautiful young women who paraded past the footlights during the many spectacular tableaux. The story, said Hill, was the playhouse, not the show.

"It is the new theatre which is the talk of the town," he wired New York. "The house is the most beautiful . . . in Chicago, and competent judges state that few theatres in America can rival its architectural perfections, the splendor of its decorations, or its facilities for comfort. The lobby is surprisingly beautiful, the auditorium is fitted luxuriantly, and the stage is commodious and perfect in [every] detail."

The glittery opening must have impressed the entire audience, the prominent businessmen George Plamondon and Alexander Revell among them. They didn't have to wait to read the reviews. The elegance of the theatre, combined with *Mr. Bluebeard*'s music and dance spectacular and especially Foy's zany routines, would be a perfect Christmas treat for their daughters, one a teenaged debutante, the other a child of seven.

A special Thanksgiving matinee was scheduled for the following day, but that was of course too early; with Christmas only weeks away there were limited options for the children and their friends to see the spectacle. The most appropriate date would have to be a day close to the end of the year during school holidays. And it had to be an afternoon performance so that festive family dinners could be held immediately following the show. The Plamondon girl would be part of a group of friends celebrating the return of a chum who had come home for the holidays from a school in Washington, D.C. And the Revell child would bring a little friend with her, along with the family maid.

There seemed to be only one day on the calendar that would fit all these requirements. That would be the afternoon of December 30, the Wednesday holiday matinee, little more than five weeks away. It would be a marvelous New Year's treat.

{4}

STRIKES, SNOW AND SHOW BUSINESS

*"That is the most flammable goddamn mess of scenery
I ever saw . . ."*
— *Will J. Davis, Co-owner, Iroquois Theatre*

IN THE WINTER OF 1903, Charles Collins and his colleagues were
delighted to note that the *Record-Herald*'s average daily circulation was 147,000 readers, jumping to just over 180,000 on
Sundays, running far ahead of its morning rival the *Tribune*.
Chicago was a notoriously competitive newspaper town and in
the rough-and-tumble rivalry between the two morning dailies,
the papers hustled after the same stories, but the way they
handled the inaugural performance of the Iroquois Theatre made
it seem as if the opening had been staged in two different cities.

On its theatre page the morning after the opening, the *Tribune* ran an elaborate photo montage of the theatre's promenade foyer, of Eddie Foy in one of his ludicrous costumes and
of the lovely young Chicago-born actress, Bonnie Maginn, a
female lead. Its lengthy feature story about the theatre and Amy
Leslie's review of the playhouse covered many columns, describing even minute details like "a curtain of deep red velour used
between scenes, a brilliantly colored autumn landscape . . . on

the act drop and a woodland scene on the fireproof curtain."
The Iroquois, the *Tribune* wrote on Sunday, "challenges comparison as to beauty with any in the world."

Charles Collins's review in the *Record-Herald*, limited to two-paragraphs in the "Music and Drama" column, was loaded with superlatives, although it seemed restrained in contrast to James Bennett's overblown fifteen-paragraph discussion of *Ulysses*. Collins described *Bluebeard* as "a dazzling succession of stage pictures, each so brilliant and unique that its predecessor was instantly forgotten, each representing the pinnacle of the stage manager's and costumer's art. . . . a gorgeous pageant . . . music and mirth are subordinated [to] a spectacle which would stir the jaded imagination of a pleasure-sated Roman emperor. Eddy [*sic*] Foy bloomed out in his old-time form and was lord high jester of the carnival."

No one reported that at the time the Iroquois opened, both Fuller and Klaw-Erlanger were in serious financial difficulty, leading co-manager Davis to go out of his way to save money wherever he could. One item on which he cut expenses was the asbestos safety curtain.

The George A. Fuller construction company, described in the souvenir brochure as "second to none in handling enterprises of magnitude, and carrying them to completion in spite of all obstacles," was in truth one of a handful of large general contractors that had both the manpower and special skills necessary to handle all aspects of building construction. With important contracts in New York, Boston, Pittsburgh, Chicago and other major cities, it was the construction arm of the United States Realty and Construction Company. On November 12, eleven days before the Iroquois was to open, with work by Fuller's Chicago employees still incomplete on the theatre's roof ventilation system and exterior fire escapes, New York City bricklayers, one thousand strong, struck all Fuller projects in the city. That included the new headquarters of the *New York Times*, the steel skeleton of which was then rising on Broadway at 42nd Street. Joined in sympathy by stonecutters and ironworkers, the bricklayers claimed they had been denied work when Fuller supplied not only fireproofing equipment, but used its own men for a job at a downtown Manhattan office building.

The strike had an immediate effect. On November 18, five days before the Iroquois was to open, Fuller announced major workforce reductions, leading to widespread reports that U.S. Realty would sever its ties with Fuller. Officials at Fuller's New York headquarters denied the reports, but confirmed that there had been considerable staff reductions, including workmen, due to "the depressed state of the building industry brought about by unusual labor disturbances." The reductions were bound to have ramifications in Chicago and other cities.

When, after several days, the New York bricklayers' strike was finally settled, Fuller became the target of a second and far more serious walkout. This time it was Local 2 of the New York ironworkers, who objected to the subletting of ornamental work on another Manhattan project. Though Fuller quickly signed an agreement with a new ironworkers union, S. P. McConnell, the company's president, acknowledged on November 24, the day after the Iroquois gala opening, that the strike against Fuller was going to expand to other cities. The Iroquois had opened for business, but the building was not yet completed.

November of 1903 also spelled trouble for two of the most powerful names in the theatre industry, Marc Klaw and Abraham Lincoln Erlanger. These two, who called themselves "booking agents," controlled, along with other partners, the vast Theatrical Trust from their offices on south Broadway. At the time, American business was going through a major metamorphosis, "from freewheeling competition to loosely knit cartels to air-tight trusts." Though miniscule compared to giants like John D. Rockefeller's Standard Oil or the Southern Pacific Railroad, the Theatrical Trust was the most powerful monopoly in the world of vaudeville and the legitimate stage. Its business practices emulated America's largest corporate combinations by "centralizing control, absorbing and eliminating competitors, [and] crushing labor opposition."

Created in 1896, by 1903 the Trust (also known as the "Syndicate") controlled most if not all of the important legitimate theatres in the country. Weeks before the Iroquois debut, Klaw and Erlanger had opened their stunning New Amsterdam Theatre on West 42nd Street in Manhattan, the largest stage in New York. It was said to have been "built expressly for musical productions . . . a monument to the musical's ascendancy to a position of artistic and financial respectability."

"Respectable" was not a word used often to describe the Klaw-Erlanger organization, which was frequently referred to as the "skindecat." Marc Klaw was a thin, cadaverous lawyer from Louisville who had worked briefly as a newspaperman and as a press agent. With penetrating eyes and a neatly cropped mustache and beard, he was "a natural diplomatist, suave and easy in his converse with men." His partner and opposite was Abraham Lincoln Erlanger, a crude little man with a billiard-ball head, who had begun his theatrical career selling tickets in a Cleveland box office. Erlanger was a punitive, rancorous bundle of energy, a bully who kept busts of Napoleon in his office and enjoyed acting like the Little Corporal. He once rudely responded to a theatregoer who complained about the two-dollar price of an orchestra seat: "In answer to your letter . . . we would suggest that you borrow a dictionary and look up the word 'impertinence.'"

These two were possibly the most feared men in what was then called "the show business." To describe them as "booking agents" was a gross misstatement. Over the years since the Trust had begun taking over leases of most of the available first-class theatres in the nation, it had consolidated a substantial amount of power. Through their network of local resident theatre owners and managers, Klaw-Erlanger had the power to decide who and what would play in the many theatres under their control. They were ruthless, often demanding and getting as much as fifty percent of a show's gross profits, as well as hefty add-on commissions from advertising, publicity, booking and other service fees. If an independent theatre operator would not agree to their terms, they could permanently darken his stage, eventually shutting him down by steadily withholding anything but second- or third-rate performers and equally undistinguished productions. They played their "good guy-bad guy" roles often, and, according to one theatre historian, extremely well. "Managers from the hinterland who'd been pulverized by Erlanger's imperious edicts could be rehabilitated by Klaw's unctuous attentions. [But] each man, in his own manner, was out for the same thing: utter domination of the American stage."

Though unknown to most of the general public, Klaw and Erlanger were detested not only by many actors and independent theatre owners, but even by some members of the press who saw them as more than another monopoly to be destroyed, agreeing with many leading clergymen of the day that the Trust was responsible for the degradation of the American theatre and the corruption of Christian morals. It was easy to dislike Marc Klaw and Abe Erlanger. They were powerful and ruthless, wealthy and arrogant. And they were Jews.

Among the prominent outspoken holdouts against the Trust were the French actress Sarah Bernhardt and Minnie Madden Fiske, "The First Lady of the American Stage," whose husband and manager, Harrison Grey Fiske, was the powerful editor and publisher of New York's *Dramatic Mirror*. In subtly anti-Semitic rhetoric, Fiske railed against the Syndicate's "greed, cunning and inhuman selfishness." But Fiske's innuendos were mild compared to the Jew-baiting of *Life* magazine's drama critic, James S. Metcalf. *Life** was founded in 1883 by three Harvard graduates as a smart humor publication with an emphasis on fine pen-and-ink sketches: Charles Dana Gibson's "Gibson Girl" first appeared in its pages. Through Metcalf, *Life* carried on a crusade against what its editors considered the general tawdriness and commercialism of the American stage and the men who controlled it. While not at first identified by name, there could be no doubt about the target of these attacks. At a time when European immigration to America was at its height and Jews by the thousand were fleeing Russian pogroms, *Life* was routinely filled with anti-Semitic articles and cartoons: male and female Jews were referred to as "Hebrews," speaking guttural broken English and were caricatured with huge hooked noses.

In one cover cartoon, "The Drama. As We Get It In New York," a short, swarthy hook-nosed man in top hat and tails tries to entice two innocent (and presumably Gentile), young ladies into his theatre to see the current attraction: "'The Immoral Woman,' a new play from the sewers of Europe . . . produced by The Jew Syndicate." A centerfold drawing in another issue depicted the usual anti-Semitic stereotypes (like those used thirty years later in Nazi Germany): three swarthy hook-nosed men in top hats and frock coats, standing before banners parodying Lincoln's Gettysburg Address: "Theatrical Trust. Of the Jews. For the Jews. By the Jews." In still another issue, *Life* presented "The Jewish Mind in these States," a full-page essay written by a founder of the *Harvard Lampoon*. A letter of complaint from an anonymous "important member" of New York's Jewish community was printed in a subsequent issue with no

---

* Henry Luce bought the name in 1936 for his unrelated *Life* magazine.

retraction or apology, but with a stilted defense of the original theme.

In 1904, without mentioning Klaw and Erlanger by name to avoid a libel suit, Metcalf told his readers, "They are not Jews of the better class, certainly not descendants of the poets, prophets and mighty warriors of Israel. In their veins runs the blood of Fagin, Shylock and the money-changers who were scourged from the temple. . . . The two Jews are well clad and have the toad-like appearance which comes from gross feeding." *Life's* scurrilous campaign continued for years.

Apart from these ugly attacks, 1903 was not a particularly auspicious one for the Theatrical Trust. Ticket sales, especially in New York City, were down, a situation attributed to hard times on Wall Street. The Shuberts, three young and aggressive brothers from Syracuse, New York, were flexing their muscle as competitors to the monopoly; a new entity, the anti-Trust Independent Booking Agency, was fueling rumors of a split within the Syndicate; the explosive Erlanger banned negative critics from his theatres and pulled ads from offending newspapers. The Trust seemed always involved in an endless string of suits or disputes with leading entertainers and producers like the prominent comedy team of Weber and Fields, who, like the actresses Bernhardt and Fiske, refused to cave in to Klaw-Erlanger's threats and demands.

There was also strong stage competition to deal with. In Chicago, drama critics generally agreed that the undisputed hit of the 1902 season was a new musical, *The Wizard of Oz,* based on L. Frank Baum's fantasy. The hit of the 1903 season, which debuted in Chicago just weeks before the Iroquois opened, was a Victor Herbert operetta, the sweetly sentimental *Babes in Toyland.* These were not Klaw-Erlanger productions. But the Trust had enjoyed considerable success with family-oriented musical entertainments like *Aladdin, or the Wonderful Lamp, The Crystal Slipper,* and *Sleeping Beauty and the Beast,* all imported from London's Drury Lane Theatre, and Klaw-Erlanger was determined to produce another big crowd-pleaser for the 1903 fall season. At considerable cost, it had signed Eddie Foy, who was not particularly fond of Klaw or Erlanger, for an unprecedented $800 a week to star in *Mr. Bluebeard,* which had been an undisputed hit in London.

Even for the wealthy Trust, the show represented a huge investment of approximately $150,000, including $65,000 just for the sets, lights, costumes and special effects, all shipped across the Atlantic. The cost did not include the expenses for two hundred New York seamstresses and others hired at the last minute the previous January for *Bluebeard*'s Knickerbocker Theatre opening. These women toiled night and day altering more than three hundred costumes and shoes to fit the American cast. "[Englishwomen] are every bit as round and quite as well proportioned," one New York fashion writer commented on the expensive *Bluebeard* costumes, "[but they] . . . are flatter chested and with larger waists and larger frames . . . [and no] English shoe will fit an American foot." The same article noted that a stage taboo had been broken in *Bluebeard*'s huge Egyptian tableau scene, which featured costumes in peacock shades of greenish-blue along with peacock feather fans: "Peacock feathers, as everyone knows, especially superstitious stage people, are supposed to be unlucky. . . ."

Klaw-Erlanger faced an even more daunting problem than anti-Semitism, competition, defections, declining revenues, mounting expenses and the peacock feather omen. Throughout 1903, Chicago, like New York, was embroiled in a continuous round of labor disputes so disruptive that they could significantly affect the Trust's profit margin by delaying the opening of their expensive Midwest investment. To add to their misery was the Windy City's notoriously uncooperative weather. The first snow of the season blanketed the area on November 5, followed by cold, bone-chilling rain. The Trust's original plan was to open the Iroquois in early October at the start of Chicago's new theatre season, but the date had to be pushed back, week after chilly week because of labor problems and bad weather. In addition to lost business there was an endless stream of negative publicity. On November 11 the public was disappointed to read the announcement: "The Iroquois Theatre will not be opened a week from tomorrow night. The new date has not been fixed but it will be either Tuesday or Wednesday, the week after next, November 23 or 24."

In addition to the Fuller strike in New York, completion of the Iroquois was held up when 3000 Chicago streetcar motormen, who had long been threatening a strike, walked off the job. City officials had warned in advance that a transit strike would seriously tie up South Side lines, causing thousands to walk to and from work in the cold.

The walkout began November 14, and, as predicted, created havoc, making it difficult if not impossible for Fuller workers living outside the Loop to get to the theatre with any regularity. Other complications for Klaw-Erlanger included last-minute delays of replacement items ranging from additional auditorium seats to stronger support cables for scenery flats and curtains, not to mention slowdowns caused by undefined "labor difficulties" among the theatre's marble finishers.

News of the continual delays was not well received in the New York offices of the Theatrical Trust. That previous summer, Erlanger had begun bullying his Chicago partners and Iroquois executives Davis and Powers, to speed up the construction and get the theatre open in time for the fall season, even if it meant handing out free tickets or bribing building officials and others to look the other way, make cursory inspections and issue the appropriate city permits. And still the theatre was unfinished. A juicy rumor making the rounds of Chicago theatre circles that fall, according to the *New York Clipper*, was that "Davis's summer of hustling has almost gone for naught."

Charles Collins had heard still another rumor, never confirmed, that Davis had stopped by the Iroquois one day while the heavily painted *Bluebeard* scenery flats were being loaded in through the stage doors. According to Collins, "Davis had a fit, [saying] 'that stuff is the most flammable goddamn mess of scenery I ever saw. . . . I won't let it go into this theatre.'" But remembering Erlanger's temper, the New York backers' sizable investment in the show, the fact that they owned a percentage of the theatre and that the *Bluebeard* opening could not be indefinitely delayed, Davis quickly relented, saying, "All right, we'll try to get along with the damn stuff." The scenery went inside.

Given everything else that was going on in Chicago at the time, these rumors were largely ignored. Press and public attention was focused on the local transit stoppage, fueled by an almost daily stream of scare headlines like, "Turn Car Barns into Barracks; Await Siege." Readers in the city and around the country saw alarming reports of a Chicago "labor war [in which] . . . lawless forces have the Western metropolis in their grip." *McClure's* magazine commented, "Only the outsider coming to Chicago, can fully realize the extent of this industrial armament—a sort of militant neutrality comparable to that of Europe."

In a city with a dark history of labor violence—the infamous Haymarket incident, for instance—the November 1903 transit strike was as nasty as it could get short of bloodshed. Violence had been predicted from the start because of management's decision to keep the cars rolling by importing strikebreakers from as far away as St. Louis and New Orleans, while union leaders vowed that the cars would never leave their barns. When the walkout began, the surface line was at first operated under police protection and crowds were banned from streets through which the trains passed. But the following day, November 15, strikers threw huge barricades across tracks, hurled stones at the cars, sliced trolley wires and plugged cable slots. A piece of military ordnance was found in the path of one train (nearly resulting in a riot when it was mistaken for a dynamite bomb), and police began clubbing and arresting demonstrators. Politics intruded almost immediately when the city council demanded to know how Mayor Harrison had the authority to let the Bluecoats ride, like shotgun guards, on city railway cars.

The third day of the walkout, as wind and rain pelted commuters and demonstrators alike, five hundred more uniformed officers were assigned to patrol the tracks after linemen, dynamo tenders and repairmen joined the strikers. On the fourth day, though peace efforts had been announced, several shots were fired at strikebreakers and police were ordered to board U.S. Mail wagons if the drivers showed any inclination to block the streetcars. By Saturday, November 22, as negotiations to end the dispute were underway, a mob of several thousand men who had gathered to intercept food wagons bound for the car barns, charged police, shouting and hurling stones. The officers drew their weapons, but drove back the crowd without a shot being fired. Then on Sunday, fierce fighting broke out once more between police and strikers, with many demonstrators being clubbed by the officers, who this time fired shots over the heads of the mob. A few days later, as streetcar union men were trying to reach an agreement with management, a commuter was accidentally shoved off a crowded downtown "L" platform into the path of an oncoming train; he was said to be the only person killed in the short-lived skirmish.

On November 25, with the intervention of city officials, the strike was settled. The railway reinstated all employees except those proven guilty of violence, and Mayor Harrison spoke for many citizens when he said that Chicagoans "had been living in a powder magazine in which men were walking about with lighted matches in their hands."

The tense labor situation meant more bad news for the Iroquois. It was bad enough that a violent transit strike had prevented people, particularly women and children, from going into the Loop, but given the "powder magazine" edginess that still prevailed, it was not surprising that audience attendance for *Bluebeard* was not what the Trust had expected.

On December 5, the *Clipper*'s correspondent wired New York that the previous week's "business has been good, but not on the capacity order, which one might have expected." Eight days later, it was the same negative story from the *Clipper*: "Business has been good but not up to expectations, considering the glories of the production."

In a final stroke of bad luck, the weather turned foul. On December 13, the mercury plunged to twelve below zero, making it the city's coldest day on record in thirty-six years. Headlines told the story: "Three Dead from Cold"; "Many Streets Cleared and Cars Run But Railroad Trains Arrive Late"; "Cold Wave Held Chicagoans in its Icy Clutch"; "L's Crawl in Snow Storm." The frigid weather, complicated by yet another transit strike involving over one thousand Chicago liverymen, or taxi drivers, also prevented people from venturing downtown. And there was plenty of other sensational front-page news to divert attention from the new theatre.

First came the revelation that thieves who operated in the city's notorious Levee district, where everything from brothels to opium dens operated openly, were "in with police." Screamed one headline: "Pay Lion's Share of Their Plunder to Men of the Department, Witnesses Declared," but no one seemed especially surprised. The public's attention was further diverted by a series of stories about daring daytime robberies, homicides, running gun battles and policemen shot down in cold blood. Not many citizens disagreed with Alderman William Mavor when he called Chicago, "a lawless city," adding, "It is the worst place for violating statutes. . . . no one respects the courts; the courts don't respect themselves."

But still, it was the Christmas season, and the sensational crime, labor and weather stories had to share space with page after page of alluring advertisements heralding the approaching holidays and the wondrous array of gifts stockpiled at local stores. Toy departments reported a brisk business in "Teddy" bears named after the president—who disliked the nickname— by an enterprising Brooklyn manufacturer who had seen a cartoon of Roosevelt holding a cub. Mandel Brothers was offering a complete dinner set of Haviland China for $35. A new Oldsmobile Light Delivery Wagon, the equivalent of today's pickup truck, could be hitched up and driven off the lot for $850. Marshall Field's had a wide selection of men's ready-to-wear hats, street models for $6.75, dress hats starting at $10. Even for the overwhelming majority who did not own cars, Mark Cross was suggesting a ladies' hand-sewn, pigskin "strap handle automobile bag" for $16.50, an unheard-of extravagance for all but the very rich.

There were attractive descriptions of novel technological products like wind-up Columbia phonographs and Kodak Brownie Box cameras, along with reports of the holiday doings of Chicago's haute monde planning the winter Bal Poudre fete. But lost among the sensational headlines and the pages of holiday cheer was the fact that Chicago had permitted the opening of a dazzling, new and dangerously incomplete playhouse—a fact known to its resident managers, owners, architect and building contractors; to city inspectors, stagehands, ushers, performers and some members of the fire department, among others. It turned out that Deputy Building Inspector Edward Loughlin, a ten-year department veteran who had never taken a civil service examination, but who had the responsibility of inspecting the Iroquois daily during its constuction, issued his final report prior to the theatre's opening in the form of a verbal statement to his boss. He said the place was completed and "OK." "The report was accepted without question as to fire apparatus, exits, equipment or appliances of any kind."

THE SONG-AND-DANCE MAN

"I risked both our lives at every crossing."
                                        —*Eddie Foy*

IF CHARLES COLLINS WAS HAPPY with his twenty-five-dollar-a-week job, Eddie Foy, with a salary that by terms of his contract would escalate to $800 a week, must been in a state of euphoria. The forty-seven-year-old song-and-dance man was closing out the year on a particularly high note. He had recently purchased a large home in New York's Westchester County, and he had returned in triumph to Chicago, the place he considered his hometown. He was the star attraction in a hit show, performing in the impressive new Iroquois Theatre and staying at the luxurious Sherman House. Best of all, Foy was spending the holiday season with his wife Madeline and their children Bryan, Charles, Madeline, Mary and baby Richard, who had come by train from New York. It was an added sweetener arranged by Klaw and Erlanger, a luxury not always experienced by an entertainer who had spent a good part of his career on the road, living out of suitcases in lonely hotel rooms.

Foy was born Edward Fitzgerald, the son of an immigrant Irish tailor, in the slums of Greenwich Village in lower Manhattan. After the death of his father, he moved with his mother and two siblings to Chicago at the urging of a relative who thought mistakenly that it might be easier for the family to make a living there. Boasting in later years that, as part of the family tradition, he could dance the day he was born, Fitzgerald became a street performer by the age of eight, doing Irish clog and acrobatic dancing for small change. At age twelve he had quit grade school and was back on the sidewalks, hawking newspapers on street corners. By the time he was sixteen, he had decided to become a professional performer and had already begun a song-and-dance routine with a friend. At first they billed themselves as "Finnegan and Fitzgerald" but later, believing that that sounded too Irish, changed the name to "Edwards and Foy."

Unable to afford even the cheapest theatre ticket, Foy would frequently lurk outside concert halls or wine rooms to catch the sounds of minstrel and vaudeville shows and other entertainment. On one occasion he collected enough money to be able to buy a balcony seat and see a complete minstrel show and was so impressed with the songs, the dancing and the comedy routines, that he remembered the experience as "one of the red-letter evenings of my career."

There was another vivid memory from his early Chicago days that overshadowed virtually everything else and that he probably would have preferred to forget. It was the Great Chicago Fire of 1871, that legend held began when Mrs. O'Leary's cow kicked over a lantern in her barn. No one knows how the fire started—some believed that a group of neighborhood hooligans accidentally knocked over the lantern while horsing around—but in any case the Fitzgerald family lived, like the O'Learys, on the South Side in an Irish district of wooden shacks which went up like kindling. Foy, who was fifteen years old, was told to take his sister's eighteen-month-old son and get out of the area as fast as he could. The family would meet again somewhere after the danger had passed. He set out for the home of a family friend who lived in a part of the city believed to be well out of range of the conflagration, because for the flames to reach the house, the fire would have had to travel through Chicago's main business district where most of the buildings were considered to be fireproof. "It never occurred to [my mother] or anyone else that sort of thing could possibly happen," he recalled. "The firemen would undoubtedly . . . stop the fire dead in its tracks, but they didn't."

Fanned by strong winds, the conflagration spread and quickly went completely out of control. With his small nephew squirming in his arms, Foy attempted to escape across the Chicago River, but the narrow wooden bridges were jammed with wagons, carriages and trucks and with terrified mobs struggling on foot to reach the other side. Like thousands of others, Foy survived the fire by fleeing to the Lake Michigan shore, and watching in helpless incredulity as the city was consumed, block by block. "Every street I crossed was so thronged with vehicles, all lashing ahead at a trot or a gallop," he remembered, "that I risked both our lives at every crossing." For days, he and the baby caught fitful naps in church pews and ate what food they could find at emergency food centers. Finally he and his nephew were able to connect with the rest of their family. All the Fitzgeralds had survived, but they had lost everything except a sofa and a feather bed.

In his theatrical career, Foy's charm, his easy manner and comedic style—considered "low" but not brash—became very popular and eventually led him from singing and dancing in second- and third-rate Western playhouses and saloons to perform in some of the most prestigious theatres in the country. He was especially loved in Chicago, which considered him one of its sons. "I savored the joy in being able to move thousands to laughter merely by a gesture, a twist of the countenance," he said. "I yearned to feel an audience's pulse, as it were, and when I had them laughing hilariously, to prolong it just by walking across the stage with that slow swagger and sad grin which had become sort of copyrighted gestures of mine."

"Everyone in a Chicago audience would know Eddie Foy," agreed a London newspaper, "an active little man . . . with an impressive face [who] could at once compel a Chicago audience to laughter at the turn of a finger or a wink of the eye." But Eddie Foy was a better actor than he was given credit for. Behind his façade—the smiles, the jokes, pantomime, songs and outrageous costumes—there must have lurked the indelible memory of those terrible days so many years before.

MIXED REVIEWS

"The music . . . is hopelessly common . . ."
—CHICAGO TRIBUNE

"The piece has no consistency as a story . . ."
—INDIANAPOLIS NEWS

"Stupendous is the word that best describes the production . . ."
—PITTSBURGH DISPATCH

AT THE TURN OF THE century, American entertainment was undergoing a significant change, much of it because of new technology, and the public's increasing rejection of Victorian notions of propriety. "Vaudeville," "Mutoscope," "peep shows," "nickelodeons," "ragtime," "jazz," "Pianola," "burlesque," "dime museums," "fantasy" films, "coon shouters" and "race records" had become or were about to become part of the new lexicon of popular American entertainment. The double-sided phonograph record was about to be introduced. Enrico Caruso, John Philip Sousa and Scott Joplin were household names.

In 1903 people were singing "Bill Bailey Won't You Please Come Home." Bert Williams starred in *In Dahomey*, the first full-length musical on Broadway written and produced by black Americans.

The first known silent film version of *Alice in Wonderland* had been released. Col. William "Buffalo Bill" Cody was attracting large crowds throughout Europe in a touring "Wild West" show, the highlight of which was a mock Indian attack on a bright yellow stagecoach whose occupants were saved by the timely arrival of the U.S. Cavalry, guns blazing. That year, over twenty-five percent of the stage productions playing in Chicago, New York and on the road were musicals, and since many of them were billed as musical comedies and several held special appeal for children, the Theatrical Trust decided that *Mr. Bluebeard* would be the perfect vehicle to open its Chicago showplace.

At the time the Iroquois box office began to issue tickets, the city's thirty-six playhouses and music halls were presenting everything from Shakespeare to minstrel shows, from *Coriolanus* to the cakewalk. It was claimed that more musical shows originated in Chicago than in any other city outside New York, largely as the result of the efforts of Joseph Howard, an enterprising and talented producer. The fact that both *The Wizard of Oz* and *Babes in Toyland* premiered in the city helped to bolster that claim.

Mr. Bluebeard and shows like it were something new; they were precursors of the modern American musical, combining comedy, song and dance loosely hung on the semblance of a story line and presented by a huge cast, many of them young women and, before the enactment of child labor laws, children. The forerunner of *Mr. Bluebeard* was not popular Viennese operetta, but British pantomime, a Christmas tradition on the London stage. To Americans who could afford the price of a ticket, a production like this was a welcome novelty. The standard one-dimensional vaudeville bill featuring at best a dozen or so variety acts and rinky-dink bands paled in comparison to casts of hundreds including attractive chorus girls, ballet troupes, ornate stage sets, large orchestras and a plethora of special effects made possible by new technology, much of it through the imaginative use of theatrical illumination. Foy commented, "The incandescent lamp opened up some wonderful possibilities for stage lighting."

These new "musical comedies" were incredibly expensive. The *Bluebeard* advertisements trumpeted a cast of four hundred, but that number included not only actors, dancers and musicians, but also stagehands, carpenters, fly men, electricians, wardrobe mistresses and others. The cost of the second act alone was estimated to be over $38,000, and *Bluebeard* was presented in three acts: four scenes in the first, five in the second, and four again in the third. In the wedding scene alone there were two hundred people on stage, most of them in shining armor. The great finale, "Truth and Light," and the Grande Ballet, "The Light of Asia," were described by Foy as "remarkable." The costumes, scenery and many of the special electrical effects had been leased by Klaw-Erlanger from the Theatre Royal, Drury Lane Company of London with the stipulation that the materials would be for "temporary use," bonded in lieu of payment of import duties, and that everything would be returned at the end of the U.S. run.

Some of the cast members were from England—notably the charming, flirtatious teenagers in the "Pony Ballet" (reflecting the vogue for diminutive chorines), and Nellie Reed, a comely young aerial ballerina. She virtually stopped the show at every performance when she flew from the stage toward the dome of the house over the heads of an astonished audience, showering them with paper carnations as she was drawn along a nearly invisible wire attached to a harness beneath her filmy costume. Her flying act was highlighted in the largest newspaper ads for the show. For all of its spectacular effects, however, *Mr. Bluebeard* was weak in both story line and song.

Opening in Chicago just weeks before the Iroquois unlocked its doors for the first time, Victor Herbert's *Babes in Toyland* was a colorful fantasy filled with appealing tunes, some, like "March of the Toys," still performed today. But that could not be said of *Bluebeard*. While the critics praised Foy and the show's production numbers, the general consensus was that *Bluebeard* was no *Babes*. Its book was a very loose interpretation of the European fairy tale in which Bluebeard, a rich, cunning monster, weds a young girl and forbids her to enter a certain room in his castle. She disobeys him and enters the room, where she discovers the murdered bodies of his former wives. In some versions of the story Bluebeard threatens to kill her also, but in the end her brothers come to her rescue.

The adaptation of the Drury Lane costume fantasy transformed this tale into a bland musical comedy with new characters added in an attempt to suit American tastes. The undistinguished lyrics were by J. Cheever Goodwin with most of the equally undistinguished musical score credited to Frederick Solomon, though typical of the time was the inclusion of music from many songwriters. Perhaps in an effort to punch up the first act with at least a single memorable tune, one number was included by the successful American songwriter Harry Von Tilzer, composer of the 1900 ballad "A Bird in a Gilded Cage," which became the century's first hit phonograph record. Von Tilzer is probably best remembered for "I Want a Girl Just Like the Girl Who Married Dear Old Dad." Von Tilzer was not his real name; in his hometown of Indianapolis he was born plain Harry Gumm; his niece Frances would one day become famous as Judy Garland. When Von Tilzer later established his own company in New York, one of his first song pluggers was Izzy Baline, an immigrant youth from Siberia, who was to achieve immortality as Irving Berlin.

In the *Bluebeard* production, the setting was moved from Europe to the exotic Near East, with the monster wishing to marry a beauty named Fatima. The queen of the fairies saves the heroine from the fate of Bluebeard's seven wives, and Fatima and her true love live happily ever after. Bluebeard was played by Harry Gilfoil, a Chicago vaudeville comedian, as a Technicolor Jekyll and Hyde in blue whiskers and green hair, by turns a cruel villain, a singer of comic nonsense songs and an impressionist who made strange noises with his mouth—a Gilfoil specialty. Stella, queen of the fairies, was the future Ziegfeld girl Annabelle Whitford, who, saddled with a long gown, spent much of her time attempting to thwart Bluebeard's cruelties. The lovely Chicago actress Bonnie Maginn ballet danced onto and off the stage throughout the performance as Ima Dasher, an aptly-named character, a part that required at least twelve costume changes.

Fatima, the young object of Bluebeard's lust, had seven ugly sisters, the ugliest of which was Anne, played by Foy, appearing in "drag," a term coined in the nineteenth century to describe the petticoats worn by actors playing women. Performing in drag had become something of a Foy trademark: he had perfected a movement in which he could twist his torso so that he went one way and the bustle of his dress went flying in another. The sight of Sister Anne apparently coming and going in two directions at once, never failed to draw laughter. Wearing an absurd red wig with a pigtail, Foy also performed a trick number with a baby elephant (played by two actors), in which he taught the little pachyderm to dance, and he appeared with the Pony Ballet girls in a skit based on the nursery rhyme "The Old Woman Who Lived in a Shoe." He also sang two songs specially composed for him: "I Am a Poor, Unhappy Maid," and a Shakespearean burlesque, "Hamlet Was a Melancholy Dane."

In virtually every city he toured, Foy received high praise, as did the show's stunning tableaux effects like "The Valley of the Ferns," "Egypt" (the number featuring the unlucky peacock feathers), "Japan," "India" and "The Parisian Rose Garden." In "The Triumph of the Fan," hundreds of elegantly costumed girls filled the stage, waving huge illuminated ostrich plume fans, as even more girls waving even larger illuminated lace-and-feather fans materialized from the flies and wings, while high above, seven aerialists, each poised on the points of an electrified glass star, twirled the sphere at the touch of their toes.

Despite these spectacular effects, some critics dismissed *Mr. Bluebeard* as claptrap, with lots of glitter and little else. The New York critics had been generally positive at the show's January, 1903, premiere, the *Herald* calling it "gorgeous . . . with spectators cheering every special effect," and the *Post* praising Foy as the star in the "most spectacular pantomime ever produced here." The *Telegram* said *Bluebeard* "showed the latest and the brightest, the costliest and the lightest, the gaudiest and the noisiest, all crowded together in affluent juxtaposition."

When the show began its road tour en route to Chicago, the *Pittsburgh Dispatch* called it "the biggest and most magnificent spectacle ever seen. . . . Stupendous is the word that best describes the production. . . . The audience could not get enough of [Foy]. Arrayed in his skirts as Sister Anne, his ludicrousness was exaggerated." In Indianapolis, the *News* commented, "Looking back on the performance as a whole, one can recall really only a bewildering mass of beautifully blended color; unique and gorgeous costumes, an endless array of sparkling lights, flashing jewels, pretty girls, handsome scenery, merry twinkling feet in a mass of dancing, and over it all a wealth of music, none of it startlingly original, perhaps, but all tuneful, pretty and fitting. . . . There is practically no story. . . . the well-known fairy-tale is only hinted at and the plot is the [thinnest] thread on which a spectacular entertainment could be hung. . . . In short, the piece has no consistency as a story, it is merely a great big spectacular show—a thing of beauty, and it does not pretend to be anything else."

When *Bluebeard* finally made its long-delayed Chicago opening, some of the city's papers expressed disappointment at the least. The *Evening Post* blamed the hated Abe Erlanger for what the critic considered a miserable book. "Oh, Abraham!" the review began, "Mr. Erlanger is unquestionably responsible for the book. No other genius could have written it. Had it not been for the many wonders to be studied in the new [Iroquois], strong men would have wept at his libretto. It is to cry. Nothing sadder than the dialogue of this affair has been encountered in the realm of burlesque for long years." And though the critic liked the quick costume changes ("One second the chorus is on in blue; the next the entire band appears in red"), he reserved his most cutting remarks for the local actress, Bonnie Maginn, the show's lead dancer, elsewhere hailed as a dainty and dashing soubrette who came "pretty near being the whole show." "Bonnie Maginn is no more," sneered the *Post*. "She of the nimble toe has grown stout. Alas, too true! The result is more or less deplorable."

The *Chicago American* was no less disdainful: "The principals . . . were principals in name only. . . . There was so much chorus and so little principal that the main impression the . . . audience carried away was that *Mr. Bluebeard* could have gone along fairly well even if Mr. Foy had stayed at home and if all the other principals had been indisposed."

Though the *Tribune* praised the theatre, its critic W. L. Hubbard disliked the play: "Of story there is little or none [and] the music of the piece is hopelessly common, save bits here and there which are filched from the classics. . . ." The *Journal* critic was more positive, citing the "striking combinations of costumes, scenery, masses of attractive choruses and elaborate stage pictures, following one after one," paying homage to Foy and to "two or three catchy songs . . . which will probably be heard on the streets soon." One of the most melodious was "Songbirds of Melody Lane." The other was a romantic song and dance put on shortly after the start of Act Two, "Let Us Swear It By the Pale Moonlight," words by Matt Woodward, music by Ben Jerome, performed by the show's dashing double octet.

But for those who held tickets for the holiday matinee, it did not matter what the Chicago critics wrote or whether the tunes failed to arouse the public's enthusiasm in the five weeks *Mr. Bluebeard* had played. There was still a sense of excited anticipation. Many who had received clothing, watches or jewelry for Christmas looked forward to showing off these gifts for the first time in the new theatre. Foy's reputation alone was enough to guarantee a cheerful and even hilarious afternoon.

THE DAY: DECEMBER 30

"We're not going . . ."—Dorsha Hayes

WEDNESDAY, DECEMBER 30, dawned clear and very cold. There was a hint of snow in the air and a thin mist of coal smoke hung over Chicago like a gray shroud from more than one million pot-bellied stoves, ovens, fireplaces and anything else not running on gas. The temperature was due to drop later in the day, making it particularly unpleasant for pedestrians because of the continuing livery drivers' strike.

Rural electrification was thirty years in the future for most of the country, and in Galesburg, Illinois, a small town about one hundred miles west of Chicago, gas lamps flickered in the home of Dorsha Hayes. Over their lamplit breakfast, the little girl and her older brother could talk of nothing but the day they were going to spend in the city beginning with the long train ride, then a visit to the fascinating department stores in the Loop, lunch with their father and mother and the thrilling culmination of the day: seeing *Mr. Bluebeard* in the remarkable new Iroquois Theatre. It would be the first theatre experience for Dorsha, the baby of the family.

Pretty fourteen-year-old Caroline Ludwig of Chicago obviously hadn't paid any attention to the *Tribune*'s November fashion piece advising women never to wear wool in the winter because "excessive bundling up" was the cause of most seasonal illness. Caroline dressed that day in woolen underwear, black woolen stockings, a flannel petticoat with two tucks and lace at the bottom, a pink-and-white striped skirt with five tucks, a white shirt with an embroidered ruffle, a brown accordion dress with matching hat and a long red woolen coat. She was going to the Iroquois with her parents and her eighteen-year-old sister Eugenie. Her father Harry Ludwig, manager of the Hallwood Cash Register Company, located relatively near the theatre, had decided to take the day off to share this family treat.

But for most people, Wednesday, December 30, was an ordinary workday. The press of business did not allow Arthur Hull to attend the performance that afternoon, but he had arranged a surprise for his children. His wife Marianne, accompanied by the family maid, Mary Forbes, would take their twelve-year-old daughter, Helen, to the Iroquois, along with their two recently adopted sons, Donald, eight, and Dwight, six.

It was much the same for John R. Thompson. The Chicago telephone directory listed him simply as "grocer," with an office and commissary at 38 State Street. But that was something of an understatement. Thompson was the prosperous owner of eight eponymous restaurants, strategically positioned throughout the downtown area on major streets: Madison, Dearborn, Adams, Jackson, Van Buren and State. Thompson was most proud of his restaurant on Randolph Street next door to the new theatre, just steps away from its imposing entrance. To Thompson, it was a case of being in the right place at the right time because that location had the potential for rich profits.

Thompson planned to work that day while his wife remained at home with the maid and their youngest child to prepare a big family dinner, but he had ordered matinee tickets in advance for the rest of his family. The party included his eight-year-old daughter Ruthie and her nine-year-old brother John, Jr., their aunts Dottie and Alice, and, wonder of wonders, his wife's eighty-year-old father, George Holloway, who had come from Georgetown, Illinois, to spend the holidays with the family. Mr. Holloway, a devout Quaker, had never before been in a theatre which he genuinely believed was the province of the Devil. Ruthie and John had never been to a theatre either, but were excited about going, and, together with their mother and aunts, had begged their grandfather to come along. Against his better judgment, he had agreed.

Business executive Charles Plamondon's attractive debutante daughter Charlotte was there with a group of her friends in what they were calling a "box party." Like Charlotte Plamondon, seven-year-old Margaret Revell, the daughter of housewares merchant Alexander Revell, was also excited about going to the Iroquois, accompanied by her friend Elizabeth Harris. The two little girls were chaperoned by the Revell maid.

Like Dorsha Hayes, hundreds of children were up early that day, bathed and dressed, excited because many of them had never been to a theatre before. Some of the older teenagers and adults planned an early lunch so that even with the livery drivers' strike, they would have plenty of time to settle in their seats for the two o'clock curtain.

In his comfortable rooms below the mansard roof of the Sherman House, Eddie Foy may have been slightly annoyed. He had wanted his wife and children to come to the matinee, but the box office had regretfully informed him that would be impossible because of the large number of ticket holders and those who would wait until the last minute to purchase the few remaining seats or decide to stand at the back of the house. The comedian decided that even if the entire Foy clan could not come, he would bring along six-year-old Bryan, his oldest son, and find the boy a seat somewhere, perhaps on a far side of the orchestra section.

Foy lunched with his family in their suite, and prepared to leave for the theatre in enough time to get Bryan settled before he had to start applying his makeup, getting into his costume and adjusting his wig.

Charles Collins had reported in at his normal hour that morning and was handling routine rewrite chores when he was summoned by his edgy editor, Al Bergener. It looked like a slow news day and Bergener said that he was interested in a piece on the flourishing practice of ticket scalping, and in particular, what, if anything, the management of Chicago's newest theatre was doing about it. Powers and Davis owned other, older playhouses in the city, but the new Iroquois would probably command the most interest among readers. And Collins, who after all had attended the opening night less than six weeks earlier, was told to try and set up an interview with one or both of the owners that afternoon. After a couple of phone calls it was confirmed that Powers was holding a box party for some friends that day, but would be happy to break away for a few moments to meet the reporter in the theatre lobby. Collins doubted that Powers would be forthcoming on the touchy issue of scalping, but he hoped for some kind of statement, not only because his editor wanted one, but because there was little going on that was newsworthy that day, and he did not want to spend the rest of the frigid afternoon making dull rounds in the Loop. Mayor Harrison was out of town for the holidays, negotiations with the livery drivers were going nowhere and both the fire and the police chiefs were involved in closed-door departmental disciplinary hearings.

♣

The Iroquois was so close to his hotel that Eddie Foy could walk there in under three minutes. With a brisk wind snapping off the lake, Foy thought the temperature must be hovering around zero. He and Bryan entered the theatre less than an hour before curtain time. Just before making the ninety-degree turn at the corner of Randolph and Dearborn, Foy must have noticed the crowd beginning to swell in front of the theatre but he had no idea that he would be performing that afternoon to one of the largest audiences of women and children in his career.

The seating capacity of the Iroquois was 1,602, with approximately 700 in the expensive "parquet," the seats down in front that looked over the orchestra pit; more than 400 in the first balcony or "dress circle," and probably just under 500 in the steeply angled upper gallery. There were four expensive lower boxes, each seating six people, and two upper boxes designed to hold four persons each, but the owners had managed to crowd eight chairs into each box.

Added to those who had purchased tickets in advance were the usual late arrivals. Some came in to buy tickets for available standing room; others had guest passes because of special connections: they were friends of the management and of actors in other productions in the city; some were off-duty employees from neighboring theatres or special VIPs like city inspectors who had done favors for Davis and Powers. Estimates varied, but because the managers wanted to make up for the earlier anemic ticket sales, there may have been considerably more than 200 standees that afternoon.

The Wednesday "bargain" matinee tickets ranged from thirty-five cents for general admission or "standing room," high up behind the last rows of the cantilevered balcony and gallery, to one dollar or more for orchestra seats. The box office counted up $1,761.50 in receipts. By curtain time approximately 1,840 or more people, most of them women and children, packed the house, far beyond its stated capacity. While most of them were Chicagoans, some theatregoers had come from as far away as New York and California and at least one had come from South America. Though it was an afternoon performance, many were dressed as if they were attending an evening soiree.

Lula Greenwald, thirty-two, of Chicago, surely attracted attention as she made her way down the center aisle with her ten-year-old son Leroy. It was not so much the striking peacock blue shirtwaist and black woolen skirt she wore, but her impressive jewelry. On her left hand, Mrs. Greenwald wore a diamond solitaire ring with her gold wedding band, on her right hand another large ring containing three opals surrounded by thirty emeralds and diamonds and on her bosom a stunning sunburst pin with an amethyst stone encircled by diamonds and pearls. She carried a chic steel beaded chatelaine handbag. Leroy sported a double-breasted blue serge coat and matching knickers, black stockings, a shirt with a stiff collar and a pearl stickpin.

As might be expected, there were many University of Chicago students in the audience. Walter Zeisler, considered one of the school's brightest students, Fred Leaton and the Reverend Henry Richardson all studied at the Hyde Park campus, while Daisy Livingston, Agnes Chapin and Gertrude Falkenstein were student instructors at the College for Teachers. Clyde Blair, the ruggedly handsome captain of the university's track team, was

on a double date with a teammate, Victor Rice and their girl-
friends, Marjorie Mason and Anne Hough. They had seventh-
row balcony seats, not far from an Ohio Wesleyan student from
Buenos Aires, William McLaughlin, who was in town to attend
a friend's wedding. A jeweled Delta Tau Delta fraternity pin
glistened in his jacket lapel. McLaughlin was the nephew of the
president of Chicago's Armour Institute of Technology.

Barbara Reynolds of Chicago had had misgivings about
going to the theatre that day, but she was there with her daughter, her sister and her sister's two sons. As she went to take her
seat, Mrs. Reynolds looked around and, for no apparent reason, suddenly blurted to her startled sister, "What a death trap!"

Myron Decker too felt uncomfortable. The prosperous
sixty-five-year-old Chicago real estate broker was with his wife
and thirty-three-year-old daughter Mayme, and he was probably doing them a favor by being there, because he had a particular horror of fire and seldom attended the theatre. But being in the Iroquois was "the thrill of a lifetime" for eleven-
year-old Harriet Bray, who had come from Indiana to see the
show. Holding her father's hand, the little girl marched happily down the aisle.

Attending the theatre was a time-honored Christmas tradition for the family of Henry Van Ingen, a wealthy Kenosha real
estate investor. Van Ingen was at the Iroquois with his wife Emma
and their five children: Grace, twenty-three; Edward, nineteen;
Jack, eighteen; Margaret, fourteen, and Elizabeth, nine. Their
eldest son, twenty-five-year-old Schuyler, had to work that afternoon, but he promised to join the family for dinner at the
Wellington Hotel after the show. The Van Ingens were prominent in Chicago and Kenosha social circles, and also in Newport, Rhode Island, where Emma Van Ingen's brother was commander of the Newport Naval Reserve.

Also from Kenosha were the Cooper brothers, Willis and Charles. Willis, active in local politics and rumored to be a millionaire, was general manager of the largest stocking manufacturing plant in the world, the Chicago-Kenosha Hosiery Company. His younger brother Charles was the firm's manager and general salesman, who in that era of continual labor unrest, had begun a profit-sharing plan for employees and was, not surprisingly, extremely popular with the rank and file. Together with a third brother, the Coopers had also founded a local undergarment factory, which would evolve into Jockey International.

Because of the Christmas break, there were an unusually large number of Chicago public schoolteachers and even some principals in attendance from all parts of the city, surrounded by hundreds of restless, excited grade- and high school students. To the teachers, the theatre must have seemed like a huge, ornate—and very noisy—classroom.

Edith Mizen, a junior at Englewood High School, was present, much against the wishes of her parents, who, believing that the theatre was no place for proper young ladies, strongly objected to her attending *Bluebeard*. But the young woman was insistent, her parents finally gave in, and Edith was seated among a group of her Theta Pi Zeta Club pals in the sixth row of the dress circle.

Up near the theatre's dome, behind the last row of the gallery seats, stood seventy-year-old D. W. Dimmick, from Apple River, Illinois, his face almost hidden behind an impressive gray beard. He had come to Chicago, he said, "to see the sights." Along with three others in his party, Mr. Dimmick was determined to stand through all three acts.

If anyone in the crowd came close to having celebrity status, it had to be Charlie Dexter, a professional baseball player who had just quit the Boston Red Sox. Two months earlier,

Dexter had taken part in the first World Series, when Boston defeated the Pittsburgh Pirates, five games to three. Dexter was not considered much of a hitter but was called "the ultimate utility man" because he played a significant number of games during the regular season at virtually every infield and outfield position.

Dexter was sitting in a box with a friend and former athlete, Frank Houseman, who may have had one of the shortest careers in the Major Leagues. The good-natured Houseman had pitched one game for Baltimore in 1886, lost it and permanently hung up his spikes, deciding that his real calling was running a tavern.

It was getting close to curtain time. With so many children in the audience, a happy, excited buzz filled the Iroquois. But everyone who had bought tickets was not there. On the train approaching Chicago from Galesburg, Dorsha Hayes's mother was having serious second thoughts about attending the performance. As the flat Illinois landscape rushed past their window, her increasing nervousness soon became apparent to her son, who asked her repeatedly, "We are going, aren't we?" Thinking that she might be worrying that his kid sister would make a disturbance in the theatre, he assured his mother that he'd see that Dorsha behaved herself.

As they drew closer to the Chicago terminal, Mrs. Hayes experienced something odd, "a heavy feeling . . . a terrible despondency . . . and out of it in sharp recurring flashes, the quickening sense of alarm—don't go." She couldn't put her finger on what it was exactly. At noon over lunch in a downtown restaurant, when her husband, apologizing for not having gotten main floor seats, reached into his jacket pocket and produced four tickets for the balcony, Mrs. Hayes suddenly made a decision.

"We're not going," she announced to her startled family. "We can't, we mustn't, not this time." She refused to change her mind, and the two confused and dejected children wandered around the Loop that wintry afternoon with their parents, ending up in Marshall Field's at just about the time the two o'clock curtain was going up. The Hayes children, not to mention Mr. Hayes, did not think that the toy department, impressive as it was, made up for missing *Mr. Bluebeard*.

The Iroquois was so crowded that Eddie Foy could not find a seat for his son, and finally was forced to park the child on a stool offstage in the wings, not far from the switchboard, a place the boy really enjoyed because of all the color and behind-the-scenes activity and excitement. Bryan loved the theatre. For him it would be another afternoon of fun and adventure.

For ten-year-old Warren Toole, it would be another afternoon of gloom and disappointment. The son of former Montana governor Joseph K. Toole, Warren and his family were visiting Chicago, probably to cheer Warren up over the holiday. The boy had been the victim of an unusual string of bizarre accidents. Four months earlier, disregarding his parents' warnings, he was playing with a gun when it accidentally discharged, seriously wounding him. Before he had fully recovered, he fell from a cart and fractured his arm. Then, just before Christmas, his pet dog, for no apparent reason, had leaped at his face and bitten him between the eyes. He could have lost his sight.

Now Warren was holed up in the family's rooms in the downtown Auditorium Hotel with his brother, bored stiff and wondering how he could entertain himself. Earlier that day he had asked his nurse to take him to see *Mr. Bluebeard*. She, in turn, asked his father, and the former governor agreed that Warren and his brother could attend the performance, but only if their mother returned in time from a shopping expedition. With the post-Christmas crowds in the streets and the livery strike mess,

Mrs. Toole came back to the hotel long after the matinee had begun. The lad was crushed.

It had to be another depressing day for him. He felt very sorry for himself. But that evening at bedtime as he knelt to say his prayers, Warren Toole would thank God for saving his life.

Charles Collins's press card got him into the theatre's ornate lobby. As arranged, the Iroquois co-owner Harry Powers came out to meet him, to discuss the subject of ticket scalping. "He was very ingratiating," Collins recalled. "Powers was Irish but had English mannerisms." As expected, the brief interview led nowhere. "He lied to me," Collins said. "He didn't tell me anything about ticket speculators except to say they didn't bother him. He was hand-in-glove with them all the time, I knew that." The young reporter had no story. Annoyed, he left the theatre to fulfill what he considered other petty assignments, including a visit to a lawyer's office and then to a presentation by a stock company press agent at a competitive newspaper, the *Inter-Ocean*.

Powers returned to the guests in his box party. The first act was half over. It was approximately 2:30 p.m.

{8}

ENGINE 13

"Are All Our Theaters Safe?"
—THEATER MAGAZINE, *January 1904*

IN THE FALL OF 1903 the Edison Manufacturing Company was prominently promoting *The Great Train Robbery*, which in 740 feet of celluloid was the first motion picture to tell a complete story. A lesser known Edison film exhibited that same year was *The Life of an American Fireman*. Ten minutes long and in less than a dozen shots, it told the story of the rescue of a mother and child from a burning house. It also showed how a firehouse operated: the men sliding down poles at the sound of an alarm, hurriedly donning coats and leather helmets, hitching up their horses and racing to the scene, smoke belching from the rolling steam pumper. As the nascent motion picture industry quickly discovered, fire fighting was a very popular film subject. Distributors learned that the exploits of these heroic men could always be expected to draw large audiences wherever they were shown.

Currier & Ives had discovered the public's fascination with firefighting decades earlier. The famous printmakers sold thousands of colored lithographs of firemen rescuing people or rushing to conflagrations. For years, these were among its best-selling prints. By the turn of the century, the covers of children's magazines, and even popular sheet music, sometimes featured illustrations of the exploits of daring firemen.

On the afternoon of December 30, at about the time Foy was in his dressing room starting to apply makeup for the two o'clock curtain and Charles Collins was heading for the theatre district, a recognized hero of the Great Chicago Fire sat in his City Hall office with some top aides, conducting a disciplinary hearing against six firemen who had been accused of publicly denigrating their chief. William Henry Musham, a balding man of sixty-five with a great walrus mustache and pride to match, would not tolerate that kind of behavior. A native Chicagoan, the son of a Scottish sailor, Musham was a muscular man of medium height and trim build. He had distinguished himself since he joined the city's then-volunteer fire department in 1855 and had once come close to death when a brick wall collapsed on him, killing a companion.

During the Great Fire, he was foreman of the first unit to arrive, working without a break from 9:30 in the evening to three o'clock the following afternoon, when he was ordered home for a few hours' rest. Six and a half hours later, with the fire still roaring out of control and his mother dying from injuries received in the blaze, he and his company went back again to battle the flames until it became obvious that the conflagration would have to burn itself out. Over the years since then, he had received a series of promotions, steadily working his way through the ranks, and eventually becoming Chicago's fire marshal.

In 1903 Musham was in charge of 1,273 officers and men in 123 companies scattered around the growing metropolis. He was a proud officer with a serious flaw. He was a poor manager of men, a disappointment to those who had once expected great things of him. "As a rank and filer," it was said, "he was admired, but as department head he became aloof and detached, and though he was considered a man of undoubted efficiency and thoroughness . . . he lacked the executive ability and tact to fill the position of fire marshal with equal success." By 1903 he had lost much of his hard-won popularity.

♦

Though the Age of the Automobile had arrived—Henry Ford had started his own business that year—and mechanized fire engines were just beginning to appear in some cities, they were not only expensive but subject to break down at inopportune times in those early years of the new century. Musham's army of firefighters still depended on horse-drawn vehicles propelled by powerful animals like Percherons, a fast-trotting draft horse perhaps fifteen hands high, the cream of the breeding farms.

Chicago had 2,790 miles of streets, of which 1,206 were paved with everything from cedar block and crushed stone to brick, granite and asphalt. Asphalt was the smoothest surface, but it provided poor footing for horses in the icy winter months. It was not so much the streets that presented a problem, however, as the traffic. There were no lane markers or signal lights, and wagons, horse carts and cable cars could go no faster than ten miles an hour. Average traffic speeds were generally not much faster than a brisk walk, particularly in the Loop where there seemed to be few rules for curbside parking. Even the electric streetcars, light carriages and the few automobiles to be seen on those congested streets could barely go even five miles an hour.

Urban working horses had a hard life, often putting in the same sixty-hour week as their owners and more than likely spending their nights in filthy stables. But things were different in the Chicago Fire Department. The big horses were groomed daily, exercised, well-fed, trained and housed in stables regularly mucked out and washed down. Within the department ranks, there was a deep and abiding affection for the powerful animals.

Engine Company 13, located at 209 North Dearborn Street, was a typical station house. Within its brick walls the horses, their names engraved or painted above their stalls, were stabled in the ground floor rear, which meant that there was no room for a kitchen. The men who made up the company's single platoon ate at nearby cafes. Over the stalls, a long flight of steps led to a second floor loft where heavy hay bales and bags of oats were winched up and swung into the building on a pivoting boom. Adjoining the loft were showers and lavatories, a polished dark wooden equipment locker for each man, and the sleeping quarters—nothing more than one large Spartan room furnished only with cots and bare mattresses, each man responsible for his own bedding. Captain "Paddy" Jennings had his private quarters and lavatory in the front. Jack Hannon, First Battalion Chief, had quarters on the building's third floor. All activity was focused below at the front of the building on the apparatus floor, forward of the horse stalls. The watch officer's desk and telegraph alarm system were along one wall, with additional equipment lockers and a two-story, chimney-like closet (for drying out fully extended hoses), on the opposite side.

Company 13's prized piece of equipment was an ornately red-and-gold-painted, highly polished five-ton LaFrance "Metropolitan" steam pumper, standing behind a relatively light, red wooden hose wagon. The $6,000 steamers were massive machines mounted on spoked iron wheels and crude suspension systems. The technology used for keeping the pumper ready for action was relatively simple. Jutting from the engine's rear were metal slip connectors, looking like flattened tailpipes, attached by a long rubber hose to a hot water heater in the basement or the rear of the building. The heater, which was kept burning around the clock, provided a steady stream of hot water, constantly maintained at or just below the boiling point of 212 degrees Fahrenheit, so that by the time the engine rolled from the station house, a head of steam was building rapidly inside its huge boiler.

When the gong over the watch desk clanged out a street alarm box number, chain barriers across the horse stalls automatically dropped and the huge dapple-and-steel-gray geldings, usually without a verbal command, were trained to trot to the front of the building and then back into their assigned positions in front of the engine and hose wagon, each animal standing just below a harness with an open collar suspended by leather straps hanging from the ceiling. As the half-dressed platoon, typically consisting of the captain, a lieutenant, one engineer and five "pipe" or hose men, came sliding down wood or brass polls from their sleeping quarters, the company's two drivers would yank on ropes and quick-hitch harnesses would drop from the ceiling onto the backs of the horses and automatically snap into place through an elaborate system of counterweights. Because of its important Loop location near City Hall, Engine 13's horses were probably kept in harness even when they were stabled.

When an alarm sounded, the engine driver, John Murphy, who had been chosen not only for his ability to control the animals but also for his knowledge of every street and alley in the sector, would quickly climb and strap himself into the "box," a high, precariously positioned leather seat above the front wheels. At the same time, Mathias Blaney, 13's engineer and the man expected to know the dimensions of every water main in his zone, would fire the engine's furnace with wood shavings or kerosene-soaked cotton. Standing on the fuel box at the rear of the vehicle, he or another firemen—there was room only for two on the small metal perch—would grab a brass rail with one hand while feeding kindling or coal into the furnace to bring steam pressure rapidly up to optimal pumping capacity, which might be one thousand gallons of water a minute.

As the big front doors swung open, the hose wagon carrying the pipe men and a "hydrant man" armed with a heavy wrench, would be first out of the station house. As the steamer pulled away, the coupling connecting the boiler to the hot water system would snap apart and a valve would automatically cap off the flow of hot water. Some firemen were convinced that their beloved horses could recognize alarm box numbers with each strike of the gong, quickly move forward to their assigned places and start whinnying to be let out. They needed little encouragement from the drivers and when the station house doors opened, the horses would charge out, and the hose wagon with the full company on board would race through the streets with its accompanying engine, bells and steam whistles clearing the way. Hook and ladder companies would be on their way from other fire stations. In rushing to the scene of a blaze, standard operating procedure in the Chicago Fire Department was to have the horses run at a full gallop for the first mile, then trot for the remainder of the distance to conserve their strength. Various fire departments specified 1,100-pound horses to pull hose wagon teams, 1,400- pound horses for the steam engines and 1,700-pound animals for hook and ladder trucks. The animals ran hard and fast and it was unquestionably true that a horse racing to a fire, pulling a heavy hook and ladder truck, once threw a shoe with such force that it smashed through a third story window.

For all the excitement and adventure portrayed in the popular pulp magazines of the time, a fireman's life was sometimes dull but always hard and dangerous, not just because of the inherent perils of the job but because men could accidentally be thrown from vehicles or crushed beneath the wheels of the lumbering, awkward equipment. Firefighters today are forbidden to ride on the backs or sides of trucks for that reason.

Each member of Company 13 was drilled in his assignment. When approaching a fire, the hydrant man would often leap from the moving hose wagon holding the end of an uncoiling pipe, sprint ahead and, with his wrench, uncap the nearest hydrant and wrap the end of the hose around it, even as the reins were being pulled to bring the horses to a complete stop. The drivers would quickly unhitch the two- or three-horse teams, cover them with blankets and lead them a safe distance away from the action.

While Engineer Blaney monitored his pressure gauges on the boiler and kept the pumps operating and the fire stoked— he would use the engine's powerful steam whistle to signal if he needed a fresh supply of coal—Captain Jennings and his lieutenant would quickly calculate the number of hose lengths needed and begin issuing orders to the pipe men through speaking trumpets as the company swung into action.

Battalion Chief Hannon and his driver, Fireman First Class Michael Corrigan, would arrive at the scene independently in the chief's buggy, and it was not uncommon to have extra horses strategically positioned at different station houses throughout the city so that winded animals could be instantly switched, pony express style, and fresh horses quickly harnessed to the light buggies, to speed the chief to the scene.

Commonly, three engines and two hook and ladder companies were designated to respond to a first alarm, and the nearest company was expected to be the first to "push out" from its station house and to reach the scene. In written reports to their superior officers, company captains and lieutenants had to state the order of their arrival and which unit came first to fight the blaze or conduct rescues. Consequently, there was considerable competition among the companies to be first on the scene.

Although it depended on horses, the Chicago Fire Department did have a complicated electro-mechanical street alarm system, consisting of cast iron boxes with miniature roofs, called "cottage style" sector alarms, mounted on poles or pedestals. To prevent false alarms, the boxes were locked, and only firemen, police, night watchmen or businessmen with nearby property had access to them. (Chicago police operated their own independent street box telephones.) After a box was unlocked, an inside lever on a metal panel bearing the instructions, "Pull Hook Down Once And Let Go," activated the alarm. Behind the lever, a closed electrical circuit began cranking a system of spring-loaded, clock-like gears, which included a code wheel the size of a half dollar with raised triangular teeth.

The code wheel corresponded to the number on the box and electronically the number would be tapped out to the fire department's central station at City Hall. There an operator would quickly confirm that the box number was correct and then put the alarm on a "sender" which would transmit signals identifying the box number's location to the appropriate station house, where the information would come in both on a ticker tape with punched holes representing the digits, and by the repeated tapping of gongs at the watch desk. The whole process might take a little more than ninety seconds from the time the ticker started or the first gong sounded to the moment the men and equipment flew out the door.

In between fire runs, there were endless monotonous chores. The men would water, feed and exercise the horses, scrub down the engine and shine its hardware, stretch out the lines to dry in the hose chimney, take part in drills, tidy personal gear, repair broken equipment, feed coal to the basement hot water heater and spruce up the apparatus floor, by, among other things, polishing the large brass gongs near the watch desk. The company was mainly confined to the station house where alcohol and card games were banned. The men might grab a quick meal nearby, treat the horses to apples and sugar cubes, and spend time taking naps, gossiping and reading their stock of books, papers and magazines. Jack London's *The Call of the Wild* was the popular novel of the moment. But the men of Engine 13, particularly officers Hannon and Jennings, might have been particularly interested in a magazine that had gone on sale in New York City that same morning. Since it was a theatrical trade publication, it was not likely to make their reading list. In the January 1904 number of *Theater Magazine* was an article warning that some playhouses were "firetraps, where, in case of fire or panic, a terrible catastrophe could result." The title of the article was "Are All Our Theaters Safe?"

"PALE MOONLIGHT"

"Fate had brought them together in a fool's Paradise."
—*Eddie Foy*

IF THERE WAS JOYOUS excitement in the Iroquois' noisy auditorium that afternoon, that feeling did not seem to extend behind the curtain. Among some of the stage crew and cast members there was a discernible edginess that had begun earlier in the week with arguments and even some scuffling among hotheads in the group. In the thirty-seven days since the show had opened, most of the cast and crew had gotten along well with one another. For a bit of diversion from dreary hotel rooms or boarding houses, cast members in particular had plenty of backstage gossip to share, some of it centering on the men who owned the show. The prominent New York theatrical producer, Daniel Frohman, had married one of his leading ladies, Margaret Illington, who was working in a Klaw-Erlanger production. With their usual insensitivity, Klaw and Erlanger held Illington to the letter of her contract, meaning that she had to work to the end of the show's scheduled run with no breaks allowed. Frohman sadly told reporters, "We will have to postpone any honeymoon trip we may wish to indulge in."

Another well-known Broadway figure was not so acquies-
cent. The powerful impresario David Belasco openly broke with
the Syndicate, saying he "had thrown down the gauntlet" by
refusing to present his show *Zaza* at the Harlem Opera House
controlled by Klaw and Erlanger. Instead of agreeing to their
demands, Belasco openly defied the Trust by announcing that
he would stage *Zaza* at Weber and Fields' independently operated West End Theatre. "Belasco Declares War," shouted one
headline. A few weeks later, Belasco was back in the news when
he filed suit against Klaw and Erlanger, demanding dissolution
of their partnership in the play *The Auctioneer*, starring the
prominent actor David Warfield.

Backstage gossip at the Iroquois might also have included
talk about the heartwarming action of the entire company of
Babes in Toyland, who had adopted a week-old infant found
abandoned one night in a box seat at New York's Majestic Theatre. The child was being cared for at Bellevue Hospital, and
the cast and crew had pledged that they would donate a portion of their salaries to the foundling's support. Newsmen commented that it was "great good luck" for an infant to be born,
or found abandoned, in a theatre, citing an incident the previous spring when a baby was born in New York's Casino Theatre, which, at the time, was not doing much business. After the
birth announcement, the theatre apparently could not handle
the huge crowds that materialized night after night.

Unfortunately, huge crowds had not materialized for *Mr.
Bluebeard* and the backstage buzz at the Iroquois that Wednesday was laced with nervous tension. Despite the *New York
Clipper*'s early reports of "good business," the cast was well
aware that Chicago attendance was below expectations. Then
on December 26, the *Clipper* confirmed their worst fears, reporting a rumor that Klaw and Erlanger would disband *Bluebeard* at the end of the Chicago run in early January and re-

place it with *Ben Hur*. Coming at the height of the holiday season, the news could not have been worse, especially for the younger cast members, including the British girls. If the report was true, they faced the prospect in the New Year of being stranded far from home with no work in sight. "We drew big crowds all through Christmas week," said Foy, "and [that] Wednesday afternoon the house was packed and many were standing. . . . I was struck by the fact that I had never seen so many women and children. Even the gallery was full."

What Foy probably couldn't see beyond the blazing lights was that the house was not merely "full," it was bursting. Not only were people standing four deep in the designated areas behind the last rows of seats but some, contrary to regulations, were sitting in the aisles and standing along the walls on both sides of the auditorium. One usher estimated that there were fully five hundred more spectators than the theatre capacity permitted.

Throughout the audience, anticipation mounted as the house lights slowly dimmed for Act One. In accordance with Powers' and Davis' standard operating procedure, most of the doors leading from the balcony and gallery had been locked or bolted by young ushers to keep out gate crashers and prevent those sitting or standing in the upper tiers from sneaking down under cover of darkness to the more expensive seats, though it was obvious there were no empty seats anywhere. Some of the door bolts, manufactured in Europe, were unfamiliar to Americans. Also, virtually all of the Iroquois' doors were designed to open in, toward the audience, and not out, toward the streets.

As the twenty-six-piece orchestra began the show's opening number, the curtain rose to the top of the proscenium arch revealing the colorful scene of a crowded marketplace on a quay near Baghdad, where a large chorus performed "Come Buy Our Luscious Fruits." Other songs followed, climaxing in the grand entrance of the grotesque villain and his retinue, singing "A Most Unpopular Potentate."

For those who might have had trouble following the thin story line, the playbill offered a scene-by-scene synopsis sandwiched between pages of advertisements promoting everything from five-cent Cremo Cigars to the Iroquois Buffet a few doors away in the Delaware Building.

The plot in Act One is simple. Mustapha schemes to separate Selim from the beautiful Fatima and sell her to Bluebeard, who arrives in the marketplace to purchase slaves. Sister Anne, played by Foy, falls in love with a roguish gent named Irish Patshaw. The scene ends with Bluebeard seizing Fatima and spiriting her away on board his yacht. The act concludes with the first of the show's spectacular tableaux, "Ballet of the Ferns" and "Procession and Weaving of the Magic Fan," a huge production number with the stage overflowing with young women and children in gossamer fairy costumes. It was all fantasy and magic, and, judging by the audience's reaction, Act One was a great success.

During the first intermission, those in the expensive orchestra section and the boxes retired to the smoking room or went to freshen up, relax on the plush settees or mingle in the promenade, while those in the balcony and gallery behind the locked and bolted doors, flowed through the upstairs promenade, restrooms and antechambers.

By 3:15, the second act of *Mr. Bluebeard* was well under way. During one of the early scenes, possibly while Foy was on stage doing his turn with the baby elephant, Nellie Reed of the aerial ballet was hooked to the thin trolley wire that would send her high over the audience in "The Triumph of the Fan." The glittering sequence was made all the more spectacular through the

imaginative use of hundreds of colored lights, a brilliant display of illumination unlike anything the audience had ever seen before. Some of the bulbs were concealed inside two narrow concave metal reflectors, twenty feet long and five inches wide, one on each side of the stage. Called "front lighting," each reflector was mounted on vertical hinges and, if unneeded, was supposed to be pivoted by stagehands using pikes, and to disappear into niches on the stage side of the proscenium arch. For the "Moonlight" number that was about to start, the brilliant lights were not needed, but a member of the stage crew, for some reason, had neglected to completely retract the "right stage" reflector, leaving it slightly extended, like the tip of a curved index finger, jutting a few inches beyond the inside edge of the huge arch, in the path of the curtains. In the usual business of moving scenery, adjusting lights, clewing lines attached to battens that supported the backdrops, manhandling snatch blocks and hundreds of other details, no one caught this error.

The man at the switchboard used a dimmer switch to reduce all lights except the one used for the "Pale Moonlight" number, featuring the show's double octet in a romantic song-and-dance routine performed in front of a painted floral backdrop of Bluebeard's castle garden. The house lights were now fully extinguished, and the stage was bathed in a soft blue glow from one of the backstage carbon arc lamps, a powerful spotlight that had for its source an electric current arcing between two carbon rods. The spot was positioned on a narrow metal light bridge about fifteen feet above the stage and the marble switchboard and within a foot or so of the theatre's drop curtains and a "tormentor," a fixed curtain that prevented the audience from seeing into the wings.

Young William McMullen, an assistant electrician in charge of the spotlight, had to be careful with that heavy piece of bulky equipment. With its large metal hood and reflector, mounted on a high pedestal, the spot, sometimes mistakenly called a "calcium light," could generate temperatures as high as 4000 degrees Fahrenheit. There were seven other spots located backstage, but they were switched off and only McMullen's was being used to create the dreamy moonlight quality for the scene.

Herbert Dillea, the company's musical director, raised his violin bow to begin one of the show's most romantic numbers. On the downbeat, the opening strains, *allegro moderato*, of "Let Us Swear it By the Pale Moonlight" filled the hushed theatre. Bluebeard's eight wives, pretty young chorines with shoulder-length hair, wearing long gowns and broad-brimmed, feathered hats, began to enter from the wings and move slowly to the center of the stage where they would meet with eight dashing cadets coming from the opposite side. Their characters, in keeping with the show's theme, had exotic nonsense names: Abulim, Mizra, Zaidee, Amina, Zara, Nadie, Beco and Zoli.

Ruthie Thompson sat mesmerized in her orchestra seat, fascinated by the glistening satin costumes in the silvery blue light. The chorus girls were beautiful and the cadets looked incredibly handsome in their Hussar uniforms, from the tips of their plumed and brocaded hats to the ornate gold piping on their jackets and trousers, down to their white boots with colored tassels. At center stage the cadets and the maidens joined hands and slowly began dancing toward the footlights singing their love song. The cadets sang and whistled, "Softly give the signal for the ladies to appear. Just a little louder, boys, perhaps they didn't hear." The girls responded: "Better give the signal, for the boys have gone away. Girls are not so good as men at whistling, so they say."

As the music was swelling and the young performers were beginning their entrances, McMullen's light suddenly began to sputter and spark. He heard "a slight crackling sound" moments before a few inches of orange flame appeared and began to spread out, ever so slowly, along the fringe of the tormentor. On the stage below, the chorus girls and boys were into their up-tempo song, swearing their love "by the pale moonlight." McMullen tried slapping at the tiny flame with his hands, but within seconds the quivering light had grown, consuming the material above his head and beyond his reach, and was beginning to catch on to the heavier curtains. He shouted to the man on the catwalk above to help.

"Put it out," he cried, "put it out!"

"Damn it, I am, I am!" The fly man too began slapping at the burning material with his hands.

On stage, the cadets sang, "We love you madly," begging the maidens for a kiss: "So make no noise but come join the boys, on condition that the moon is shining bright."

The girls responded, "The reason we allow this liberty, is because you wear a smile that says it's right." And together they sang, "Let us swear it by the pale moonlight."

The audience was engrossed in this romantic musical scene, but on either side of the castle garden set, stagehands, grips and those on the catwalks above were pointing and a voice from beneath the light bridge called out with some urgency, "Look at that fire! Can't you see you're on fire up there? Put it out!"

What had been small orange-yellow flickers were beginning to spread to the draperies above those already dissolving into flame.

In front of the footlights the double octet had begun its dance.

"Look at that other curtain," someone yelled. "Put it out!" But the flames had suddenly grown larger and were beyond reach. Black smoke was starting to rise.

Another light operator, W. H. Aldridge, heard no crackling sound but thought he saw "a flash of light, about six inches long, at the place where the 110 volt line connected" to McMullen's lamp. "As I looked," he said, "a curtain swayed against the flames . . . in a moment the loose edges of the canvas were ablaze. . . ."

Down below, the music continued, effectively muffling the backstage hubbub, and few people in the audience realized what was happening. Madeline Dupont, in the role of Mizra, saw "a little bit of flame on the first drop curtain. It was just above the lamp reflecting on the 'Moonlight' girls. I . . . got in my place and the boys came out and sang their lines. Then . . . going downstage I saw the flame getting larger."

Daisy Beaute, playing Zara, danced onto the stage, as did the octet's leader, Gertrude Lawrence, who recalled, "I was . . . going to meet my partner when I first saw it [but] I went on working as usual, down to the front, and paid no more attention to it because I thought it would soon be out."

William Sallers, the house fireman, had serious doubts about that. Sallers was on his usual rounds to make sure no one in the cast and crew was smoking and as he made his way up the stairs from the basement dressing rooms, he spotted the flames. Instinctively, he yanked some tubes of Kilfyre from their wall hooks, ran quickly up the vertical steps of the light bridge and began tossing the powder up at the growing blaze. The platform was only eighteen inches wide, so to attack the fire he had to straddle a thin side railing, holding fast to the metal rail with one hand while trying to hurl the contents of the Kilfyre tubes with the other. But it was too late. The flames were beyond his reach.

Herbert Cawthorn, playing Irish Patshaw, watched Sallers using first one canister and then another and another. It seemed to Cawthorn that the fireman was too excited and that he was swinging the tubes too widely so that instead of reaching the flames the white powder was flying in the opposite direction. Sallers later explained that if he seemed excited it was because seasoned firemen had to act "in double quick time, [where] a fraction of a second counts a whole lot." But many whole seconds were rapidly slipping away, even as Sallers began calling for the theatre's asbestos curtain to be lowered. From his position in the wings, Cawthorn could see the double octet still going through its "Pale Moonlight" number in front of the footlights and he was sure that the actors had no idea what was happening.

He was wrong.

Jack Strause, one of the handsome cadets, made his entrance, walked four steps and danced eight, bringing him to the side of his young partner, Daisy Williams, playing Nadie. They saw the flames at the same moment and, as they went through their routine, Strause felt Daisy's arm stiffen, but she went on dancing as if nothing unusual was happening.

In the audience, the first few observant spectators were becoming aware that something was wrong.

Walter Flentye, of Glenview, Illinois, believed it was sometime after three o'clock when "the octet was singing there in the pale moonlight, that I noticed a kind of hesitation on the part of the actors, and pretty soon I saw a few sparks begin to come down about the size of . . . a Roman candle."

On stage, Ethyl Wynn, as Zaidee, could just make out the faint ringing of bells for the asbestos curtain to drop. The shouts and the bells were muffled by the music. As she danced past Daisy and Madeline, Ethyl whispered some words of encouragement. "The curtain will fall, the bells have rung," she said under her breath.

Moments later, Daisy whispered to Jack Strause that she was feeling faint. At about the same moment, Frank Holland, another cadet, whispered to *his* partner, "Don't stop. Something's happening, but don't stop singing or dancing."

In the orchestra pit, musicians were beginning to wonder how soon the curtain would drop. Herbert Dillea, violin in hand, no-

ticed what looked like "a red light" near the proscenium arch during the second verse of the song. "The moment I saw the glare," he
said, "I knew there was a fire and in whispers I ordered the members of the orchestra to play as fast as they could. . . ." He swung
his bow and the tempo picked up. But most of the orchestra had
spotted the red glow and some musicians were becoming rattled.
In the string section, Ernest Libonati, a violinist, had his eyes on
the fire from the start; he kept looking up from his sheet music at
it. The bassoon player near him reacted less calmly; he put down
his instrument and exited through the orchestra pit door beneath
the stage. Other musicians quickly followed.

Depending on where they were sitting or standing, some
members of the audience saw the red glow simply by following
the gaze of the chorus girls and boys who were glancing up. At
first, many were simply puzzled, but others were becoming
alarmed. Most of the children in the front main floor rows remained in their seats, watching the glow spread across the top
of the proscenium arch as if it was one of the show's magical
effects. For many long moments the audience was silent.

A late arrival, Mrs. James Pinedo, was one of those standing in the aisle at the extreme right of the orchestra section.
From there, she had an unobstructed view into the wings on
stage right where the fire had begun. She clearly saw the first
sparks and the men using their hands to slap out the flames. "I
quietly turned around to see if there was any fire escape or exit
in case there should be a fire," she said, but "I did not move
because I was afraid of starting a panic. I simply turned my
head and saw what I supposed was an exit. I couldn't tell."

Those in the upper gallery who saw the red glow had no
idea at first of what was happening, until bits of burning fabric
began fluttering down around members of the double octet who
were still trying to go on with the number. But it was becoming
obvious that some of them had fallen out of step with the music

and others seemed to have lost their voices. Most were terribly frightened and like Daisy, one or two of the chorus girls, were feeling faint. Lester Sackett, a doctor from Elgin, Illinois, thought that "those girls remaining there with the fire dropping all around them and still dancing in an effort to quiet the audience" was the most heroic thing he had ever seen.

In the gallery, when the elderly Mr. Dimmick, the man with the long snowy beard, heard a boy near him call "Fire!" he told him to keep quiet: "If you don't look out you'll start a panic." A similar thing happened to a Chicago schoolgirl, Ruth Michel, who was sitting with three friends in the second row of the gallery when she saw "a man at the side of the stage making motions with his hands. I didn't know whether he was coming in at the wrong time or not, and then I saw a spark come from above the stage. Then another spark fell down and one . . . in our party said, 'We'll get out of here,' and a man rose and said he would knock our heads off if we got out, so we sat there."

Twelve-year-old Willie Dee was the eldest of four children sitting down in front in the parquet with the Dee family nurse, Mrs. G. H. Erret. Willie was the first of his brothers to spot the trouble and he immediately told Mrs. Erret to take them out. She hesitated, because she thought the flames were part of the show. Willie did not wait; he grabbed his nearest brother, Alerton, by the hand and hurried up the aisle toward an exit.

Backstage, fear and confusion was growing exponentially. The stage manager, William Carleton, could not be found—he had gone to a nearby hardware store—and Joe Dougherty, a stagehand, was trying to handle the curtains from near the switchboard. But Dougherty was substituting for the curtain man who was hospitalized that day, and in all the confusion, he could not remember which drop should be lowered. The asbestos curtain ran on an endless loop of wire-reinforced rope but he wasn't sure which rope controlled what curtain.

High above him, Charles Sweeney, assigned to the first flying gallery, had seized tarpaulins and, with some other men
wielding wooden battens, was slapping at the flames.

"It got out of our reach," he said. "It went along the border
toward the center . . . then it blazed all over and I saw there was
no possibility of doing anything." Sweeney dashed up six flights
of stairs to a roomful of chorus girls whom he led down to the
small stage exit. In the rush to escape, most of the girls dropped
everything, including their purses, and left the building wearing
only flimsy costumes or tights. Other men raced downstairs to
rescue girls in the dressing rooms below the stage level.

High up in the theatre's gridiron, the Grigolatis, sixteen
young German aerialists—twelve women and four men—who
operated their "flying" wires, had a frightening birds-eye view
of the scene. Clouds of thick black choking smoke were rising
toward them and some blazing pieces of canvas the size of bed
sheets were falling over the stage and the footlights. From his
vantage point at stage level, William Sallers, the fireman, saw
the same thing and knew instinctively that the theatre was gone.

The Grigolatis had only seconds to act. One, Floraline, some
distance away from the others, suddenly found herself engulfed
in flames from a burning piece of scenery. Before the others
could reach her, Floraline panicked, lost her grip on the trapeze, and fell with a sickening thud onto the stage behind the
burning castle garden set, nearly sixty feet below. She lay there
unmoving. By the time her companions could unhook themselves from their harnesses and scramble down some metal scaf-
folding to the stage, Floraline had vanished and they could only
hope that someone had carried her out to safety. In all the confusion, no one had thought about Nellie Reed, still attached to
her wire.

In a fifth-tier dressing room, five young female dancers were sitting and talking, when they heard shouts of "Fire!" In the rush to get out, Violet Sidney twisted her ankle. The other girls ran, but Lola Quinlan stopped to help her friend, dragging Violet down five flights of stairs and across the back of the burning stage to safety. In the process she badly injured her hand and scorched her face. Violet's face was slightly burned.

Sallers, using his bare hands to tear down some of the burning fabric, was shouting for someone to lower the fire curtain and "pull the box"—but there was no box. The flames were spreading rapidly to other drops and the mass of scenery flats hanging in the theatre's loft. Sallers was so preoccupied that he didn't notice that both his hands and face were red and blistered. "The [girls] were frantic and the men not much better," he recalled.

Other voices could be heard calling for the curtain to come down but nothing was happening. Joe Dougherty and others were still confused about which curtain should be dropped and more precious seconds were being lost. The stagehand assigned to "pull the box" where no alarm box existed, was ordered to run as fast as he could through the cold muddy streets to notify Engine Company 13.

Inside a first-tier dressing room, Eddie Foy, in his tights, misshapen shoes, short smock and red pigtailed wig, was preparing for his novelty act as the Old Woman Who Lived in a Shoe. "I heard a commotion outside . . . my . . . room," he said, "and my first thought was, 'I wonder if [the stagehands and extras] are fighting again?' But then the noise swelled . . . and suddenly I became frightened. I jerked the door open and instantly I knew there was something deadly wrong." He glanced over the railing outside his dressing room and saw the smoke and flames. "My first thought," he said, "was for the boy. He was standing in the first entrance, and I rushed down screaming 'Bryan, Bryan!' and I got right to him."

As Foy raced down the steps to find his son somewhere in the darkness beyond the footlights, terrified voices were shouting "Fire!" and for 1,800 or more people packed inside the "absolutely fireproof" Iroquois, reason suddenly gave way to blind, animal panic. Keith Pickerell of Kenosha saw it from his box seat. "Men were fighting with women," he recalled. "They tore aside children to push through . . . They fought like demons."

Eddie Foy would later say, "Fate had brought them together in a fool's paradise."

THE INFERNO

"For God's sake, don't trample on me."
                                    —*A victim's last words*

CHARLOTTE PLAMONDON SAT rooted in horror to her box seat, watching the fire spread. It began as a "wreath of flames," she said. "It crept slowly along the red velvet curtain. We . . . all noticed it. So did the audience and I could see little girls and boys in the orchestra chairs point upward at the slowly moving line of flame."

Some people had risen to their feet, others were running, tripping and climbing over seats to get to the back of the house and side exits. Many standees were blocking the aisles and, because the theatre was new and unfamiliar to them, most of the audience had no idea where to turn. They did know which aisle they had come down and, without the navigational aid of exit signs, most of what was rapidly becoming a mob was trying to get out the same way they had come in. It was surreal: the shrieks muffled by the music and the chorus boys and girls continuing to sing and dance while pieces of burning scenery cascaded down like crimson snowflakes and terrified families were quickly being torn apart.

Eddie Foy had grabbed his son and was rushing to the stage exit when he suddenly felt he had to stop and go back. "Something told me that I was selfish . . . all those women and children out there . . . would be helpless, trodden under foot in a panic. Something told me I ought to go down and see what I ought to do, so I threw my boy in the arms of a [stagehand] and said, 'Take my boy out of the theatre,' and when I went back my object was to get the curtain down and calm them; my whole thought was, If they get into a panic they are all killed. I paused a moment to watch [Bryan] running toward the rear doors. Then I turned and ran on the stage, through the ranks of the octet . . . still doing their part though the scenery was blazing over them."

On the stage, chorine Madeline Dupont thought that the octet had completed only one chorus of the "Moonlight" song when the half-dressed comedian burst in. As Foy reached the footlights, Daisy Williams, who had at first "braced up," according to her partner, "did a few more steps and collapsed." Jack Strause and a second chorus boy quickly carried her off. Others in the octet began to faint, overcome by fear or the black smoke swirling about them. Near hysteria, Charlotte Plamondon saw some of the girls fall and be bundled off the stage. "I saw the men in the cast and some stagehands lift them to their feet and carry them to the rear," she said. "By this time the [flower garden] scenery was a mass of flames."

Panic-stricken, Frank Holland, one of the chorus boys, bolted from the footlights, squeezed through the stage exit and, his Hussar tassels and gold braid flying, sprinted through crowded downtown streets to the safety of his hotel.

From the second-tier balcony outside her dressing room, actress Annabelle Whitford could see clearly what was happening. When the first pieces of burning scenery began to fall, she knew she was in great danger. Her costume included an eight-foot train of lacy fabric that "would burn like cinder." She threw the train over her shoulder, and hurried down the iron stairs.

Alone on the empty stage, a blazing backdrop behind him, scenery flats in the loft above crackling and glowing red, black smoke beginning to billow around the top of the proscenium arch and bits of canvas raining down like burning confetti, Eddie Foy behaved in a way that many thought was heroic. Dodging some burning brands, he stepped to the edge of the footlights, partially clothed in his ludicrous costume, and begged what was left of the audience to remain calm. "Don't get excited," he shouted, "sit down, it will be all right, there is no danger, take it easy."

Remarkably, some of those in the parquet down front took their seats once again. Some even sat down momentarily in the gallery. Josephine Petry, farthest away from the stage in the top row with standees four deep behind her, got up to leave but, she said, when Foy spoke out, "Some people said, 'Keep your seats.' I got up and someone beside me said: 'Sit down, there's nothing the matter.'"

From the stage, Annabelle Whitford saw it differently. "The audience was shrinking back in fascinated horror," she said. Others were running for their lives, leaving behind a trail of coats, scarves, boas, purses, hats, opera glasses and other belongings in a mad dash for safety. Some tried to push past others, forcing their way up the aisles. Others remained sitting or standing, rooted to the spot, transfixed.

Eleven-year-old Lester Linvonston of Hyde Park, seated down front, was awe-struck. He saw Foy "dashing on stage and catching a piece of burning paper which had sailed down from above." "See, I'm a good catcher," the comedian lamely joked to anyone within earshot. "I was so interested in watching Foy," Lester said, "that I didn't realize what was happening."

Heavy black smoke continued to pour from beneath the arch over the stage.

When the double octet's performance suddenly stopped, the music stopped too. Many in the pit were scrambling to get out, stumbling over chairs, instruments, stands and piles of sheet music. But Herbert Dillea and a handful of his musicians bravely remained.

From the edge of the stage Foy glanced down and urged the musical director to play: "An overture, Herbert, an overture. Play, start an overture, play anything. Keep your orchestra up, keep your music going." The six musicians struck up the overture to an earlier Klaw-Erlanger fairy tale production, *Sleeping Beauty and the Beast*.

Alone on the burning stage, larger pieces of flaming scenery dropping around him, his wig now singed and smoking, Foy's mind whirled with fragments of unanswerable questions. "I thought of my boy again," he said. "Maybe this man didn't take him out. Why hadn't the curtain come down? What would happen to the women and children? Could [I] stop a stampede? Where in God's name was the stage manager? Did anyone know how to bring that damned iron curtain down? Why couldn't someone just cut the wire?"

Once again he tried to address the auditorium, but this time he did not tell people to keep their seats. "Take your time, folks," he pleaded. "Don't be frightened, go slow, walk out calmly. Take your time." But he dropped his voice to say to some stage-hands on the brink of fleeing, "Lower that iron curtain, drop the fire curtain! For God's sake, does anyone know how this iron curtain is worked?"

"The crackling of the timbers above increased," Foy said later, "and I repeated [for the last time], 'Get out—get out slowly.'" But now no one was listening. His eyes swept the semi-lit auditorium. In the parquet, frightened people were moving quickly up the aisles in a somewhat orderly fashion. But what he could make out in the balcony and gallery terrified him. In

the upper tiers, people were in "a mad, animal-like stampede."
Under the screaming and yelling a sickening rumble reverberated throughout the house.

♦

Lester Linvonston hadn't budged. In childish wonderment, he
could not stop staring at Eddie Foy. Oblivious to the flames and
the terrible noise that now reached every corner of the auditorium, Lester stood in an aisle, completely fascinated by the man
in the funny costume and smoldering wig, standing on the edge
of a burning stage. And then, for a fleeting moment or two,
something else caught the youngster's attention.

"Almost alone and in the center of the house," he said later,
he watched "a ballet dancer in a gauzy dress suspended by a
steel belt from a wire. Her dress caught fire and it burned like
paper." It was Nellie Reed, the British prima donna of the aerial
ballet.

Somehow Lester managed to escape from the theatre. A
cousin, sitting a few feet away, never made it out.

Ruthie Thompson's family had also, she said later, "joined
the yelling crowd. I turned back once to grab my aunt's hand,
and saw the black shapes of people's heads silhouetted against
the solid wall of flame that now reached above the proscenium
arch into the ceiling. Those flames were like waterfalls, and
they came faster than people could move along in the crowd."
Ruthie was swept along by the adults in her group, her feet only
occasionally touching the floor, "seeing little, hearing only
screams and shouts," as men, women and children, most of
them now separated from one another, made a wild dash for
any exit they could find.

August Klimek and his cousins, who had arrived late with
his mother, were so enthralled with the first act that they were
still wearing their overcoats when the fire broke out. "All of a

sudden sparks began to fall above the curtain and everybody got up," said August. "We were stunned. Eddie Foy came out and tried to compose the crowd. But my mother said, 'Let's go.' Normally someone our age would want to stay and see what happened, but we went right with her." She told the children to hold hands.

Klimek could hear the pleading cries of mothers and children who had been separated, calling to each other. "We didn't attempt to leave by the door on the ticket stub," he said. "We went to the door we came in. That was still open. If we had to get out the door intended for us we never would have made it because it was locked. And as we left through the open door I could see people starting to assemble around the locked exit, trying to get it open and pushing against each other. We would never have gotten out alive."

In the gallery, Ella Churcher was sitting with her mother and nephew in the fourth row from the front. She could see Foy gesturing, but with all the noise it was impossible to hear what he was saying.

"I couldn't hear his words," she said, "but his motions were to sit down and keep our seats, and we did so until I saw the red curtain come down."

The red curtain! Was it the safety curtain? Most of the backstage crew had by now fled, but obviously someone had figured out the way to lower what was thought to be the asbestos shield. It was inching its way down on a steel cable between wooden guide tracks. As if in slow motion, the curtain descended and then, incredibly, less than twenty feet above the stage, it suddenly stopped, one end jammed on the light reflector projecting out just beyond the proscenium arch, the other end sagging down to within five feet of the stage. The wooden guide tracks tore apart and the curtain that was supposed to have been reinforced with steel rods and wire, began to billow out over the orchestra pit and the first rows of seats like the spinnaker on a sailboat, pushed by the draft coming from the open stage exit that was mobbed by members of the cast and crew.

Some stagehands tried to dislodge the curtain and yank it down. John Massoney, a carpenter working as a sceneshifter, tried, but it was beyond his grasp. The theatre's engineer, Robert Murray, also attempted repeatedly to jump and dislodge the edge of the curtain, but it was beyond his reach too. It was a foolhardy effort because if Murray had lost his footing while he was jumping, he could easily have missed the edge of the stage and plunged into the empty orchestra pit. After a few failed attempts, realizing it was a lost cause, Murray ran down to the basement and told his crew to shut off steam in the boilers heating the theatre, bank all fires to prevent an explosion, and collect their belongings and get out as fast as they could. Then he helped a group of frightened chorus girls in one of the basement dressing rooms to escape by pushing them, one at a time, up through the theatre's coalhole into the alley. One or two were dressed in street clothes, but most escaped wearing only their smudged costumes. Some wore even less as they emerged into the frigid air. After that, he said, "I made a trip around the dressing rooms [calling], 'Everybody out down here?'"

As he rushed back up the stairs to the stage level, the engineer saw a young woman whose costume and tights were shredded and burned and whose skin was horribly blistered. Nellie Reed had somehow become unhooked from her wire but was seriously injured and obviously in great pain. She "was up against the wall, scratching it and screaming," said Murray. "I grabbed her and went out to the street," where he handed her to some rescuers and then remembered he had left something behind. He reentered the burning building, retraced his steps to the boiler room and found what he was looking for—a toolbox. Then he made it out through the alley coalhole.

Her long filmy train draped over one shoulder, the terrified fairy queen, Annabelle Whitford, crossed the burning stage heading for the scenery dock. "What had been a mystic fairyland had turned into a blazing inferno," she said. "The heat was stifling, the smoke suffocating. In another minute we who were backstage would have been in panic if the stagehands hadn't broken open the big double scenery doors with a heavy steel trapeze standard."

The act of flinging open the iron doors undoubtedly saved the lives of the remaining cast and crew but sealed the fate of the audience in the upper tiers. Employees and subcontractors of the Fuller Construction Company had not only failed to connect the controls for the roof's ventilating systems at the switchboard but had nailed shut the vents over the stage and left open the vents above the auditorium, creating a natural chimney. The curtain billowed out over the orchestra pit and front rows of seats, and the blast of cold wind that rushed in through the scenery doors instantly mixed with the super-heated air fueled by flames consuming forty thousand cubic feet of scenery. The result was a huge deadly blowtorch which one fire official later described as a "back draft."

A churning column of smoke, flames and chemical fumes burst through the opening between the stage and the jammed fire curtain, whirled above the orchestra seats and whipped into the balcony and gallery located just below the open roof vents.

John Massoney, the sceneshifter, described it as "a great sheet of circular flame going out under the curtain into the audience." To Foy, "It felt like a cyclone, it was so quick." He narrowly escaped being in its path because he was standing to the side of the stage. In the balcony and steep gallery, those who were stampeding for the exits or who had become separated from loved ones, never had a chance. The fireball was suffocating and had enough force to blow doors open.

Moments earlier, Mrs. Pinedo had been sitting quietly in a vacated seat at the edge of the orchestra section, pulling on her rubbers. "I have never seen an audience who were saner than these women and children," she recalled. "They sat perfectly still . . . while those sparks changed into flames. They were perfectly calm . . . Then I saw the big ball of flame come out from the stage . . . and I thought, 'Now's the time to get out.'"

Seconds after the fireball seared or asphyxiated those in the upper levels who had remained in their seats or were caught in the aisles, the last of the stout two-inch Manila lines holding up the scenery flats gave way. With a roar that reverberated throughout the building, tons of wood, rope, sandbags, pipe, pulleys, lights, rigging and nearly 280 pieces of blazing scenery, crashed to the stage. The combined mass struck with the force of a bomb, instantly knocking out the electrical switchboard and plunging the auditorium into total darkness.

Screaming, wailing adults and children clawed and fought their way toward the exits by the light of the inferno raging behind them, which seemed to grow in intensity by the second. Mothers and children were wrenched away from each other and trampled underfoot by those behind them. Skirts, dresses, jackets, vests, trousers and other articles of clothing were ripped to shreds as "a human whirlpool" of people tried to get through the exits and escape the advancing flames and asphyxiating smoke and fumes. The jamming at the doorways was horrible.

Out of desperation, some whose clothing had caught fire jumped from the first balcony to the orchestra floor. Many died instantly. Others were paralyzed and suffered agonizing deaths when they landed on seat backs or arm rests.

A momentary burst of bright light flared suddenly from the stage. The fire had engulfed the jammed safety curtain and in a matter of seconds, it, too, dissolved in flames. The curtain, it turned out, was not made of one hundred percent asbestos but of some cheaper material chosen by the theatre's co-owner, Will Davis.

The conductor and the rest of the orchestra had long since fled, leaving behind heaps of discarded instruments and over-turned wooden music stands. Now it was Foy's turn to get out. Still standing at the edge of the stage, he thought first of vault-ing over the orchestra pit to try and escape through the Ran-dolph Street entrance, but, desperate to find Bryan, he made his way around the burning pile of wreckage on the stage and left through the scenery doors, hoping to locate his son in the mill-ing noisy throng in the alley. "I got out as quickly as I could," he said.

Those in the side boxes fared better than the others because the fireball missed them. Charlotte Plamondon was in a state of total panic and confusion. Later she had only a vague recollec-tion of leaping over the box railing, being caught in the arms of a man who might have been a theatre employee and being pushed bodily along one of the aisles. It was there, she said, that she heard "a scream of terror . . . I shall never forget . . . men were shouting and rushing for the entrance, leaping over the pros-trate forms of children and women and carrying others down with them." Behind her was a sheet of flame that "seemed to be gathering volume and reaching for us." She found herself jammed against a pillar in a side aisle. "I know I was almost crushed to death, but it didn't hurt. Nothing could hurt, with the screaming . . . the agonized cries of women and children ringing in your ears."

August Klimek, still in his overcoat, had reached the bot-tom of the stairs and was almost at an exit when the house went black. In the darkness his cousin George stumbled and fell. In reaching down to help him to his feet, Klimek's mother dropped her mink muff. A few minutes later, as they stood in

Randolph Street, shivering as much from shock as from the
cold, his mother announced that she wanted to go back inside
to retrieve the muff; she said she remembered where she had
dropped it.

"We begged her not to go," said Klimek, and she finally
agreed not to make the attempt. "We stood there waiting to see
what would happen. We couldn't hear a sound from inside the
theatre. It was all quiet."

Backstage, it was bedlam.

Just before the switchboard went dead, a terrified young
elevator operator, Robert Smith, his face a ghastly white, remained at the controls of his backstage lift, making repeated
trips up and down through clouds of smoke to help cast members escape. When the fire started, he brought down a load of
hysterical chorus girls from the first level.

Waiting for them on the stage floor was Archie Barnard, an
electrician who headed a group of stagehands. As the women
burst out of the elevator, some were so frightened and disori-
ented that they began to run back toward the burning stage. Barnard and his group quickly formed a makeshift human chain and
began herding, guiding, pulling, pushing and, in some cases, bodily
tossing the young women from man to man until each girl was
safely out the stage door. On his second trip, Smith ascended to
an area so thick with smoke he could hardly see or breathe. He
found one girl on the sixth level and then rescued another load of
women from the fifth. By the time he made it down with them,
Smith noticed that part of Archie's clothing and his hair were
smoldering, but the electrician remained calm and continued to
guide the young actresses to safety in the alley.

Smith's third trip was his last. He worked his way through
the smoke to some women so terrified that they had to be
dragged into the elevator, where flames had now reached the

controls. His hand badly burned, Smith descended with this last carload and saw them safely out of the building. It was only then that he, Barnard and the rest of the impromptu human chain fled the theatre.

In the darkness, those of the audience who were among the first to reach the exit doors discovered to their horror that these were locked and that the stairways were barricaded with metal accordion gates. Some of the young ushers had deserted their posts at the first cry of "Fire!" and the few who remained, stubbornly followed management orders, and would not, or could not, open the barricades. One, Willard Sayles, said he had been given explicit orders to lock the wooden inner doors to the auditorium once the performance had begun. "We had not got instructions as to what doors we were to attend to in case of fire," he said. "The only time we got instructions was the Sunday before the house opened [when the head usher] told us to 'get familiar' with the house. There were no fire drills or anything of the kind."

When the fire broke out, Clyde Blair, the powerfully built University of Chicago track star, left his overcoat and hat, grabbed his girlfriend Marjorie and maneuvered her through the pushing, shoving mob toward an exit, followed closely by his friend and teammate Victor Rice and Rice's date, Anne Hough. "The crush at the door was terrific," said Blair. "Half the double doors opening into the [promenade] were fastened. People dashed against the glass, breaking it and forcing their way through. One woman fell down in the crowd directly in front of me. She looked up and said, 'For God's sake, don't trample on me.' I stepped around her, unable to help her up, and the crowd forced me past." Blair never saw the woman again.

A resourceful eleven-year-old girl in the third row of the orchestra, Winnie Gallagher, almost immediately became separated from her mother in the rush for the exits. Thinking quickly, Winnie climbed onto one of the plush seats and, using them like stepping stones, jumping from seat to seat, kept out of the crowded aisles and managed to reach an exit. There she was nearly crushed in the mob but somehow was able to get out of the theatre.

Even more resourceful was Emil Von Plachecki, a husky twenty-four-year-old civil engineering student, one of the standees in the gallery. As the fireball swept into his area, "everyone started to scream," he said. "I felt my face burning. It felt like breathing a hot blast from a furnace." He pursed his lips and held his breath, and when he found that stairways leading from the gallery were blocked, suddenly remembered the washroom he had visited before the performance. It had no exit but it did have a skylight. Using superhuman strength he hardly knew he possessed, the chunky young man pulled himself up, seventeen feet above the floor, hand over hand, on a stout window cord.

Grasping the cord in his left hand, Von Plachecki punched his way through a glass skylight reinforced with wire mesh and hauled himself onto the theatre's snowy roof, where he bound his bleeding right hand with a tourniquet made from his clothing and waited in the cold until he was rescued by ladder. He had intended to find a ladder and lower it into the restroom so that others might escape, but he was too weak. Von Plachecki was rushed to a pharmacy where oil was poured on his blistered face, head and arms and his lacerated hand was treated.

D. W. Dimmick, the plucky, bearded seventy-year-old Apple River man who minutes earlier had hushed a child to prevent a panic, found himself feeling his way along a wall toward an exit when "the whole front of the stage seemed to burst out in one mass of flame. From all over the house came shrieks and cries of 'fire!' I started at once hugging the wall on the outside

of the stairway," he said. "As we went down the platform where
the first balcony opens, it seemed . . . that people were stacked
up like cordwood. There were men, women and children in the
lot. By crowding out to the wall we managed to squeeze past
the mass of people who were writhing on the floor, and . . .
blocking the entrance. As we got by the mass on the floor, I
turned and caught hold of the arms of a woman . . . pinned
down by the weight resting on her feet. I managed to pull her
out and I think she got down [safely] . . . I tried to rescue a man
who was also caught by the feet, but, although I braced myself
against the stairs, I was unable to move him."

There were many heroic acts that afternoon. Georgia Swift,
a young society woman badly shaken and bruised, had been
sitting in the orchestra section. "When I reached the back of the
auditorium," she said, "the aisle was choked with people who
had fallen. I looked down to avoid stepping on them and as I
did, my eyes were caught by those of a little boy about seven
who was on the floor and unable to rise. He had large, brown
eyes and was so neat he looked like a little gentleman. He fascinated me. It was all in a second, I know, but as he saw me
looking at him he said, 'Won't you please help me, please do?' I
stooped to raise him if I could, but the crowd was too thick and
the rush too strong. I seized him under the arms and was then
knocked over to my knees in the aisle. I struggled to my feet but
the weight of the crowd was such that I could not turn back,
and I was carried on through the door. The little boy was unquestionably trampled to death, and the memory of those eyes
will haunt me [forever]."

Modern forensic science has identified two phases of death.
Somatic death is the cessation of the vital processes. Molecular
death is the progressive disintegration of the body tissues. For

most of the victims inside the Iroquois, the end of life would have been classified as somatic death, which, tragically came by varying degrees.

At the first sign of fire, minutes before the blast of smoke and flames burst from under the safety curtain and into the auditorium, the adrenalin in virtually every man, woman and child present, whether members of the audience or those backstage, would have begun pumping in the space of a millisecond. The two pyramid-shaped adrenal glands, one atop each kidney, are not among the body's larger organs—each is about two inches in diameter—but in situations of sudden stress like the theatre fire, they would instantly have prepared the body for "flight or fight."

When one becomes frightened, the adrenals release large quantities of the hormone epinephrine into the blood system, which instantly help the body adjust to sudden stress by increasing the rate and strength of the heartbeat, raising blood pressure and speeding up the conversion of glycogen into glucose, providing a burst of energy to the muscles. For those trying to battle their way to the exits, this adrenalin "rush" would have propelled them on in their desperate attempts to escape. But once the victims had become trapped in the doorways or hit by the blast of fire, other bodily processes would have rapidly occurred.

Some people were immediately overcome by inhaling poisonous gasses or fumes containing deadly carbon monoxide produced by the incomplete combustion of wood or paint. Fumes and smoke from the scenery may also have contained equally deadly cyanide. The degree of saturation of these chemicals in the bloodstream, together with soot clogging the air passages of the lungs, could have produced a quick death with no physical signs of disfiguration, as was the case with some of those caught in their seats. If they survived the smoke and flames, their next biggest risk was dying from shock or burn injuries as bodily fluids rushed to the skin. If fluids are not replenished quickly enough, organs can die for lack of blood. There is also what is known as "delayed death" from smoke inhalation. Lungs badly damaged from chemical burns caused by poisonous gasses can fill with so much fluid that the victim dies days or weeks later.

Then there were those seared by the flames. For them, the end would have come quickly. The body exposed to fire often assumes what is called the "pugilistic attitude," in which the flexor or bicep muscles contract so that the victims' arms in particular are outstretched and fixed in an attitude commonly adopted by boxers. This "pugilistic attitude" is evidence of exposure of the body to intense heat. "Among the bodies," one journalist would note that day, "a strange uniformity was observed. In nearly every case the victim's left arm was held stiff and close to the side, while the right arm was stretched out as if warding off peril."

Those who were trampled or were piled on top of one another in the doorways died in still another way—by traumatic or crush asphyxia, a particularly horrific end. "The victim of such crushing would have experienced the sensation of tremendous pressure on the body, pressure sufficient enough to fracture ribs. If the person was conscious, he might have felt as if his head were about to explode or his eyes pop out." Those victims of the Iroquois who lost consciousness immediately were the fortunate ones. Slow asphyxia can take two to three minutes to kill.

Such was the fate of those trapped inside what had been advertised as "the best theatre on earth." But even as men, women and children died by the hundreds and the piles of bodies grew higher inside the building, scenes equally devastating were occurring outside, in Couch Place. It would soon come to be known as "Death Alley."

{11}

DEATH ALLEY

"I heard the roar as the crowd came after me."
                              —Anna Woodward

*"Nobody came down the stairs. They never lived to
reach it."*

                              —John Galvin

PETER QUINN, CHIEF SPECIAL agent for the Atchison, Topeka
and Santa Fe Railroad, was returning to his office that afternoon after attending a trial in the Criminal Courts building. As
he reached the intersection of Randolph and Dearborn streets,
his attention was caught by a man running from the theatre's
entrance, hatless and coatless despite the frigid weather. Quinn
saw the man collide with pedestrians as he rushed up to a police
officer and said something which made the Bluecoat dash away.
More out of curiosity than anything else, Quinn followed the
running man into the alley behind the theatre, lost him and was
about to turn and leave, when he heard noises coming from the
stage door, which was opened just a crack. He heard women
and children on the other side screaming for help. They were
pressing against the door, begging to get out. Using some small
pocket tools, Quinn was able to remove the hinges and order

those inside to back away. The door fell in, releasing, one by one, possibly one hundred members of the show's company. "We could not realize the awfulness of what had happened," he said.

❀

Fireman First Class Michael J. Corrigan, a ten-year veteran of the department, was sitting comfortably inside Engine 13's station house that bitter Wednesday afternoon, idly looking out the front window at piles of snow in the street, when someone ran up, rapped on the glass and began gesturing. Because of street noises Corrigan couldn't hear him, and raised the sash. "What are you saying?" he asked the stranger, who did not seem particularly agitated.

Seconds later, Corrigan wheeled about and shouted to his superior officer, Paddy Jennings, "Let 'em out, captain, there's a fire at the Iroquois!"

In less than ninety seconds, Engine 13's heavy steamer, rumbling behind its hose wagon, had pushed out of the station house and was racing the short distance to the theatre, all horses at full gallop and all the company's men dressed in standard issue rubber coats, hip boots, mittens, scarves and leather helmets bearing the company's numerals above the crown. Thirteen was the first unit to arrive, pulling up near the alley behind the theatre where heavy black smoke was billowing from the stage and scenery doors.

Corrigan arrived a minute or two later, whipping the horses for Battalion Chief Hannon's buggy. As they wove through traffic and approached the congested intersection of Clark and Randolph, Hannon, who understood the implications of a fire in the incomplete theatre and the need for additional assistance, may well have ordered Corrigan to halt the rig for a moment and pull the alarm at Fire Box 26 in front of the Sherman House.

In Room 607 on the second floor of City Hall, directly above the mayor's office, gongs immediately began clanging.

Engine 13 had hooked up to a hydrant near the Couch Place alley and its men were deploying cotton-jacketed rubber hose lines and rigid suction hoses ringed with wire bands coupled to the steamer. When Corrigan leaped from his rig he could see "smoke and people coming out [the stage door], some with their clothes on fire. False wigs and beards were burning." As black smoke clouded the alley, other firemen with fire axes and pike poles were hacking away at the Iroquois' lower exit doors and windows whose iron shutters seemed to be rusted tight.

It was approximately 3:33 in the afternoon. For all anyone knew, the fire may have been burning for ten minutes or more. Other units were pulling up in Randolph Street, snarling traffic and attracting large crowds of the curious. Men in derby hats and overcoats and boys in knickers and long socks were pressing in to see what was going on.

In front of City Hall, Fire Marshal Musham jumped into his buggy and was driven quickly to the theatre. The six firemen who were facing disciplinary action dashed toward the Iroquois on foot. Police Chief Francis O'Neill was also on his way. The Bluecoats had received the initial word from an officer on theatre patrol who called in from a Randolph Street box as the first hysterical men, women and children burst out of the theatre, their clothing torn and disheveled, some of it on fire.

Standing at the box office to purchase tickets for a future performance, John Galvin saw the center doors of the lobby foyer and the outside entrance doors blown open by what he described as a gust of hot air. "I looked into the foyer and saw people running toward the entrance," he said. "I realized at once what the trouble was and went to the lobby doors and tried to open [a] door there [but] it was locked on the inside . . . I tried to pacify people from rushing or crowding, but it was no use . . . there were probably a dozen cleared the door before the crush came. The first person to go down [was] . . . a rather stout woman, who seemed to be free, when somebody stepped on her skirt. She turned to gather up her skirts and she was borne down by the crowd and then they piled on top of each other." Galvin kicked in some glass door panels and tried to pull people out through the openings. "I was expecting a big crush in the vestibule," he said. "I thought there would be a jam on that stair, but nobody came down the stairs . . . not a soul. They never lived to reach it."

The stout lady may have been Anna Woodward, a gallery occupant, who saw the fire start and instantly decided that "if there was going to be a panic it would be wise for me to beat it to the street." She weighed close to 180 pounds, not including the thirty-seven pounds of winter street clothing most women wore, nineteen pounds of which hung from their waists. Miss Woodward tried to go through an exit door but found it closed and "a man standing on the outside refused to open it." A boy renting opera glasses confirmed that ushers not much older than himself refused to unlock the exits, telling theatre patrons to remain in their seats.

"I was leaving quietly up to this time," Anna Woodward said, "but when he refused to allow me to pass out peaceably I determined to get out if I had to make all sorts of noise." She was not only physically imposing, but aggressive. As the music and singing continued on stage, she walked another ten feet or so along a passageway, smashed open a beveled glass partition with the steel tip of her umbrella, and got out of the auditorium. When she was halfway down the stairs, she said, she "heard the roar of the crowd as it came after me. They overtook me, knocked me down, and but for the fact I was close to the door I think my chance of life would be almost nothing. As it was, I think I walked the last ten feet to the exit on the bodies of those who had fallen."

The hatless, coatless man who had been about to purchase tickets at the box office dodged traffic as he dashed across Randolph Street to notify a patrolman. Because of the concentration of city and county municipal offices, department stores and theatres, many officers were assigned to foot patrol in the vicinity. Summoned by a chorus of police whistles, they immediately converged on the theatre, arriving there minutes ahead of the engines and hook-and-ladder trucks. Some policemen dashed inside accompanied by civilian volunteers and reporters and helped in the early stages of the evacuation. Others halted traffic around the theatre and blocked off Randolph Street from two sides. Within hours there would be hundreds of Bluecoats in and around the theatre and, because of the large number of female victims, some of Chicago's thirty uniformed police matrons were also pressed into service.

Inside the theatre's office, racking tickets for the evening performance, Fred Brackenbush, assistant treasurer, heard what sounded like a "fierce storm" striking the back of the house. "There was a wind and a terrible racket," he said. Seconds after he went into the box office, the face of the *Bluebeard* company's business manager, Thomas Noonan, appeared at his ticket window.

"Get your money out quick," Noonan snapped.

Because of the crowd pouring down the stairs, the box office door could not be forced open, and Brackenbush, temporarily trapped, had to kick out a metal window grill and scramble over the counter with the theatre's cash box. He ran to a corner cigar store in the Delaware Building and put the strongbox in the shop's vault. He thought by the time he returned to the theatre that most of the people had gotten out safely.

The first news of the fire was spreading through the downtown area and beyond, and within minutes, Randolph Street was jammed with horrified crowds who had broken through police lines, anxious to know what had happened. Among them were many frantic people whose relatives had gone to the Iroquois that afternoon. As the crowd grew, all traffic was halted except for police, fire and rescue wagons. Apart from some telltale wisps of smoke, there was almost no evidence of fire on the Randolph Street side.

Inside the theatre, oblivious to the burns to his hands and face, house fireman William Sallers was shoving members of the cast and crew out the scenery doors and into the crowded alley. By now, he believed, Engine 13 should have arrived and he stepped outside and began shouting for Captain Jennings. "I thought I could get him on the stage," Sallers said, "and that [he] could prevent [the fire] from getting into the audience. The captain, he was there. When I looked around, I saw the flames coming out the door I had left. I knew that anybody who was in there was gone. I knew there was no chance to get out."

In the frantic minutes that had been lost because the Iroquois had no alarm system or telephone, before Engine 13 and the other units began arriving, the "best theatre on earth" had been transformed into an oven. In collecting valuables after the fire, police found at least a dozen watches, all of which had stopped at about the same time, 3:50 p.m. That meant that, incredibly, seventeen minutes had elapsed from the time the gongs first began to clang in City Hall. That would account for the jamming at the exits and for the reason why relatively few people were seen exiting the theatre. Eyewitness reports varied.

William Grover, manager of the high-rise Unity Building more than a block away, calculated that perhaps as much as seven minutes had gone by from the time flames first burst through the theatre's skylight before any person left the Iroquois. "My office on the fifteenth floor commands a view of the entire [theatre]," he said. "I was startled by a loud explosion and concussion that rattled windows, and returning to the window I saw a sheet of flame shooting from the roof. I watched that fire seven minutes, and in that time not a soul came out of the front doors . . . then the flames died down and people began to come out in scores. After that, it was a steady blaze until it was put out."

Grover's field of vision was the front of the theatre on Randolph Street and did not include the side bordering on Couch Place. There, in the narrow alley separating the Iroquois from the Northwestern University building, another horrible scene was taking place before the eyes of petrified students. Though it was the Christmas holiday, some of them were in the building that day, along with a group of painters and workmen who were repairing damage to some classrooms from an earlier fire. What they witnessed was further evidence of the rushed, incomplete job done by the Fuller Company and its subcontractors. The highest fire escape was simply a metal platform with no ladder to the ground. Though the theatre had been open for nearly six weeks, no one had bothered to complete the work.

One of the Northwestern undergraduates was George Dunlap, 22, of Chicago, who said, "I was passing one of the classrooms where the painters [were working], and I looked [across the alley] and saw fire coming out of the theatre exits and people fighting to get out, but they were so jammed in, nobody was getting out. I called the painters to let us put some of their planks [or ladders] across [to] the fire escapes."

"Run it out, run it out," one of the painters shouted; he and other workmen shoved a twenty-six-foot ladder across the alley to rest on the railing of a fire escape platform. They watched in horror as a man, "crazed with fear . . . started to cross the improvised bridge as flames burst out of the exit beneath him."

As he began edging his way across, the ladder slipped from an icy window ledge of the university building and the man plummeted screaming to his death on the slushy cobblestones fifty feet below.

After the ladder was lost, three wide boards were pushed across to the theatre and the painters anchored them with their knees. "Come on, come on," they shouted to sixteen-year-old Hortense Lang, who was pulling her terrified eleven-year-old sister, Irene, by the arm. The two girls were the first ones to make it across the plank bridge. "I was going to jump," Hortense sobbed, "but I thought of my mother. I just grabbed [Irene] by the hand and waited for the planks. I don't know how we crossed." They and their mother, who had also escaped unharmed, were later reunited in the Northwestern building where they held hands and wept for an hour.

Rachael Gorman of the Sisters of Charity was especially courageous. She crawled a foot or so out on the boards, steadied herself by holding on to a window frame, held out her arm and helped some people to safety. The plank bridge worked for a while, but it could not handle the crush spilling out of the theatre. "We went over and tore people loose," wrote the student George Dunlap, "and the painters helped them across the planks. We did that until the curtain on the stage let out a terrible roar, and no one came out the door . . . We got thirty-six people out and laid them on the floor" in the classrooms. Some of the women's clothing had been torn away or was in flames. Not knowing what else to do, the young student pulled tubes of Kilfyre from their wall hooks and tossed the powder on the burning clothes.

"When I threw it on their burns they stopped screaming," he said. He guessed it was because the powder kept air from reaching their wounds. One survivor later admitted that she was temporarily outraged at the young student because, even though the chemical powder smothered the flames around her waist, some of the stuff accidentally got tossed into her mouth as she was screaming.

When what sounded like a bomb went off inside the theatre, those at the university's windows on different floors watched helplessly as people trapped in the theatre tried to escape. What they saw was beyond imagination.

Those who swarmed from the exits and were pushed to the edge of the iron railings discovered there was no place to go. The highest platform had no steps, and on the other landings, if anyone attempted to descend through the blinding smoke, they were forced back by flames bursting out of lower exit doors and windows. Compounding the horror was that those who made it to the fire escapes found it impossible to turn back because of the crush behind them. Some of the trapped men, women and children tried crawling across the planks but in the smoke and confusion, most missed their footing and plummeted to the street. Others, whose clothing was on fire, simply gave up and jumped from the railings.

The boards and ladders began falling away and as the fire increased and flames shot out of the doors and windows along the theatre's wall, many were burned to death in full view of the students. From some of the higher Northwestern University windows they looked into the theatre at what appeared to be one solid wall of flames. In the inferno, they could see men, women and children running about. The victims did not look human. One witness described them as "crawling things."

Mrs. F. R. Baldwin of Minneapolis and her mother, both of whom had been seated next to one of the fire escapes, had taken only three or four steps before the crowd from behind flung them through the open door. Miraculously, neither mother nor daughter was seriously hurt. But as she rose to her feet, Mrs. Baldwin saw "a girl lying on one of the fire escape platforms

with flames shooting over her through [a] window." Something
else would forever haunt her: "One man, who had jumped from
a platform [about six feet off the ground], had not taken two
steps before a woman who jumped a moment later from a height
of about forty feet came right down on him, killing him on the
spot."

Couch Place was "a smoking, flaming hell . . . too narrow
for effective aerial ladder work." In that narrow alley, swarm-
ing with people, William Sallers at last found Captain Jennings,
told him that people were cut off, and helped Engine 13's pipe
men drag the nozzle end of a hose line up the lower iron stairs.
"The water came at once," he said, "and I hollered, 'Play away,
Thirteen!'" The pressure was reduced slightly so that firefighters could drench those victims whose clothing was on fire. If
the full force of the stream had struck them, it was feared that
the victims might have been pushed back into the flames.

"[Firemen] heard pounding from behind iron-shuttered
doors and windows. They tried to wrench them open with axes
and claw bars. Above them . . . people (many of whom were
being burned alive), were pushed onto the unfinished fire escape platform which led nowhere, body and after body thud-
ded onto the cobblestones." At first, the firefighters tried using
nets to catch the jumpers, but the mesh was woven of black
material and, in the dense smoke, impossible to see. They were
useless. Countless numbers of people leaped from the fire escapes that afternoon and the ones who survived did so only
because they landed on the bodies of those who had preceded
them. No one had exact figures of how many people made it
across the improvised plank bridge, but 125 victims were removed from the slushy cobblestones in Couch Place that afternoon.

Ruthie Thompson had no memory of being carried out of
the theatre through the scenery doors but, like something out

of a nightmare, she recalled "waves of black cloth streamed over me. For one moment I thought I was dead. But I wasn't even hurt." Ruthie had fallen to the ground and crawled beneath the raised edge of the theatre's carriage step. For what must have seemed an eternity, the child had remained wedged into a small opening, while a "torrent of people had swept over me . . . I crouched there until no one else came out and then I stood up and looked around." She would always recall seeing "panic-stricken people, firemen, hoses, swarms of humanity . . . running up and down the alley."

In a Northwestern classroom, George Dunlap had run into an unexpected problem. Before blankets and sheets had arrived from nearby department stores, "there were many female victims lying on the floor, naked. Some guy kept gawking at them. I told him three times to get some cans of Kilfyre hanging in the hall. He didn't go. I got mad and swung a half empty can and it struck him on the forehead and down he went. I figured I had killed him; he lay there a long time." When police arrived and Dunlap explained what had happened, one officer was so outraged that he went for his revolver, threatening to shoot the unconscious student. Dunlap stopped him by saying that the young man was already dead. The officers hurried on and the student who had been knocked out later regained consciousness and disappeared.

One survivor remembered how inside the theatre "the desperate crowd was screaming and pulling off their burnt clothing." The stronger ones, she said, managed "by strength and endeavor to edge their way out around the jams at the doors — which opened inward." The victims "were piled in a pyramid and others were falling on them. It was an awful sight."

The "stronger ones" were mostly men. One member of the audience, D. A. Russell, Pittsburgh manager of the National Life Insurance Company, said, "Not a man, as far as I could see, made any effort to save any one but himself." That was an overstatement. Many men helped women and children out of the theatre that afternoon at considerable risk to their own lives.

When the fire broke out, the ballplayer-turned-saloonkeeper Frank Houseman started for an exit on the east side of the building, but he immediately ran into trouble. He told an usher to open the door, but the usher told him to "'Wait till the drop curtain comes down.' By this time the crowd was getting wild and pushing against the doors. The stage was blazing and the smoke rolling out into the body of the theatre.

"'For God's sake, open the doors!' I shouted.

"The usher didn't move. I grabbed the fellow and threw him as far as I could and burst open the door. All I thought of was opening that door, because people at that time were crowding close to me and screaming . . . and I don't remember just how I got that door open, but anyway it opened and carried the crowd out. I felt the latch and found it was like the one on my ice box at home. 'This is easy,' I said to Dexter, who had broken open another door.

"I tried to do what I could around there for the people being trampled on, trying to pull them apart, and start them on their way if they were not too badly hurt, until [others] began jumping from the fire escapes above . . . I could not do very much of anything, [except] to pull out the people being trampled upon [and] put them to one side." Houseman remembered one other thing: he and Dexter had shared a box with a man and a young woman. He told the man, "'You'd better bring out the lady.' But the man answered, 'I guess I know my business,' . . . and they stayed behind. God help those two."

By the time Houseman's friend Dexter got downstairs from the box, he could see Eddie Foy "trying to keep the crowd quiet and the orchestra leader playing his fiddle, facing the audience, and nodding to them to sit down. People were running around,

I didn't know what to do, and I ran into a crowd of little children. I saw some draperies . . . and I opened them. I didn't know where I was going, and I found myself up against some iron doors. I didn't know how to work them. The only thing I could see was a crossbar . . . and I started to beat at it.

"By that time the people were pushed up against me, and I didn't know whether I would be able to get it open or not. I had all the poor little kids around me, and I beat [at the bar] until it finally went up, and as it did the people behind me—we went out into the alley. I turned back and saw a wave of fire sweeping over the whole inside of the theatre." Houseman thought he saw Foy being burned in the flames seconds before the crowd pushed him out.

Harriet Bray, the little girl from Michigan City, Indiana, considered herself lucky to get out. When the fire began, her father had grabbed her hand and, with the aid of a stranger, the three made their way through the intense heat and smoke to one of the fire escapes. Harriet remembered the human stampede, people jumping over bodies and the terror when her father discovered that the fire exit door on their level was jammed.

"My father and this other fellow pounded and banged until the door opened. From there we descended down the fire escape only to find that the last flight of steps was also jammed."

Her clothing and hair singed, Harriet waited for her father to jump the remaining twelve feet to the ground and then catch her in his arms. "By then, the firemen were on the scene. I'll always remember crawling beneath the legs of the horses who pulled the fire equipment and how they stood motionless in the face of all that chaos."

Captain Edward Buckley of Engine 32 was credited as being the first officer inside the theatre who began evacuating victims from the front of the building. It was there on Randolph Street, not far from the entrance, that one of his men bent low over a woman to catch her last words. "My child, my poor little boy. Is he safe? Tell me he is safe and I can die."

"He is safe," said the fireman, forcing back tears. The woman died and the fireman covered her body with a blanket and carried it away. He knew nothing about her son.

INSIDE A VOLCANO

"Oh dear Jesus, have mercy on their souls."
— *John Campion, Deputy Fire Marshal*

AERIAL LADDERS WERE USELESS. As soon as they arrived, fire companies on the Randolph side had dragged hoses into the front entrance, through the elegant promenade and up the arched staircases, trying to get to the burning auditorium while rescue efforts were underway by other firefighters, police and volunteers. A passerby, Arthur McWilliams, Purdue University, Class of 1902, first saw "people, mostly children . . . running out of the theatre, some with their clothes on fire. Frightened, flaming people ran down [the] street like wild animals. I was in the middle of the first rope line to enter the theatre to try to rescue those inside. We held a rope and each others' hands as we groped into the dense smoke. The first fireman in the line encountered the first little bodies and shouted back: 'There must be a dozen dead in here!' He came out carrying two little scorched bodies, one on each shoulder."

What McWilliams and the others discovered inside was sickening.

As they groped their way up the grand staircase toward the auditorium, the smoke was so thick that lantern light could hardly penetrate it. But here and there, they could catch glimpses of piles of corpses in doorways. Firemen tugged hose lines up and over the bodies, in some places stacked within two feet of the top of the door frames. From some of the tangled human piles they could hear moans. The stench of burnt flesh was everywhere, mixed with the odor of charred hemp, cloth and paint.

Police, firemen and volunteers, moving along slowly, crouching close to the floor, their noses and mouths covered with handkerchiefs, saw that where some corridors converged, bodies were piled ten feet deep. There were victims everywhere, some horribly disfigured and many whose clothing had been torn from them in the mad rush to escape. Some among the uniformed ranks wept as they worked and others were so unnerved that they had to be relieved of duty.

One civilian, William Corbett, a Chicago building contractor who helped carry out some of the victims, tried to dislodge the body of a boy from one of the piles of the dead, only to have the child's skin peel off in his hands.

Police and firemen heard moans as they frantically struggled to untangle masses of bodies, raising hopes that some victims buried under the dead might still be alive, but the task was overwhelming. One of the Bluecoats told Chief O'Neill that they couldn't do it; they couldn't untangle them. But the chief responded that they *had* to get the bodies out of the way to get down to those who were still alive. He told his men to grab hold of a dead man and pull him out. Two big firemen seized the body by the shoulders and struggled and pulled until it was free. Then another body was removed. And another. And another.

Again there was a terrible moan from somewhere in the tangled mass. "For God's sake," O'Neill cried, "get down to that one who's alive!" A policeman pulling at the heap gave a shout. "I've got her, chief. She's alive all right!"

It was a girl, about eighteen years old. She was moaning softly as they released her from the mound of bodies. A fireman picked her up and hurried away to a first aid station, cradling her in his arms.

"There must be more alive," shouted O'Neill. "Work hard, boys!"

From the moment they had entered the auditorium, Musham and O'Neill began issuing a string of orders. O'Neill demanded more lanterns, blankets, doctors and nurses and all available police vehicles. Musham called for additional men and fire equipment and for every available ambulance, wagon, carriage, dray and delivery truck to be sent to the theatre. By now there may have been as many as twelve engines and five hook and ladder trucks on the scene.

As the news spread, the public response was immediate and overwhelming. A nearby medical school sent one hundred students to help the doctors arriving at the theatre. A hardware company two doors down from the Iroquois emptied its stock of two hundred lanterns. Marshall Field's, Mandel Brothers, Carson, Pirie, Scott and other department stores sent piles of blankets and sheets, rolls of linens, packages of cotton and big delivery wagons, and immediately converted their ground floor restrooms and lounges into emergency aid stations. Neighboring hotels and businesses did the same. Montgomery Ward dispatched one of its huge new electric motorized delivery vans, but, even with its gong ringing, it could not navigate through the crowds jamming the streets and had to turn back. Police commandeered whatever vehicles they could.

J. B. Evans was driving a horse-drawn wagon on Randolph Street near the theatre when the fire broke out. Leaving a helper in charge of the vehicle, Evans rushed to the lobby as the first

survivors reached the ornate entrance. "People coming out kept
wedging in the doorways owing to the terrific pressure of those
behind, trying to [escape]," he said.

"The crush in the doorway was indescribably fierce, and
defeated the efforts of even those in front to get to the street.
With a number of other men who gathered there, I tried to pull
persons out of the center of the jams at the doors, so as to start
the throng ahead. Each time we would release a person from
the opening a score of people would be shot through, and then
the crowd would jam again. It seems scarcely credible the way
the people were wedged in the door openings. Sometimes it required the combined strength of several of us to pull them out.
The clothing of the women was torn to fragments. . . . One was
stripped to her undershirt in the efforts to haul her out."

In minutes, small restaurants, buffets, saloons and street-
front stores in the vicinity of the theatre had been turned into
improvised aid stations as medical personnel and civilian volunteers began showing up in large numbers. Chicago's central
telephone exchange was overwhelmed with emergency calls.
"The estimate of those who lost their lives started at a small
number," recalled the poet Edgar Lee Masters, then practicing
law in Chicago. "But every few minutes added to the list. When
it reached sixty the [people in the] street and the city were hor-
ror-stricken, but then it began to mount to a hundred and beyond. . . ."

In Marshall Field's toy department, Dorsha Hayes, whose
mother had refused to let her family attend the matinee, was too
young to understand what was happening. Her parents became
aware that something was dreadfully wrong when they noticed
distracted sales clerks whispering among themselves and then
abandoning their counters and crowding at the store's windows
to look out at the street. As the news quickly spread from floor to
floor and department to department, the Hayeses finally learned

what a close call they had had. Dorsha would say in later years that her mother could never explain her premonition.

Behind the theatre, Corrigan worked in the slushy, water-soaked alley, helping hysterical victims to get down fire escape steps past open iron shutters where flames were still visible. After that, he went to the top floor of the auditorium "and got [dead] people down; I had to throw some of them down. It was hot and smoky . . . we cleared the balcony floor. . . . people were jammed in [the exits]." They extended a ladder from the fire escape to the Northwestern University building, and were able to carry a few corpses out that way. Then Corrigan went back into the building and "found a girl lying under the seats. She suddenly stood up, [bolted] for the door and ran straight over the ladder and we were paralyzed. The workers shouted, 'Get her! Get her!'" When they did, "they threw a blanket over her—she was as black as could be and nearly all her clothes were torn off. "

Corrigan reported back to the company inside the auditorium. As he was using the pipe to put out sparks, his "leg slipped between some of the bodies. The captain said, 'Let's get going,'" but Corrigan said he felt "something alive near my feet." The captain lowered his lantern to look and told Corrigan to shut off the pipe and "get going." There was a woman near his feet, but she was not alive. "She was burned," Corrigan said, "right across the face and chest."

Because the hardware store lanterns were not powerful enough to light the blackened auditorium, the Edison Company rushed over forty arc lamps and, when they were turned on, rescuers were stunned anew by what they saw. Deputy Fire Marshal John Campion looked around and crossed himself. "Oh, dear Jesus," he said, "have mercy on their souls."

Some of the audience had died sitting straight up in their seats facing the stage, their eyes staring blankly ahead. Others bore no burn marks or bruises; they had apparently suffocated quickly from the smoke and fumes. Many women were found with their heads resting on the seat back in front of them. A young boy had been decapitated. One woman was doubled over backward across a seat back, her spine severed. It was hard to count the number of people who had been trampled; one person's face bore the imprint of a shoe heel and other faces were missing any recognizable features. Clothing, shoes, walking sticks, opera glasses, pocketbooks and other personal belongings were strewn about. Some of the bodies were burned beyond recognition.

As workers struggled to make their way around a mound of tangled dead, a fire officer burst out in horror to a reporter, "Good God, man, don't walk on their faces!"

Scores of victims were wedged in doorways. A husband and wife were locked so tightly in one another's arms that they had to be removed together. A woman had thrown her arms around her daughter in a vain effort to save her. Both were unrecognizable. And there were so many children. Onlookers wept as they watched the small bodies carried from the theatre. Many of the victims' hands were clenched and outstretched, as if trying to ward off the inevitable. All the plush on one of the settees in a passageway was burned away, except for one spot where two dead children were found with the kneeling body of their mother, who was leaning over them in a desperate effort to save them from the flames.

At the edge of the auditorium, a fireman emerged from a cloud of smoke with the body of a small girl in his arms. He groped his way toward what had been the grand promenade. Musham ordered him, "Give that child to someone else and get back in there." The fireman, obviously dazed, kept walking. Another senior officer, irritated, said, "Hand off that child to someone else."

As the fireman came closer, the marshal and his aides could see streaks of tears on the man's blackened cheeks. "I'm sorry, chief," the man said, "but I've got a little one like this at home. I want to carry this one out."

Musham told him to go ahead. The marshal and the other officers stepped aside, and the weeping fireman carried the little body carefully down the slippery steps of what only an hour before had been the Iroquois' glittering promenade.

With the aid of the arc lights, Deputy Chief Campion searched the theatre's smoking interior while his men continued hosing down hot spots that periodically burst into flames.

"Is there any living person here?" Campion shouted.

There was no answer.

"If anyone here is alive," he shouted again, "groan or make some sound; we'll take you out." He looked around at the burned seats, the paint-blistered walls and the twisted pile of metal that littered the stage.

The devastated theatre was silent.

One of the small fires flared out. Campion turned to his men and reluctantly gave the order to "fall back."

In possibly less than a quarter of an hour, five hundred or more lives had suddenly and violently ended in what had been thought to be the grandest, safest theatre in Chicago, if not in the nation. Hundreds more had been injured. The number of dead was greater than those who had perished in the Great Chicago Fire. Just hours earlier the Iroquois had glittered like some luxurious palace, but as the Associated Press would report that evening, "from the galleries, [the theatre] looked like a burned out volcano crater."

The Chicago Fire Underwriters Association later estimated that approximately seventy percent of those who perished were in the gallery and nearly thirty percent in the balcony. Comparatively few on the main floor lost their lives.

Many newspapermen were hard pressed to put into words what they had seen that afternoon. A Reuters man, in a dispatch to the *Manchester Guardian*, tried to explain to his British readers how so many could have died so quickly: "Through some mischance the iron shutters of the emergency doors were locked, compelling the [audience] to make for the ordinary rear exits. These people converged at the doors. They came from three directions—those making their way from the body of the house, and those in the balconies who had come down the east and west staircases.

"The struggling mass was in the form of a huge writhing T, the converging point beginning where the upright meets the horizontal. The impact of the rush of those coming down the stairways as they met together and butted against the stream moving from the stalls was terrific. Women and children went down as if swept by a discharge from a Gatling gun."

But it was Police Chief O'Neill who best put into words the otherwise indescribable human tragedy he had witnessed that day. O'Neill had lost four sons to diphtheria and within a month would lose a fifth to meningitis. "The victims," he said, "looked like a field of timothy grass, blown flat by the wind and rain after a summer storm."

THE CHARNEL HOUSE

"The good Lord never intended him to burn.
— *Mrs. George Thompson, Housewife*

CHARLES COLLINS WAS DUMFOUNDED by what he saw. Ninety minutes earlier he had been at the theatre talking with one of its owners about ticket scalping. Now as the afternoon sun began to sink, long shadows descending over the Loop and slanting through the tracks of the elevated line, he was standing inside police barricades in muddy Randolph Street which was choked with fire engines, wagons, halted trolleys and crowds of bystanders watching an endless procession of blanket-covered bodies being removed from the Iroquois' once-grand entrance.

He never remembered the cold. He stood, numbly staring at the blanket- and sheet-wrapped forms laid out on the curb, some dumped into the slush.

"The bodies," he said, "extended about one hundred yards on either side of the theatre's entrance. A long line of horse-drawn vehicles waited to haul the dead or dying to hospitals, morgues or funeral parlors." The throng in Randolph Street, he thought, might have swelled to as many as five thousand people.

"They were gazing at the theatre, absolutely quiet, hushed as if they were in awe. There was total silence."

A few men, but mostly women and children, much of their clothing missing and some horribly injured, had been carried next door into Thompson's Restaurant, which in the space of fifteen minutes had cleared dishes and flatware from its marble-topped tables and become a first aid receiving and triage station.

Collins had first learned of the disaster in the *InterOcean* building, where a clerk behind an advertising display counter had casually mentioned that "a fire alarm has come in from the Iroquois." Collins immediately asked to use a telephone and told Central to ring the *Record-Herald* at Main 3315. Al Bergener, the editor, calmly confirmed the report. Yes, he said, there had been an alarm and there seemed to be trouble. He told Collins to come in. But by the time the reporter had hurried the four blocks to his paper, the editor was no longer calm. "It's bad, very bad," he yelled to Collins. "You'd better get over there." Collins left the building on the run, irritated that he had been so rushed that he had forgotten to bring a notepad, and that Bergener, a "fidgety, fox terrier type," had given him no specific assignment or instructions except to "get over there."

"I must find survivors," he told an officer as he entered Thompson's.

Behind the glass of Thompson's window with its large lettering: "Serving Lunches and Dinners," was a sight both unimaginable and stomach-churning. Men, women and children were piled along walls and stretched out on table tops as doctors, nurses and medical students frantically worked to revive the injured and clear away the dead to make room for the new arrivals streaming in. The shouted orders of physicians were punctuated by shrieks of pain. Clothing was cut away and burns dabbed with olive oil and swathed in cotton while oxygen, small quantities of brandy and other resuscitation aids were given to those who were unconscious but still breathing: mechanical respirators were still three years away. Nurses and students held pocket mirrors under victims' nostrils to detect any breath of life. If all efforts failed, the body was quickly wrapped in a blanket and slipped beneath the table to make way for the next victim.

"Some were charred beyond recognition, some only scorched and others black from suffocation; some crushed in the rush of the panic, others . . . the broken remains of those who leaped to death. And most of them were in the forms of women and children," reported one eyewitness. "So fast came the bodies for a time that there was one steady stream of persons carried in . . . there was the figure of a man with broad shoulders and dressed in black whose entire face was burned away, only the back of his head remaining to show he ever had a head; yet below the shoulders he was untouched by the fire. There lay women with their arms gone, or their legs, while one had [her] side burned off, with only the cross shoulder-bone remaining. She had worn a pink silk waist and black skirt; the fragments of the garments still clung to her like a shroud . . . There was a little boy, with a shock of red-brown hair, whose tiny mouth was open in terror and whose baby hands were burned off so that his tiny wrists showed like red stumps."

Collins went into Thompson's back kitchen where a female employee was sitting in a corner calmly peeling potatoes, presumably for that night's dinner. A distraught father was there being treated for burns. Collins jotted the man's name on a small piece of paper he had found. The father, who had become separated from his daughter as they fled the theatre, was weeping uncontrollably as he described his child. Collins tried to reassure him that she would eventually turn up safe.

Minutes later, Collins crossed Couch Place, stepping in the mud over snaking hose lines and around slippery pools of frigid water, to visit a first aid station set up in a paint shop opposite the theatre. Through the window he saw "a very bright and intelligent girl of seven or eight who was walking around with a little olive oil on the bridge of her nose, which was slightly scorched." In the paint shop, the child, who appeared too dazed to cry, told the reporter she had lost her father. On a hunch, Collins asked some nurses if he could carry the child back across the alley to the restaurant. Sure enough, the weeping man inside Thomson's kitchen was her father and the two were tearfully reunited. Collins left them alone and never saw them again.

In Thompson's restaurant, William McLaughlin, the Ohio Wesleyan student from Buenos Aires, lay dying. A young medical student attending him noticed the Delta Tau Delta pin in his lapel and said, "I'd better take off your frat pin, old man; someone might take it if you go, you know."

"No, I guess not," replied McLaughlin, his life slipping away. "It's been a friend of mine for quite a while and I'd not like to have it taken off now; just let it stay on to the finish." The pin remained until the young man died hours later in a hospital.

❦

There were many heroes that December afternoon. Among them was the Reverend J. P. Muldoon, Auxiliary Bishop of Chicago, who had been passing by the theatre when the fire broke out. Without hesitating, the bishop had rushed inside, stripped off his coat, climbed over bodies and entered the smoke-filled gallery to begin administering the last rites even as flames were licking the walls of the auditorium. He was repeatedly asked to leave for his own safety and finally had to be forcibly removed by authorities who feared that one of the walls might collapse. Muldoon was later commended by the Pope for his selflessness.

Dr. H. L. Montgomery, one of the first physicians to work on victims inside the theatre, said:

"I was with the Army of the Potomac during the Civil War. I rescued one hundred and fifty people during the Chicago fire. I have seen the wreckage of explosions. But I never saw anything so grimly horrible as this."

In the confusion, there were some men who entered the darkened theatre posing as rescue volunteers, but who had another agenda — to rob the dead. The press dubbed them "ghouls," and most were chased away by O'Neill's men or arrested on the spot for pocketing money and jewelry and even attempting to pry rings from victims' fingers.

Sadly, not all the thieves were civilians. George Dunlap, the Northwestern undergraduate who had first helped to set up the plank bridge, would never forget what he happened to see that afternoon. "I worked day and night carrying out bodies," he said. "I still can't get over seeing some policemen taking money out of women's pocketbooks and throwing the pocketbooks away."

As the afternoon drained into a dreary twilight, hundreds of terrified people materialized, not just outside the theatre but also at makeshift aid stations and at hospitals, morgues and newspaper offices, pleading for any information about loved ones they knew had been in the audience.

Collins had a deadline to meet. His final stop of the day was the Sherman House, where Eddie Foy was describing the tragedy to a large group of reporters. Collins reported that Foy was "hysterical" and suffering from superficial burns. "I never saw anything happen so quickly as that fire," the comedian said, weeping. "It was like a flash in the pan, and the entire theatre was in flames, men were screaming and women were fainting. It reminded me of the Chicago fire. You know I was through that." Foy said that after he found his son in the freez-

ing alley and they set out for the hotel, a kindly spectator offered to lend him his overcoat. Foy's wife was just leaving the
hotel to go to the theatre with two of his children, and he remembered getting greasepaint all over his wife's face as they
tearfully hugged. In a daze at the hotel, he had handed the bor-
rowed overcoat back to the Good Samaritan, but to the end of
his life Foy regretted not getting the man's name so that he could
write him a personal note of thanks.

By the time Collins returned to the *Record-Herald*, "the city
editor, Leigh Reilly, was much too busy to listen to play-by-play
talk. He merely said to me, 'write escapes and rescues' and
handed me a batch of Chicago City Press Association reports. I
remembered everything I saw," said Collins, who began writing his "father-daughter" reunion piece before tackling the wire
copy. It was strangely quiet in the city room that night; Collins
considered himself fortunate to be assigned to the rewrite desk.
It allowed him to stay at the paper while other staff men were
given the exhausting, depressing job of seeking victim identifications at morgues, funeral homes and hospitals in different
parts of the city. "Many of the reporters," he said, "worked all
that night, all the next day and the following night," piecing
together elements of the story and adding names to the growing
list of victims.

Within the city's nine newspapers, the *Tribune*, *Record-
Herald*, *InterOcean*, *Chronicle*, *Examiner*, *Daily News*, *Journal*, *Post* and *American*, a story began to circulate that evening
which would become a legend among generations of Chicago
newspapermen.

It was said that Walter Howey, a reporter for the City Press
Association, was on his way to City Hall when the fire broke
out. The Press Association, which covered metropolitan stories
and distributed its copy to the city's papers through a system of
underground vacuum tubes, prided itself on beating the local

competition. The story went that as Howey neared Courthouse Square, he heard bells clanging and saw firemen rushing to the theatre after the horse pulling their wagon was injured in a collision with another vehicle. Normally, the firemen would have tended to their horse, and the fact that they hurried off without doing that caught Howey's attention. He raced after the firemen and reached the Iroquois just in time to see the first frantic adults and children come stumbling out the front doors, many in tears, some bruised and bleeding and others able to give brief but coherent accounts of what had happened minutes before.

Without hesitation, Howey dashed to a nearby saloon, slipped a friendly bookmaker twenty dollars for the exclusive use of his telephone, and called his editor with the stunning news, brazenly adding that he had taken charge of the situation and all available Press Association people should report to him at the scene. Then, to further insure that he had an exclusive, Howey handed some pocket change to a neighborhood kid with instructions to purchase a package of straight pins, run to every public telephone in the vicinity and stick a pin into each phone wire, effectively rendering the instrument inoperable, thus foiling other newsmen.

From the Press Association's office in the Western Union building, carbons of Howey's stories were immediately walked across the hall to the Chicago AP bureau, where telegraphers could transmit in Morse Code at thirty-five words a minute. The Iroquois disaster, which would keep the wire service men working through many days and nights to come, traveled over a 34,000-mile network to the service's 648-member papers. People in foreign countries knew details of the tragedy before many Chicagoans awoke the next morning to the terrible headlines.

For some journalists, the story became personal. The AP's Frank Moore, who had been called in from his regular beat at the stockyards to cover the disaster, was asked to go to a city morgue that evening by friends whose daughter had attended the theatre. "She was burned so badly I was unable to recognize her," Moore said. "Her folks never got a positive identification but they buried her, thinking that it might be their daughter."

One very weary Western Union telegrapher who had worked without stopping throughout the afternoon and evening sending out endless details, returned home late that night to learn that his wife was among the victims.

The *InterOcean* reported: "With tears in their eyes, and with faltering voices, thousands of people thronged the [newspaper] last night, inquiring for missing relatives and friends, trying to secure one little article of information of missing ones, and hoping against hope they would receive favorable replies. More often than not, the news was bad."

But there were the fortunate few.

Found crouching beneath the theatre steps, Ruthie Thompson had been lifted up and carried to a nearby aid station where she met her Aunt Abby. Like Ruthie, Abby had made it to safety through the stage exit. Ruthie's little brother John had been swept up by a kindly man inside the theatre who had lifted him high in the air and passed him to other adults, hand over hand, over the heads of the screaming, struggling mob and out through the theatre's front doors. Aunt Dot had escaped through the front lobby. Stranger still, Grandpa Holloway had somehow made it out the stage entrance and was found waiting patiently at the edge of Couch Place, watching Engine 13 pump tons of water into the smoking interior.

Ruthie's father George Thompson first learned of the fire from a passerby while he was walking near his State Street office. Oblivious to the heavy traffic and slippery cobblestones, Thompson dashed into the middle of State Street, ran the length

of the block, turned down Randolph and elbowed his way
through the crowd at the theatre's entrance, screaming, "Get
out of my way! My children are in there!"

He was blocked by a cordon of uniformed officers. A fireman whom he recognized stopped him and said sadly, "No,
Mr. Thompson, you can't go in. There's not a soul alive in there
now."

Out of breath and crazed with fear, Thompson made his
way past the dead and dying to the rear of his restaurant and
clambered up a steep flight of steps to the bakery. He saw that
a ladder had been rigged from one of his windows to the theatre, helping a few people to escape. He was about to cross over
it into the smoking building when an employee, a heavy-set
baker, restrained him. "Let me go," Thompson shouted. "My
children are in there!"

"No," said the baker. "No one is alive in there now."

Thompson could not contain himself. "You're fired!" he
screamed.

"Then I'm fired," said the baker. "But you can't go in there."

At that moment, the restaurant manager appeared at the
top of the stairs and gasped, "All of them got out! They were all
in here and they've gone to your office and are waiting there."

"When father burst into the office," Ruthie said, "my two
aunts and I fell on him, weeping hysterically. My brother . . .
cried too. The only calm person was my grandfather, who was
sitting in a straight-backed office chair. He merely waited until
the storm was over."

That night at home, as they recounted their experiences,
Aunt Abby reminded them that their grandfather had "always
thought the theatre was the province of the Devil, and the first
time he set foot in one, all hell broke loose.'"

"My mother shook her head," said Ruthie. "'Don't you realize,' she said calmly, 'that the good Lord never intended *him*
to burn?'"

LEFT: Main entrance of the Iroquois shortly after the fire broke out. Trolleys and other vehicles are stopped in Randolph Street but there is no sign of fire apparatus. (*Author's Collection*)

BELOW: Intersection of Randolph and Dearborn Streets showing theater entrance to the right of the Delaware Building, the rear of the theatre to its left and the Northwestern building across Couch Place alley. (*Courtesy Chicago Historical Society*)

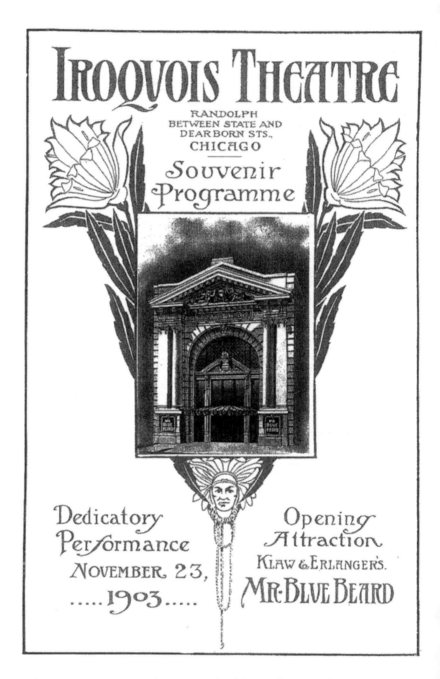

The Iroquois opening night souvenir booklet. (*Billy Rose Theater Collection, New York City Public Library for the Performing Arts, Lincoln Center*)

RIGHT: A full-page *Chicago Tribune* advertisement for the show, showing the ballet girl "floating above the heads of the audience." (*Author's Collection*)

LEFT: Newspaper cartoon of Foy appearing in "drag" with the Pony Ballet girls in "The Old Woman Who Lived in the Shoe" routine from *Mr. Bluebeard*. (*Collection of Armond Fields*)

ABOVE: The Pony Ballet. (*Billy Rose Collection*)

LEFT: Nellie Reed, star of the aerial ballet, lost her life in the fire. (*Author's Collection*)

BELOW: Bonnie Maginn, *Bluebeard*'s lead dancer. (*Author's Collection*)

The scene onstage when the fire started [the X to the left marks the position of the faulty spotlight]. The actors continued to perform the double octet as burning fabric fluttered down. (*Author's Collection*)

LEFT: Carter H. Harrison, Mayor of Chicago, hurriedly returned from out of state when he learned of the disaster. (*Author's Collection*)

BELOW: Clyde Blair, Captain of the University of Chicago Track Team, escaped from the theatre with his friends. Other students were not as lucky. (*Courtesy Chicago Historical Society*)

Eddie Foy, the star of *Mr. Bluebeard* who tried to calm the audience, became an international hero overnight. (*Collection of Armond Fields*)

ABOVE: Smoke obscures the planks spanning Couch Place from the Northwestern building (*left*) to the theatre (*right*). At least 125 people jumped or fell to their deaths on the cobblestones below. (*Courtesy Chicago Historical Society*)

LEFT: Charles W. Collins in 1903, the cub reporter who covered the theatre's opening and returned to report on the disaster. (*Author's Collection*)

ABOVE: A typical engine company, Chicago Fire Department, circa 1903. (*Courtesy Chicago Historical Society*)

RIGHT: Couch Place, the morning after the fire. The plank bridges can be seen spanning muddy "Death Alley" while a fire engine next to the scenery doors pumps tons of water out of the theatre's basement. (*Courtesy Chicago Historical Society*)

Without the benefit of spot photography to record the tragedy, newspaper
sketch artists were used to depict the terror in "Death Alley" behind the
theatre. (*Author's Collection*)

LEFT: One weeping fireman told his boss, "I'm sorry, Chief, but I've got a little one like this at home. I want to carry this one out." (*Author's Collection*)

BELOW: The *New York Times* described the victims as being caught in a human "whirlpool" and the *Roman* correspondent said that they perished "as if swept by . . . a Gatling gun." (*Author's Collection*)

LEFT: Many half-dressed chorus girls escaped from the theatre's basement through a coal hole in Couch Place, helped out by one of Chicago's thirty police department matrons. (*Author's Collection*)

BELOW: The scene on the sidewalk at the Randolph Street entrance as Collins saw it. Some victims lay in the slush. A few steps away in the background is Thompson's Restaurant, which instantly became a first aid receiving station. (*Brown Brothers photograph*)

Civilian volunteers, including the first arriving newsmen, helped to carry victims down the staircases of the theatre's Grand Promenade. (*Author's Collection*)

ABOVE: The Iroquois' once-opulent interior. The fire started on the right-hand side of this photograph about 15 feet above the stage floor. It was from here that Eddie Foy repeatedly begged the audience to be calm. (*David R. Phillips Collection*)

BELOW: One newspaper diagramed the jamming at the gallery exits. (*Author's Collection*)

ABOVE: As they groped their way toward the auditorium the smoke was thick and impenetrable to lanterns, but as it lifted fire and policemen could see piles of corpses in doorways. (*Courtesy Chicago Historical Society*)

BELOW: A line of victims awaiting identification. Blankets and sheets had been rushed to the theatre by major department stores. (*Author's Collection*)

ABOVE: View of the balcony, alley side. Many of those in the balcony and gallery were trapped where they sat, in plush seats stuffed with hemp. (*Author's Collection*)

BELOW: Flame-swept orchestra pit and front row seats. Many on the main floor escaped because the fireball that shot from the stage under the jammed curtain swept over their heads. (*Brown Brothers photograph*)

RIGHT: The scenery and rigging crashed to the stage with the force of a bomb, instantly knocking out the switchboard and plunging the house into darkness. (*Author's Collection*)

BELOW: The stage in ruins. A sudden illumination came from the stage when the safety curtain, jammed halfway down on a lighting fixture, burst into flames. (*Author's Collection*)

ABOVE: A main exit from the balcony where victims piled up in the jammed doorways. (*Author's Collection*)

BELOW: The Grand Promenade of what had been advertised as "The best theatre on Earth." (*Author's Collection*)

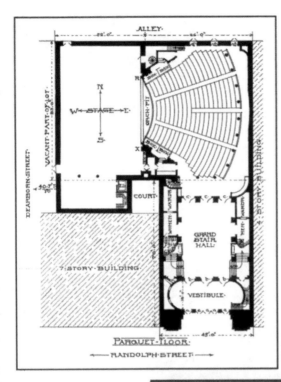

Left: A diagram of the parquet floor of the Iroquois shows the location of the Grand Stair Hall, the main floor seating and the stage. (Courtesy Theater Historical Society)

RIGHT: A door to a fire escape that could not be opened. Many died here. (*Author's Collection*)

ABOVE: Top alley exits. The paint-blistered ceiling and walls of the gallery where Emil Von Plachecki said that it felt "like breathing a hot blast from a furnace." (*Author's Collection*)

BELOW: Converging stairways and a confusing mirrored door that was not an exit led to many fatalities here. (*Author's Collection*)

ABOVE: Inspection teams of city aldermen and other officials visited the theatre immediately after the fire. Many of them blamed one another for the tragedy. (*Author's Collection*)

BELOW: A passageway leading to a blind exit, where over 200 were found dead. (*Author's Collection*)

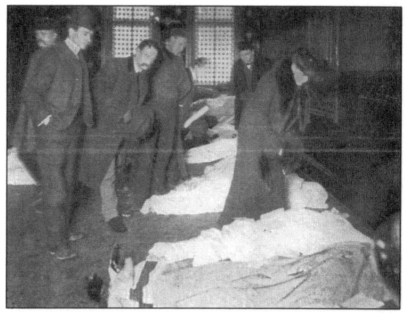

ABOVE: This news photo was captioned "Looking for her children among the dead." (*Courtesy Chicago Historical Society*)

BELOW: One of the theatre's accordion gates that was locked to prevent those in the upper tiers from occupying empty seats in the more expensive downstairs parquet. (*Author's Collection*)

Officials inspecting the width of one of the main doorways leading from the balcony. (*Author's Collection*)

ABOVE: The incomplete roof ventilation system, which was nailed down above the stage, forcing smoke, flames and toxic fumes into the audience. (*Author's Collection*)

LEFT: One of the locked doors that was smashed open as the audience attempted to get out of the theatre. (*Author's Collection*)

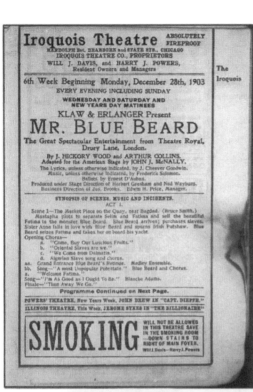

LEFT: Partly burned program for Mr. Bluebeard. Note "Absolutely Fireproof" in the upper right corner. (*Courtesy Chicago Historical Society*)

BELOW: The Iroquois entrance the day after the fire. Note the absence of police or fire vehicles. (*Courtesy Chicago Historical Society*)

ABOVE: This "extra" also contained a small announcement from a trans-Atlantic steamship company. (*Author's Collection*)

LEFT: Fireman Corrigan said: "People were jammed in the exits. We got a ladder and extended it from the fire escape to the [Northwestern University building]. We got a few [fatalities] out." (*Armond Fields Collection*)

HIS SUNDAY DINNER.

BLESSED ARE THE POOR IN SPIRIT

LEFT: John T. McCutcheon drew a series of front page editorial cartoons about the tragedy, but none moved Chicagoans and out-of-town readers so much as this, which appeared during the first week of 1904. (*Author's Collection*)

RIGHT: The *Record-Herald*'s Ralph Wilder also captured the anguish. The caption of this page one cartoon, "The Vacant Seat," said it all. (*Author's Collection*)

SECOND READER

The coroner's inquest was held in Chicago's City Hall. The owners of the theatre, Will J. Davis (ABOVE) and Harry Powers (BELOW) were among 200 witnesses who testified. (*Courtesy Chicago Historical Society*)

Mayor Carter Harrison (ABOVE) was a star witnesses. The Iroquois architect, Benjamin H. Marshall (BELOW), said he studied every theatre disaster in
history to avoid errors in the design. (*Courtesy Chicago Historical Society*)

ABOVE & RIGHT:
Mayor Harrison,
who was vilified
by many of the
nation's newspa-
pers, moved
quickly to tamp
down criticism of
his administration,
with little effect.
(*Author's
Collection*)

WHO IS RESPONSIBLE?

ABOVE: Chicago building inspectors were ridiculed. This cartoon shows one official grabbing for a free pass to the show, oblivious to the obvious dangers. (*Author's Collection*)

BELOW: In some funeral parlors, victims were laid out neatly on floors and over New Year's 1904 thousands of friends and relatives stood in the cold waiting their turn to make identifications. (*Author's Collection*)

ABOVE & RIGHT: Years before the fire occurred, New York's *Life* magazine attacked the Theatrical Trust in a series of vicious anti-Semitic cartoons including this detail (*above*) from a centerfold which parodied words from Lincoln's Gettysburg Address. In the cartoon at right, the "hooknosed theater owner is inviting passersby to see 'The Immoral Woman'. . . . Produced by The Jew Syndicate." (*Author's Collection*)

{14}

THE NEW YEAR

*"I dropped on my knees and prayed that God
might spare them . . ."*
—*Clinton Meeker, Chicago Postal Worker*

BOISTEROUS, ROWDY CHICAGO, for the first time in its history,
prepared to welcome the New Year in silence. "The greeting
for the day was seldom spoken," said Collins.

On the morning of December 31, those who had not heard
the newsboys' cries of "Extra!" the previous evening or had
learned of the tragedy by word of mouth, awoke to stunning
banner headlines and long and incomplete lists of the identifi-
able dead and injured. The news was as incredible to the citi-
zenry as it would seem nearly one hundred years later when the
World Trade Center towers collapsed in New York.

The *Tribune* spread across its entire front page a list of the
dead, along with 200 names of injured people, some of whom
were not expected to live. It ran also a box identifying thirteen
morgues holding remains. "Of the dead," said the newspaper,
"less than one hundred were identified last night. Of the uni-
dentified, nearly all were so badly burned that recognition was
impossible. Only by trinkets and burned scraps of wearing ap-

parel will the bodies of hundreds be made known to their families. Never has [the city] received a blow so instantaneously shocking."

There was scarcely a neighborhood that was not touched in some way by the tragedy. Instead of the usual sounds of celebration ushering in the New Year of 1904, the predominating sounds in Chicago were the tolling of church bells and the soft patter in empty streets of horses' hoofs, muffled by new fallen snow. "Wheeled traffic," said Collins, "seemed devoted to the transportation of flowers to homes with black crepe on the doors." Black crepe seemed to be everywhere.

Hundreds of men and women held silent lonely vigils in zero temperatures that last day and night of the old year, waiting to identify lost relatives and friends laid out in neat rows, each covered with a blanket. At the rear of one funeral home, 182 bodies lay four rows deep on the floor and three rows deep in an annex.

Mayor Harrison hurried home by train from a trip to Oklahoma, and declared a week of official mourning, banning all unnecessary noise, including band music, the tooting of horns and train, boat and factory whistles. Flags were flown at half mast. The Board of Education announced a delay in the start of the new semester out of respect for the more than forty teachers and principals who had perished in the fire. Most shops closed for much of the week, the exception being some Loop stores which remained open for a half-day to provide funeral accoutrements like candles and crepe.

The striking livery and hearse drivers at first adamantly refused to help transport the dead to morgues or to participate in funeral processions. But they quickly reversed their position, declared a ten-day truce and returned to work, many of them refusing payment for their services. Hearses suddenly materialized from everywhere: white ones for children, black for adults. "On the weekend," said Collins, "thousands of carriages moved slowly toward cemeteries."

"This frightful thing was over before the city knew that it happened; the news . . . left paralysis behind," said the *Tribune*. "Chicago," reported the *New York Clipper*, "enters upon the New Year silently, dumb with the shock of disaster and speech-less with the anguish of sudden and awful calamity . . . Lives sacrificed to some one's carelessness."

Thousands of Americans had drowned that year and died in railroad accidents, but the 600 or so who had lost their lives and the hundreds of others who were injured in a place of amuse-ment touched a nerve in America and throughout much of the world. Of those who attended the matinee performance, 150 of the dead were men, three times that number were women and, most heartbreaking of all, 150 were children. Half of all those who perished came from Chicago. Other than the terrible natu-ral disaster of the Galveston hurricane in 1900, nothing in the new century came close to the Iroquois catastrophe in the con-tinental United States. The horror cut across class lines. Bank-ers and railroad executives searched morgues along with clerks and domestic servants, among them the few blacks who had been in the theatre that day.

The combined technologies of wireless and cable had sig-nificantly reduced the time it took information to travel, with the result that from Honolulu to The Hague, the whole world seemed to pause to react emotionally to every detail of the di-saster in the American Midwest. Telegrams of condolence flooded into Washington from foreign capitals and heads of state, many from nations whose citizens were leaving by the thousand to begin new lives in America. The list included the King and Queen of England, the Czar, the Kaiser, King Victor

Emanuel of Italy, the president of the French Republic and leaders of the Scandinavian countries. Lord mayors of many British cities sent wires. Theodore Roosevelt telegraphed Mayor Harrison to express the nation's sorrow. Because it was the era of the so-called "shrieking headline," the president's brief message of condolence was sometimes buried below lurid headlines like the one carried by the *Albuquerque Morning Journal*: "Death's Rich Harvest Reaped in an Instant; Bodies of Dead Crushed to Pulp in Mad Panic."

On that New Year's weekend and into the following week, Chicago's overworked priests, ministers and rabbis held perhaps 300 funerals, each with its own personal story of horror and grief. In some cases, entire families were buried together. One of the city's most respected rabbis became ill from exhaustion after conducting fifteen funerals in that one weekend.

The Holst house was still festooned with Christmas decorations and a large sign that read "Peace on Earth, Good Will Toward Men." Mary Holst was buried together with her thirteen-year-old son and her daughters aged ten and eight, all at Forest Home Cemetery. Only Mary's husband and six-month-old son were left in the house.

At Oakwoods Cemetery the entire family of Dr. M. B. Rimes, his wife and three children, were buried in one large common grave. Mrs. Louis Lange wept uncontrollably at the funeral of her two children, Herbert, seventeen and Agnes, fourteen. "We were four of the happiest mortals in all Chicago until that awful thing blasted our lives forever," she sobbed.

A holiday reunion had turned into horror for friends of Wheaton's prominent physician and civic leader, Dr. Charles S. Owen. He and his party of eleven friends and relatives, eight of them from Ohio, had been seated in the first row of the balcony. All of them perished in the fire and Owen himself died of his injuries hours after the New Year began. Fourteen women fainted at a triple funeral in Evanston's Second Presbyterian Church for Mrs. F. S. Butler, her son and adopted daughter.

Clinton Meeker, a registry clerk in the Chicago Post Office, had lost everyone: his wife, two sons and two daughters. A friend had phoned him the afternoon of the fire to ask whether any of his family had gone to see *Mr. Bluebeard*. Meeker said that, as far as he knew, none of them had gone anywhere. But he got home to find only his mother-in-law there. "Where are Mabel and the children?" he asked. When she replied that they had gone to the Iroquois Theatre, "I dropped right down on my knees," Meeker said, "and prayed that God might spare them." Over the New Year weekend he identified the bodies of his wife and two daughters, but still searched for his sons.

At the morgues, "men showed less hope and courage as a rule than the women did. Mothers rushed breathless down the long rows of victims searching for their children, but often fathers, sons and brothers turned from the doors, lacking the courage to go in. In some morgues lay whole families, and in other cases a father or mother sat alone at home with the remainder of the family dead." Some people arranged for their physicians or dentists to accompany them to make identifications. Many who made the sad pilgrimage to private funeral parlors in the evening were told, with extraordinary insensitivity, to "come back in the morning."

The exact casualty figures were difficult, if not impossible, to determine. An unknown number of the audience who might have been counted among the dead, injured or missing, had been removed from the scene by family members, had somehow managed to get home on their own or, dazed or in shock, had wandered around the Loop for hours before they were discovered. Adding to the difficulty of identification was the fact that victims were being warehoused in different parts of the city, not just in the city morgue and makeshift facilities. This led to days of extraordinary confusion and heartbreak.

Among the first to arrive at Jordan's Funeral Home was George E. McMauglan, attorney for the Chicago and Rock Island Railroad, who had come to look for his daughter Helen. A friend who had been in Dearborn Street when the fire erupted had later discovered Helen's body in Thompson's Restaurant. He had attached a card with her name to the body, and, leaving it in the temporary custody of a physician, had gone to telephone McMauglan. But when he returned, the body had been removed and the distraught father and his friend searched all night without finding it.

Civil authorities were swamped with telephone calls, as were the newspapers. Most of the questions could not be answered. "Have you found a small heart-shaped locket set with a blue stone?" was a typical question. At one morgue a woman asked, "Have you heard anything of my daughter Lily? She was seated in the first balcony. . . . you would know her by her brown hair. She wore a white silk shirtwaist and a diamond ring I gave her for Christmas. I went to the theatre but I couldn't get near it, and they said they were still carrying out bodies. She was my daughter—my only one!"

Hours after the fire a man who had been pronounced dead in Thompson's suddenly revived to find himself wrapped in a blanket inside a wagon hauling a load of bodies to a funeral parlor. He was able to push two of the dead off his chest, sit up and weakly cry out for "more air." He was immediately removed and transferred to a hospital by ambulance.

Rita Wild, a Chicago schoolteacher, successfully escaped from the theatre unassisted and went home on her own with what were described as some burns. She was examined by her family physician, who said she would recover. The young woman died of shock four days later.

Some children made it home by themselves. Two frightened little Aurora girls, aged twelve and fourteen, walked into the offices of a manufacturing company not far from the theatre. They said they were staying with an adult family friend and had been allowed to attend the performance on their own. Somehow they had escaped from the theatre, but were so shaken that they didn't know what to do. Their story touched an employee who took them to a train station and bought them two tickets to Aurora.

They were among the fortunate ones. Theodore Shabad, twelve, had gone to the show with his fourteen-year-old sister Myrtle. Though he was badly injured, Theodore somehow fought his way out of the theatre and staggered eight city blocks in the bitter cold to the office of his father, attorney Henry Shabad. Once inside he collapsed and never regained consciousness. Myrtle was found dead in the theatre.

Dr. D. W. Alexander's son Boyer was found decapitated. He was identified by a pocket watch in his clothing. The watch had been a birthday gift from his father. John Dryden returned home after identifying his wife's body; on the parlor piano was a sheet of music she had been playing just before leaving for the theatre. The title of the piece was "Absence." Myron Decker, the Chicago real estate man who had a particular horror of fire and rarely attended the theatre, had perished along with his wife and daughter. Another victim was Barbara Reynolds, who had muttered to her sister, "What a death trap," as she entered the auditorium.

Clyde Blair, the university track team captain, muscled his way out and escaped with his friends, but other University of Chicago students were not as fortunate. The gifted Walter Zeisler, the Reverend Henry Richardson, Fred Leaton, Daisy Livingston and Gertrude Falkenstein — all lost their lives.

Willie Dee, the twelve-year-old boy who, against his nurse's wishes, decided to leave the Iroquois at the first sign of danger, successfully escaped with his brother Alerton. But his twin brother Edward was killed where he sat and the nurse who had hesitated was trampled to death along with Willie's baby brother.

Edith Mizen, who had attended the performance against her parents' wishes, was the only member of her group to escape unscathed. Another member of the Theta Pi Zeta Club survived with terrible burns and all Edith's other friends died in the theatre.

Harry Ludwig, the businessman who wanted to make the matinee a family occasion, perished with his wife Sadie and their daughters, Eugenie and Caroline, the teenager who had carefully bundled up against the weather. The cash register company where Ludwig was the manager opened its doors to care for at least fifty injured. All afternoon Ludwig's staff worried about him. By six o'clock that evening, when he hadn't returned for his overcoat, they suspected the worst.

The community of Kenosha, Wisconsin, was staggered. The members of the prominent Henry Van Ingen family became separated as they tried to escape. The parents survived with burns. But their five children — Grace, Edward, John, Margaret and Elizabeth — all died in the fire. The wealthy real estate man and his wife eventually recovered from their physical injuries but were psychologically shattered. They never returned to their home, but moved to Tarrytown, New York, where they lived for the rest of their lives.

The popular Cooper brothers of Kenosha decided to remain in their seats rather than risk the stampede for the exits. Their bodies were found near each other. Both had been asphyxiated.

Charlotte Plamondon and the Revell girl and her little friend survived. Alexander Revell heard about the fire while he was in his store, jumped into a cab and made a mad dash to the theatre. Luckily, he quickly found his daughter, her friend and the maid in the street, all uninjured. After Revell arranged to get them away from the scene, he stayed on to help carry out some of the victims. So did Will Davis, who was heard to mumble, as he stared at the rows of covered bodies on the sidewalk, "This is what cuts." Charlotte Plamondon and all of her party escaped from their box, but without their coats "The first thing we did was rush to the shops to buy wraps," she said.

The elegantly dressed and bejeweled Lula Greenwald and her ten-year-old son Leroy lost their lives. Two months later, a bizarre plot to steal Mrs. Greenwald's jewelry was confessed to Chicago police by a New York man, John Mahken. In the confusion following the fire, Mahken concocted a grisly scheme to hire an undertaker to bury her body, which Mahken identified as that of an aunt living in Montreal. He told police that he visited Jordan's funeral home "and cried as real as any person would that lost a dear relative. I identified the body and a sheet was placed over it. I then went to where the unclaimed valuables were, and there I broke down again and wept." Mrs. Greenwald was buried and Mahken was waiting to collect the jewels when her husband, after days of searching through records, had the body disinterred and made the identification.

Ethel Blackburn was the seventeen-year-old daughter of Harry B. Blackburn, who worked at Marshall Field's. In the panic, father and daughter became separated. Blackburn escaped to the Randolph Street lobby and then went back to look for his child. It was a brief search. Blackburn found his daughter's badly burned body on a staircase. Overcome with grief, he wrapped her in his overcoat, carried her out and took a taxi to the Northwestern railroad station where he caught the first train to Glenview. Within thirty minutes he had brought Ethel back home.

Another man used his overcoat as a shroud; he wrapped his wife's body in it and carried her to Evanston, where the circumstances of her death first became known days later after he applied for a burial permit.

More than twenty-four hours after the disaster, a haggard man boarded a Cottage Grove Avenue cable car. In his arms, partially wrapped in a piece of canvas, was the body of a little girl with blond curls. As he took a seat, the conductor eyed him suspiciously, approached and tapped him on the shoulder. "I'm sorry," he said, "but the rules of the company do not permit the carrying of bodies in this manner. I must ask you to leave the car."

Without the slightest change of expression the exhausted man slowly rose, cradling the child in one arm. With his free hand he pulled a large revolver from his pocket, pointed it in the conductor's face and said, with little emotion, "This is my daughter. I have looked for her all last night and all of today. I have not been able to get a cab or a carriage. I am taking my baby home to her mother, and I intend to take her on this car. Now go on." The car proceeded on its way.

Reporters covering the morgues noted that while there were occasional outbursts of hysteria when a positive identification was made, most people were silent as they filed past row after row of the dead, searching for familiar faces, articles of clothing or other personal belongings. Six bushel baskets of items found in the theatre were collected by the police, including at least two large barrels of shoes. For days, officials sifted through the charred interior of the theatre looking for rings, pins and lockets, using sieves and gold pans, the mining methods employed in the California gold fields.

The tragic stories were endless.

One grandfatherly man was heard to say as he left a mortuary, "Just think! I bought the matinee tickets for the children as a treat and insisted they take their little cousin with them." A younger man, waiting in line to view the bodies, gave way at the last moment. "I went to the theatre with my wife," he wept. "We had only been married a year. When the rush came I was torn away from her, and the last thing I remember is of hearing her call my name. Then I was lifted off my feet . . . and later found myself in the street." He never saw her again.

A few days after the fire, a man was seen on Randolph Street, across from the entrance of the padlocked theatre, pacing back and forth in the cold and mumbling to himself. Now and then he sat on the muddy curb as the traffic rumbled by, looked over at what had been the Iroquois and broke into hysterical laughter. It was said he had lost his wife and children in the fire.

In the days before long distance calls became common, tragic details were briefly transmitted in scores of telegrams. Typical was one exchange between the friends of Harriet Harbaugh, a schoolteacher in Savanna, Illinois, who, with a friend named Rose, was spending the holidays with her sister Mary, a Chicago kindergarten teacher:

SAVANNA, ILL., DEC. 31—Miss Mary Harbaugh, 6653 Harvard Avenue, Chicago. Is report of Harriet's death true? Wire answer. F. S. GREENLEAF

CHICAGO, DEC. 31—F. S. Greenleaf, Savanna, Ill.: Harriet unconscious at Samaritan Hospital. Rose at St. Luke's. Mary dead. MRS. WARNER.

In rural Galesburg, the family of Dorsha Hayes was safely at home, but the town was reeling from the news that its postmaster, F. A. Freer, had lost both his wife and daughter, Alda

Henry, in the fire. Postmaster Freer had caught the midnight fast mail train to Chicago and wired his family the following morning, "Have found Alda dead; Mamma not yet found; will wire you later. PAPA."

Even at sea one could not escape the tragedy. The liner *Lucania,* bound from New York to Queenstown, was fifty miles off the Irish coast when it received an AP dispatch by Marconigram with details of the disaster, which was immediately posted in the ship's smoking room. The novelty of receiving the day's news on the high seas must have quickly worn off among the passengers, many of them from Chicago.

At least one person at sea would not learn of the tragedy for weeks, if not months. On the afternoon of December 30, Ralph Taylor sailed from a South American port for China. His parents, Mr. and Mrs. J. M. Taylor of Chicago, his twelve-year-old sister Reine and their maid had attended the *Bluebeard* performance and all had died. Taylor could not be reached because only his parents knew the name of his ship.

Eddie Foy became an international hero overnight. Virtually every account of the tragedy mentioned his name and included all or part of his story of how he had tried to stop the panic. All but two of the nearly 350 people who worked in the *Bluebeard* production survived, the exceptions being Nellie Reed, who died from burns in Cook County Hospital, and the German aerialist who had plunged from the rigging. Some of the company, including Foy, suffered burns and other injuries. The comedian thought it was a miracle that so few of the company had died, and said so in testimony before a special investigative committee and also in a strangely worded note dated January 5, 1904, perhaps written to one of the cast members: "The catastrophe at the Iroquois was a miracle. I consider[ed the Iroquois] a perfect theatre and I don't think that from the time the fire started till the stampede took place and people were smothered in the gallery, could not have exceeded ninety seconds [*sic*] . . . It was not a fire but a miracle."

But Chicagoans did not consider the fire "a miracle." For days, the front pages of the city's newspapers crowded out other events with stories of the fire; the fluctuating casualty figures; photos of the theatre's scorched interior and of police and other officials standing next to exit doors where the greatest loss of life occurred; editorial cartoons; artists' sketches of the fire in progress, and heartbreaking photographs of many of the victims, often made all the more tragic because of the angelic poses which were common in children's portraiture of that time.

Forty-three-year-old Mayor Harrison issued a string of edicts, closing first all theatres and places of public amusement with the exception of the Chicago Auditorium which had a steel fire curtain, and then extending the closure to dime museums, dance halls and other public buildings. Even hospitals were not spared; some were told to stop admitting patients until the building department could make safety inspections. Thousands of people were affected.

A coroner's inquest was launched to determine the exact cause of the fire, and a special blue ribbon committee of architects and builders was appointed to interview survivors and report directly to the mayor. But despite these quick responses, despite his assurances of immediate improvements in public safety and his personal and obviously genuine solicitude for the bereaved, Carter Henry Harrison, Jr., a Reform Democrat, the city's thirtieth mayor and the first to be born in Chicago, would quickly find himself at the center of a controversy that would continue into 1904, and, at least for some of the victims' families, to the end of his political career.

Among those who would never forget was Max Remer, a teenage courier who had wept all the way home on the trolley the evening of the fire. He had just finished delivering the last batch of messages in the Loop when he saw policemen and men in derby hats trying to divert traffic from clogged Randolph Street. He made his way through jammed streets and sidewalks to help with the rescue efforts. "We tried to get as many out and to go back for more," he said. When the dirty, dishevelled and tear-stained boy arrived home late for dinner that night, his father was furious. His mother drew a warm bath and gave him a change of clothes. It was only then that in halting words he told his parents what had happened. As his younger brother recalled, Max tried to compose himself to talk about a "horror no fifteen-year-old should have witnessed."

But age made little difference to the reaction of witnesses, summed up by D. W. Dimmick, the elderly bearded man who had made it safely out of the theatre from standing room in the gallery, and survived to return to his rural Illinois home. "I came from Apple River to see the sights of Chicago," he said, "and I have seen all that I can stand."

THE BLAME GAME

"Chicago is in the hands of a government of monkeys."
—*Rev. Franklyn Johnson, University of Chicago*

THE FINGER-POINTING HAD actually begun well before the fire, and given the dynamics and realities of Chicago politics, it was ugly. Weeks before the Iroquois opened, the investigative journalist Lincoln Steffens, in his landmark muckraking series, "The Shame of Our Cities," had painted an unflinching and damning portrait of Chicago under Carter Harrison.

"It is absurdly backward and uneven; the fire department is excellent, the police is a disgrace, the law department is expert, the health bureau is corrupt, and the street cleaning is hardly worth mention," he wrote. "All this is Carter H. Harrison. He is an honest man personally, but indolent; a shrewd politician, and a character with reserve power, but he has no initial energy. Without ideals, he does not know what is demanded of him. He does not seem to know wrong is wrong, till he is taught; nor to care, till criticism arouses his political sense of popular requirement. But think of it, every time Chicago wants to go ahead a foot, it has first to push its mayor up inch by inch. In brief, Chicago is a city that wants to be led, and Carter Harrison, with all his political ambition, honest willingness, and obstinate independence, simply follows it."

Municipal corruption was a given. Police, aldermen, building inspectors and others followed Harrison's hands-off attitude. "Boodling," or payoffs, was a word often heard and printed in the papers. Bookmaking was openly carried out in corner cigar stores. A state law required that saloons be closed on Sundays, but Harrison did not enforce it. So open were the bordellos that the sisters who ran the city's notorious, elegant Everleigh Club were emboldened to publish and distribute a slick brochure complete with photographs, advertising the brothel's many amenities.

The press, despite critical editorials, went along with much of this. The *Tribune,* for example, in its war on vice, specifically attacked the Everleigh brochure, but night clerks who needed to round up reporters quickly were instructed to first call the club. It was said that reporters treated the "nightly shootings, robberies, kidnappings and occasional scandals involving playboys" of the seamy First Ward red-light Levee district, including everything short of murder, "as amusing recreational reading." The press corps, which in 1903 numbered nearly 600, was not held in particularly high esteem by the mayor, who often found himself criticized and ridiculed by many of the local dailies.

Harrison once described the *Tribune's* Charles Powers, who was then delving into the mayor's political life for a series, as "a reporter of the old school, none too clean, physically or morally. . . . For years," said the mayor, "Powers had worked on City Hall assignments . . . neither then nor now are newspaper men with an itching palm left out of consideration when a good thing is sprung in council or legislature. The [aldermen] long ago learned that having them on the payroll pays off."

The mayor, who earned $833 a month, was no less critical of most of the city's aldermen—whose monthly stipend was $125, and many of whom were saloon keepers, owners of gambling houses and undertakers—often referring to them as "a motley crew" and "gangsters." In turn, members of the press and social reformers pointed to the corruption of the aldermen as a reflection of Harrison's own ineptitude. The city's pioneering architect Louis Sullivan once called Chicago "this flat smear, this endless drawl of streets and shanties, large and small, this ocean of smoke . . . Seventy years ago it was a mudhole—today it is a human swamp."

"Nearly everything was a lie in the city," recalled Edgar Lee Masters. "Harrison [believed the] vices could not be eradicated and they could only be driven from one cover to another and in the face of numerous [reform] committees . . . who implored him to enforce the law, he let the city have as it would, concerning himself with order and the proper protection of the citizens." However, in permitting the Iroquois Theatre to open when it did, the popular mayor appeared to have concerned himself with neither.

Because of the long-running feud between Harrison and most of the city's seventy aldermen, the tragic consequences had been set in motion at least seven weeks before the theatre first opened its doors to the public. At that time the mayor charged that "petty grafting and wholesale grafting were rife in [virtually] every Chicago municipal department," a sensational charge even in a city used to sensational stories. "If," said Harrison, who was then serving his fourth consecutive term in office, "I could fire all the men I suspect of 'grafting' they would all be jumping out of every window in City Hall. This hall is full of 'graft, big and little.' You know it and can't prove it. I've got eighteen months left, and I'll get some of them yet."

In the wake of the Iroquois disaster, the mayor accused aldermen of not acting fast enough on the critical study submitted by Building Commissioner George Williams two months
before the tragedy. Harrison declared that "if anyone was to
blame [for the fire] they were" because they had suspended action on a new city theatre ordinance, saying that it needed further "examination." Harrison said that on October 19, the city
council had ordered "that any action against the theatre violations be stayed until the judiciary committee reported on the
amended ordinance." A resolution was passed calling on the
mayor to name three aldermen who, together with the city engineer and building commissioner, would constitute a committee for the purpose of drafting new ordinances controlling construction of theatres, and report back to the council within three
weeks.

In his defense, Harrison said he had submitted to the council such a document on November 2, eight weeks before the
disaster, based on information from Commissioner Williams,
but that it had been referred back to the judiciary committee,
which at the time the Iroquois fire occurred, had "practically
agreed upon amending ordinances, giving time to the theatres
to comply." In not taking immediate action against the numerous theatre violations, said the mayor, the council, not he, was
responsible for the dreadful disaster.

Box office employees at other theatres blamed the "Free
List" of tickets commonly given out by Chicago playhouses
"constructed and conducted in violation of municipal laws."
One theatre official said, "When a manager hands out passes to
officials he subsidizes them. A pass is nothing more or less than
compensation for some service . . ." Those who failed to pay a
"tribute," he said, " often suffered certain persecution."

Theatre owners Davis and Powers rushed to provide an
implausible excuse in a statement issued to Chicago papers.

When the blaze first broke out, they said, the house fireman "threw the contents of the [Kilfyre] which would have been more than enough, if [the product] had been effective, to have extinguished the flame at once, but for some cause inherent in the tube of Kilfyre it had no effect." Then they blamed the victims: "The audience was promptly admonished and importuned by persons on the stage and in the auditorium to be calm and avoid any rush." They added that "the exits and facilities for emptying the theatre were ample to enable them all to get out without confusion."

They concluded this specious statement saying that "no expense or precaution was omitted to make the theatre as fireproof as it could be made, there being nothing combustible in the construction of the house except the trimmings and furnishings of the stage, and in building the theatre we sacrificed more space to aisles and exits than any theatre in America."

In an exemplary example of poor timing, to say nothing of bad taste, Will Davis' wife, the actress and singer Jessie Bartlett Davis, joined the fray from Philadelphia, where she was performing. She, too, blamed the theatre victims for the disaster, claiming that it was the *actors* whose lives were regularly in danger. "It is the fault of the public that such things occur. In these swift days the public is not satisfied with good, quiet shows," she declared. "They must have lots of excitement, color and light, with the result that every actor takes his life in his hands when he goes before the footlights." She added, "I do not understand how the asbestos curtain failed to work. Mr. Davis drilled his men every day in the use of the apparatus and in the dropping of the curtain. Never before was there any hitch."

The claim that the Kilfyre had failed to work was immediately challenged by one alderman who said the theatre's management had been explicitly warned about the inadequacy of the product after a member of his staff, a former veteran city fireman, had visited the theatre. One day before the tragedy, said the alderman, a member of the theatre's management was warned by the former firefighter that "[t]he fire apparatus you have here would do no more good than a bucket of water in a sawmill," but the fireman "was told to mind his own business; he was not running the theatre."

Powers was accused of buying cheap, inferior material for the asbestos curtain in order to save money. The local manager of the Johns-Manville Company said that a pure asbestos curtain would have "stood the test" of the Iroquois fire. "If it had been woven properly it would have sufficient tensile strength to withstand any wind pressure, provided it was properly supported at the top and sides." Johns-Manville wasted no time in distancing itself from the episode, taking out a prominent ad in at least one theatrical paper: "Asbestos Curtains That Stop Fires . . . are pure asbestos interwoven with brass wire. The Iroquois Theatre curtain was not one of ours."

"The . . . curtain was not asbestos at all," declared Gustave J. Johnson, a chemist and member of the Western Society of Engineers. He said he had examined a piece of the fabric after the fire and found that while it contained some asbestos, "it was largely wood pulp. By mixing pulp with asbestos fiber, the life of the curtain is prolonged, the cost is cheapened and the wire foundation can be dispensed with. . . . It results in a curtain that may get inside city ordinances but is of no value in a fire."

Robert McClean, editor of *Inland Architect*, charged that "the theatre was not equipped with a curtain such as is demanded in the city ordinances." Chicago fire insurance underwriters accused the city of failing to comply with established building ordinances and failing to enforce them; this was not, the underwriters said, the insurance industry's responsibility. The theatre, it turned out, was not insured.

Benjamin Marshall, the Iroquois architect, who was on a business trip to Pittsburgh when the fire occurred, caught the first train back to Chicago. Shocked by what had happened, he said he could not understand the loss of life because there had been so many available exits. He announced, however, that in the future he would cease his lavish use of interior wood trim and heavy, flammable curtains. Boldly, or foolishly, he defended the use of drapery to mask the exits; this, he said, was to "improve the interior look" of his new theatre. He added that in his design there was an electrical switch near the box office that could have turned on the auditorium lights, but the staff was apparently unfamiliar with its location.

The Klaw-Erlanger organization was blamed at once for its use of highly combustible scenery imported from England; later the Theatrical Trust would be accused of disregarding the safety of its patrons by violating city fire regulations. *Life* magazine mentioned Klaw and Erlanger by name in the caption of a cartoon showing the skeleton figure of Death holding the keys and standing in front of the locked entrance of the Iroquois through which hands of the victims could be seen struggling to open the doors. The magazine was unsuccessfully sued for libel.

Chief Musham was blamed for not demanding that Fireman Sallers inform him of the incomplete fire apparatus inside the theatre. In his defense, Musham said that although he did not require Sallers to report to him on the condition of the sprinklers and the fire apparatus, it was still Sallers' responsibility to do so. Musham said there "were so many fires in Chicago during the time the [Iroquois] was fitted out I was kept busy day and night and overlooked the matter." His statement about "so many fires" was in direct contradiction to a *Record-Herald* story quoting him saying on December 31, "Five minutes before the first alarm came in from the Iroquois, Deputy Fire Marshal Campion and myself were congratulating each other on our luck this winter. Chicago had been freer from bad fires up to yesterday than any previous cold season in years."

As the arguments swirled, the fire department's attorney Monroe Fulkerson launched his own investigation and John E. Traeger, the city coroner, prepared for an inquest involving hundreds of witnesses. He promised that the guilty would be brought to justice. Virtually everyone connected to the Iroquois was blamed for something. Local unions blamed the theatre management for ignoring them and—possibly taking advantage of layoffs by the Fuller Construction Company—trying to save money by hiring unskilled workers. The Chicago Federation of Labor said the theatre had refused to hire well-paid, experienced workmen, and that it had proof that William McMullen, the operator of the light that caused the fire, was just "learning the trade."

Oliver Sollett, one of the city's largest contractors, said that "bribery and graft were responsible, that in addition to the theatre having no place to emit smoke and fumes, that chairs were placed where specifications called for aisles" and that the exits were too small to allow patrons to escape. A prominent local architect, Robert S. Lindstrom, announced that "every theatre in Chicago is virtually a death-trap," as were public meeting halls.

The Fuller Company was blamed for, among other things, not completing the apparatus controlling the skylights above the stage—which might have vented most of the smoke and flames through the roof rather than into the balcony and gallery—and by leaving the skylights nailed down with scantlings, or wooden timbers. These accusations against Fuller were extremely serious; the contractor made matters worse by attempting to tamper with the evidence. On the day after the fire, while the theatre was surrounded by Pinkerton detectives and city police, Fuller workmen gained access to the roof from an adjoining building and removed the scantlings, opening one of the skylights before city inspectors and other officials could examine them.

Their illegal activities flew in the face of a statement issued by Fuller's Western manager, W. A. Merriman, immediately after the fire. Merriman, who nearly lost his wife and three-year-old daughter in the blaze, said, "The Iroquois Theatre was built with safety as the first consideration. All the building ordinances were adhered to in every detail . . . I do not hesitate to state that there was no theatre building in the country which was freer from danger. The exits were numerous and all the work our company performed was absolutely fireproof . . . After making a careful inspection . . . since the fire I find that the structure, as erected, still stands." That the building was still standing was true, but the fact remained that hundreds had died because of the incomplete ventilation system and the unattached fire escapes.

The press, not just in Chicago, was unanimous in its condemnation of the theatre owners and the city administration. Harrison's closing of Chicago's theatres was criticized as too little and too late. One day after the fire, the *Tribune* reflected the anger, shock and disbelief of the city, if not the nation: "The theatre had just been built and inspected. It had been built by artisans whom, in our moments of national pride, we call the cleverest in the world. It had been inspected by officials whom recent public indignation was supposed to have awakened to some sense of public duty. It was a modern building, constructed with modern requirements. It was said, and it was supposed to be the fact, that the building was not only a fireproof one but that every device which human ingenuity, spurred by a desire to guard human life, could think of had been installed—that abundant precautions were taken, and that the theatre, at least, was safe. Yet, that is the theatre which has gained a terrible celebrity.

"The dead cannot be called to life, but the other theatres of Chicago can be inspected in light of the dread illumination of the Iroquois fire."

The *New York Herald* took the historic view: "Not since the burning of the Ring Theatre in Vienna in 1881 when about nine hundred people were killed, has any disaster occurred in its magnitude and horror with the destruction of the Iroquois. It is necessary to turn to the great cataclysms of nature, like the eruption of Mont Pele which overwhelmed Martinique, for anything to match it for sudden and wholesale dealing of death."

Carter Harrison quickly moved to tamp down criticism of his administration and the theatre management by choosing certain aldermen to make speeches urging public calm and moderation at the first city council meeting since the fire. The *Inter-Ocean*, for one, noted the tactic, describing Harrison's "precautions" as "puerile," "futile" and "craven": "From the living, [the mayor's] neglect of his plain duty for days, months and years needs no elaborate criticism or special censure. Carter H. Harrison is judged, censured and condemned by the dumb lips of five hundred ninety-one dead."

As the days passed, the *Chicago Tribune* expressed mounting indignation: "In all justice it must be said that the chief responsibility rests upon the city administration, which, either through carelessness, sloth, or ignorance, or because it had incapable and corrupt servants, or from a mistaken sense of security, chose to let these theatres run themselves as they saw fit, without any reference to any measures for the protection of human life.

"The managers must take their share of the blame, for, while they may be accused of nothing more than criminal carelessness and unreasonable confidence in the assurances of architects and builders that their theatre was 'fireproof,' they cannot escape censure. Nor can the owners, architect, and builders of the theatre . . . be acquitted in the public mind of a full share of the responsibility for the disaster."

"Tardy Zeal in Chicago," headlined the *New York Times,* whose readers included many of the most powerful names on Broadway. "How does it come to pass that so many, or any, theatres could open their doors and do business month after month under conditions of such obvious violation of the law that a casual inspection would discover the fact? Is this official nonfeasance or just ordinary 'graft'? The trouble is less with the law than with laxness in its enforcement, and the persons primarily responsible for the Chicago horror are the city officials of Chicago."

One of the oldest and smallest newspapers in a territory seeking statehood joined the angry chorus. The Santa Fe *New Mexican,* with the "shoot from the hip" mentality of what was still considered the Wild West, was both outraged and outspoken when it came to meting out fit punishment: "The more the Iroquois Theatre is being investigated, the more strongly it appears that absolute, highly criminal and other carelessness on the part of the owners and managers of the building and theatre caused the awful deaths. Hanging is too good for the men responsible."

Life magazine—no relation, as we have said, to the Luce publication—ever on the attack against the Trust, cited the obvious: "The [Iroquois] was new and was called fireproof . . . [This] is a story of a cheap asbestos curtain that would not come down, of exits and fire escapes by which people could not get out, of laws not enforced and precautions neglected; a dismal story of preventable disaster."

Nineteen hundred and four began with nearly every major U.S. city announcing plans for immediate inspections of theatres and enclosed public places. Authorities quickly padlocked some facilities, including the New York playhouse owned by

Weber and Fields. Thousands of actors and others associated with the theatre, not just in Chicago, suddenly found themselves without work.

The disaster was editorial fodder for foreign newspapers, especially in Great Britain. The *Times* of London said, "It is stated . . . that the fire escapes of the theatre had not been completed and that caused the loss of many lives. If this is true, it indicates absolutely unpardonable carelessness on the part not only of the proprietors of the theatre, but of Chicago city authorities." The *Globe* asked "[h]ow the Chicago authorities came to permit such an awful death trap to be constructed." The *Pall Mall Gazette* commented, "The scheme of exits appears to have been practically worthless," and the *London Daily Mirror* commented that "the horrible disaster . . . has startled and shocked the whole world. No word-painting can convey the faintest idea of such a tragedy, which leaves us benumbed and silenced."

Chicago's religious leaders were outraged. The Iroquois tragedy inflamed the passions of usually mild-mannered clergymen, many of whom spoke for their angry, confused and frightened congregants. The city is in the hands of "[a] government of monkeys," declared the Reverend Franklyn Johnson of the University of Chicago. "It is ridiculous for those men in office to spring up now with the cry of 'Punish the guilty' while they are the guilty ones. It is time for intelligent people to wake up and see in whose hands the safety of their lives is entrusted."

"Let no guilty man escape," thundered Bishop Samuel Fallows of St. Paul's Reformed Episcopal Church, who happened to have been walking past the Iroquois at the time of the catastrophe and so was able to attend immediately to the injured and dying. "God forbid that I should see such a sight again. I have been on a bloody battlefield but I have never seen anything half so gruesome."

Rabbi Moses Perez Jacobson, of K.A.M., Congregation Kehillat Anshe Ma'ariv, (Congregation of Men of the West), conducting the funeral for the two Shabad children, called the fire "one of the great calamities of the age." Another rabbi at a memorial service said, "This fire was not an act of God but due to criminal ignorance, neglect and recklessness."

So intense was the condemnation of the city's leaders that the mayor's sister collapsed in her pew at St. James Episcopal Church after the Reverend James Stone said in his sermon that "Easy-going indifference to the proper observation of law [was] the municipality's prevailing and astounding sin." The Reverend George Wright of St. Luke's Hospital declared, "The essence of the calamity . . . is a revelation of the spirit of greed for gain and utter political corruption which leads men to be shamefully unmindful of their duty." His remarks were echoed by Mrs. Corrine Brown, principal speaker at the Chicago Social Economics Club, who spoke for many women when she declared that the fire was the result of "man's greed."

Mayor Harrison was under attack from all sides. Some local papers ran an almost daily series of front-page cartoons lampooning him as an oaf and a buffoon. He attempted to respond to public pressure, but his actions, no matter what, were loaded with political and economic consequences. Because of the closures, 6000 Chicago performers and theatre employees were out of work in the first two weeks of 1904, (as were theatre professionals in other cities), and with many of Chicago's theatres dark, business leaders, including downtown restaurant owners and others, were alarmed at the prospect of an economic disaster.

When theatre managers and others lined the corridors of City Hall to urge the mayor to withdraw or at least postpone the closure order, they received what was described as "a frosty reception." Harrison let it be known that other public places would also be inspected, including dance halls, houses of worship, office buildings and department stores. Police made the first of many arrests, starting with twenty carpenters, stagehands and even members of the "Pale Moonlight" double octet, some of whom were charged with involuntary manslaughter. The entertainers were actually held on a technicality so they might serve as witnesses. The same involuntary manslaughter charge was brought against the theatre's co-owners, Davis and Powers, and Building Commissioner Williams, all of whom were placed under arrest.

The arrest warrants were issued by Justice George Underwood at the insistence of Arthur Hull, the Chicago businessman who had lost his wife and three children in the tragedy, and whose wrenching comments were wired to every corner of the globe. "It is too terrible to contemplate," Hull said. "I can never go to my home again. To look at playthings left by the children just where they put them, to see how my dear dead wife arranged the details of her home so carefully, the very walls ring with the names of my dear dead ones. I can never go there again.

"My wife and my children, all I ever had to live for, are gone. All that remains is for me to try to make someone pay for this carelessness. A few carpenters and stagehands have been arrested. Men who sang in the chorus are in jail. Such an investigation is a cruel mockery. The men who are responsible are allowed to walk the streets untouched while a few laborers are punished. The authorities must understand that those who have suffered will not wait for them to dally along. There must be no politics or favoritism in this investigation."

The press paid close attention to the mayor's every move. As he and aldermen began an inspection tour of the theatre on January 1, reporters recorded that Harrison unknowingly "trod on a lock of human hair which had been torn from the head of some victim of the disaster." With the exception of the basement, where firemen were still pumping out brackish water and police were searching in vain for more bodies, the mayor examined everything from the rigging loft to the fire escapes. The place was crowded with photographers and their boxy cameras shot everything from the ruined stage and auditorium to the locked accordion gates and doors where so many people had become trapped. The blistered walls, overturned chairs in the orchestra, piles of fabric on the floor of what had been the Grand Promenade—all were recorded for posterity.

Benjamin Marshall accompanied the mayor on the tour. At one point the mayor noted the failure to comply with the ordinance requiring that exits were to be indicated by printed signs. He asked especially why some of the exit doors had been covered by damask curtains. Marshall's response about improving the appearance of the house was not well received, nor was his explanation that the exit signs "were being made, but temporary signs were not being used because it was not desired to mar the beauty of the interior with them."

This rather stupid explanation evoked an immediate angry response from one alderman, who snapped, "This theatre was opened on November 23. It has been running fully five weeks. In Heaven's name, how long does it take to make signs?"

Charles Collins reported an element of the architect's motivation in the theatre's design which, if true, was at once both revealing and disturbing. In Marshall's plan, the same staircase reached both the main auditorium and the first and second balconies. This violated Chicago city ordinances requiring that both balconies have separate stairways and street entrances. Ignoring these regulations was a fatal error: many lives might have been saved if those in the upper parts of the house could have exited using their own stairways rather than having to crush into the jam of people converging into the same vestibule from different sections of the theatre.

Collins learned that the single grand staircase was designed to appeal to the class-consciousness of the theatre-attending public. This idea was reinforced by a sentence in the opening night souvenir booklet: "To see and be seen is the duality of advantage presented for patrons of the Iroquois."

This phrase—"to see and be seen"—resonated with Collins. He had heard that when Marshall was showing off the new theatre to a group of friends before the opening, he had said, with considerable pride, "Do you notice that sections of the first and second balconies enter by the same marble staircase? The purchasers of cheap seats will look just as prosperous as the others when they go up those stairs, and people like it better than to have to go outside and enter by separate entrances. Then, when friends see them coming down the marble steps, [the friends] do not know whether they came from the first or second balcony."

Apart from this unattractive appeal to snobbery, the design elements of the balcony promenade and grand staircase were criticized as confusing, especially in a panic situation. Coming out of the balcony was a promenade extending around the foyer. To go down to the lobby, balcony patrons had first to walk up four steps, turn left, and then descend the grand staircase. The wall near the top of the stairway was also confusing. While it appeared to be a double door, one half of it was actually mirrored glass on a fixed wooden frame.

As newspapers all over the country denounced the safety standards of the Klaw-Erlanger Theatrical Trust, the partners tried frantically to disassociate themselves from the tragedy. In a January 4 letter published in the *New York Times*, they complained, "A paper in this city is willfully and maliciously endeavoring to create the impression in the public mind that this firm is the responsible owner of the Iroquois Theatre, Chicago. The facts, which are easy to access to any one, are that Marc Klaw and A. L. Erlanger each own twelve and a half percent of the stock of this theatre, and have never owned any more." They added that they had " every faith in the integrity and competency of Messrs. Will J. Davis and Harry J. Powers, who are also stockholders, and the resident managers of that house, and we believe that when calmer counsels prevail and the proper investigation is completed, it will be found that nothing was left undone that could have been foreseen to safeguard the public from that lamentable disaster."

The press, however, refused to buy any defensive arguments from city officials or the theatre owners. A national magazine, *The Independent* (formerly *Harpers Weekly*), put it succinctly: "It would appear as if there had been a conspiracy of catastrophe in the case of the Iroquois Theatre."

It was against this backdrop of fear, grief, rage, charge and countercharge, accusation, denial, innuendo, contradiction and confusion that the city of Chicago would witness one of the longest, strangest, most emotional and dramatic legal battles in its history.

{16}

THE INQUEST

"Evidence of gross neglect was brought to light today."
—Monroe Fulkerson, Attorney,
Chicago Fire Department

ON SUNDAY, JANUARY 3, six days before *Mr. Bluebeard's* Chicago run would have ended and the company disbanded, nearly 150 members of the troupe boarded a train for New York, all of them downcast and most nearly destitute. In the baggage car was a white coffin containing the body of Nellie Reed. Mrs. Ogden Armour of the Chicago meat-packing family contributed five hundred dollars for the dancers to settle hotel bills, but most of the young women had lost clothing and other personal items, and all needed money for food. Each was owed half a week's salary, which would not go far. "Here I am, one thousand miles from home, no prospects of another engagement this season and only five dollars in the world," one girl said. Another responded that she owned only three dollars to go home with; she had lost her savings of twenty-two dollars in the fire.

Klaw-Erlanger furnished one-way transportation back to New York City. Those heading east would quickly discover that, because of the Iroquois disaster, the theatre world had changed overnight. Cities across America and Europe were taking a closer look at fire safety in public places and some were following Chicago's lead and closing down playhouses.

Broadway was the strongest barometer of change. On New Year's Eve, one Manhattan theatre manager stationed eleven firemen throughout his house, other New York theatres began refusing to sell "Standing Room Only" tickets, and at a performance of *Parsifal*, management had stationed no fewer than forty-eight uniformed police officers inside the New York Metropolitan Opera building. On January first in New York, a new city fire commissioner had taken office promising a crackdown on theatre safety violations, a politically wise pledge since New York's outgoing fire commissioner had told the press that some Broadway theatres were worse firetraps than the Iroquois. At least four playhouses were closed immediately.

Oscar Hammerstein, owner of the Victoria Theatre, proclaimed that because of the Iroquois fire no children would ever be admitted to one of his playhouses. He added that he considered a female with a child to be one of the most dangerous combinations that could be found inside a theatre. He apparently did not foresee that this exceedingly odd statement would anger many women.

Klaw and Erlanger announced that they would no longer produce "extravaganzas." This was a promise that was kept for less than a year.

Theatre managers in Paris expressed amazement that this tragedy could have occurred in Chicago, "where it was supposed at last that a really fireproof theatre had been realized." An official at the Comédie Française wondered why, if the Iroquois was a copy of the Comédie, it had no iron curtain, which he believed would have averted the disaster. Visiting the French capital, Bertha Palmer, the wife of Potter Palmer and the *doy-*

enne of Chicago society, when informed of the fire, "put her hands to her head in horror as if to shut out further details of the catastrophe. 'Don't say any more,'" she cried to a reporter, "'it's only names, names, names, I want.'"

Berlin papers, expressing horror and sympathy, reported that the fire department had announced it would immediately make a fresh study of protective arrangements at theatres. This was followed in a matter of days by an order from Kaiser Wilhelm closing the Berlin Royal Opera House until it could be adapted to meet new safety standards. In Vienna, where many members of the American colony had come from the Midwest, sympathy for Chicago was combined with especially painful memories of the Ring Theatre disaster, one of Europe's worst calamities in the previous century.

In London, theatre managers said they expected that the news from Chicago would "keep thousands away" at the height of the British pantomime season. "Audiences at performances that appeal . . . to women and children are likely to be cut in half," said one manager, adding that virtually every theatre and music hall in Europe would be affected. The chief of the London fire brigade asked for a detailed report of the disaster and the head of the British fire prevention system wired for plans of the theatre, remarking that "the piles of dead in certain places in the passages indicate faulty construction." The London County Council, the licensing authority for 350 places of entertainment, said it regarded a large number of structures in the British capital as dangerous and that the Iroquois tragedy would strengthen their hand in requesting not only permission to destroy the firetraps, but also an increase in the budget for fire personnel and equipment.

The Continent was gripped by fear. On January 3 alone there were three stampedes showing "how powerfully the Chicago theatre holocaust ha[d] affected the minds of people. There was panic in a circus in Nantes, in a church in Prussia and in a hippodrome in Antwerp, in each case following an alarm of 'fire.'"

♣

In Chicago, some female members of the double octet, held as material witnesses, had been furnished bonds that secured their temporary release. They could not leave the city because they had to testify at the coroner's inquest. Male members of the group remained behind bars, but not for very long.

The inquest began in Chicago's City Hall at 9:30 on the cold morning of Thursday, January 7, exactly one week and one day after the disaster. Two hundred witnesses were expected to testify over a six-day period, with teams of stenographers poised to record every word in pen and ink.

Those who had been summoned to appear were a strange mix. Members of the *Bluebeard* audience who showed no outward physical signs of their ordeal sat with others swathed in bandages and gauze hiding terrible welts and burns. Emil Von Plachecki, the young man who had punched his way through a skylight, was so covered in bandages that only his eyes and mouth were visible. Wealthy and socially important Chicago families shared benches with unemployed actors, passersby, theatre officials, uniformed policemen, comedians, building inspectors, dancers, wardrobe mistresses, bereaved relatives, stagehands, firemen and domestic servants. Nearly every stratum of Chicago society was there, waiting together in anterooms until, one by one, they would be questioned in the large city council chamber. The press was of course present in the person of reporters and photographers with their bulky cameras and flash pans. The public was admitted to the gallery of the hot, stuffy

room, reeking of cigar and cigarette smoke, prompting com-
plaints from at least one survivor, Mrs. Pinedo.

Coroner John Traeger and his six-man panel heard a bewildering number of accounts, all vivid and terrible, some involving acts both of cowardice and bravery, and many others contradictory. Some stagehands testified, for instance, that it was
the explosion of a backstage calcium light tank filled with hy-
drogen that was responsible for the blaze. The stage manager
insisted that the flames shot out from the electrical switchboard,
though it was hardly likely he would have known since he was
absent when the fire first broke out.

Some said they were sure that a spark from a short circuit
in the carbon arc lamp had started the fire; others said a gust of
wind had brushed a curtain against the super-heated light. There
were those who swore it was not a curtain that first caught on
fire but a piece of gauze. Some witnesses testified that it was not
the swinging light reflector but the wire used for Nellie Reed's
aerial ballet that blocked the descent of the asbestos curtain. A
few members of the audience said that what came down was
not the asbestos curtain at all, but the theatre's main drop.

There was conflicting testimony about the ushers: some said
they had refused to unlock exit doors, some that they had all
fled after the first sign of trouble, and some maintained that all
the ushers had steadfastly remained at their posts. The backstage elevator boy was accused of being one of the first to flee,
but Eddie Foy and many girls in the chorus called him nothing
less than a hero. Foy too contradicted himself, at first telling
reporters that when the fire began he was just offstage in the
wings and actually saw it happen, but then testifying that he
was in his dressing room at the time preparing for his next act.

Some people swore there had been an earlier fire in the theatre when it first opened; others could remember nothing of the

sort. There was mention of a quickly extinguished backstage fire when the show played in Cleveland. But that was denied by other members of the troupe.

Even the death toll was disputed. The coroner's official list, used at the inquest, contained 565 names; previous police reports of 591 dead had been declared inaccurate because of the shifting of bodies from one mortuary to another. The figure eventually rose to 602, but there would always be a question about the exact count.

Before the inquest commenced, Monroe Fulkerson, the attorney in charge of the fire department's investigation, heard startling admissions. The theatre's business manager, Thomas Noonan, a man who had previously escaped notice, admitted that even though it was part of his responsibility, he had never instructed the men under him about what to do in case of fire, and had not assigned anyone to manage the fire apparatus. He admitted that two ground-floor exits on Randolph Street were locked and that the north fire exits, three each from the orchestra section and the first and second balcony floors, were bolted. Noonan admitted that he had never discussed with the head usher George Dusenberry, or any of the other ushers, how to prevent loss of life in case of a panic. He assumed, he said, that the head usher "knew his business." All he told Sallers, the house fireman, was just to "comply with city ordinances."

Questioned about the operation of the roof ventilators, Noonan replied that there were three men in charge of the apparatus: in addition to Dusenberry, there were the house electrician and the building's engineer. But Dusenberry denied responsibility. He said, "My duties were in the auditorium . . . and the ventilators were worked from the stage." Both the electrician and the engineer said they had been given no authority to operate either the ventilators or the skylights.

Noonan's testimony, said Fulkerson, was the single most important piece of evidence since his investigation began, because it so clearly showed "incompetence and negligence." He went on, "Evidence of gross neglect was brought to light today. Fifteen witnesses who worked on the stage stated they never received any orders from the management as to what to do in case of fire. There never was a fire drill in the theatre, nor was any one of the stagehands informed as to the location or use of fire apparatus and the operation of the ventilators over the auditorium and stage." He concluded, "Everything which should *not* have been done was done apparently, and things which *should* have been done were left undone."

As the coroner's inquest began, a "deluge of suits" was lodged against the theatre, its management and the city of Chicago. The first of the actions, seeking ten thousand dollars, was filed by Ivy Owens, administrator of the estate of Amy Owens, one of the schoolteachers who was killed, and her mother, Mrs. Francis Owens. The city's liability immediately became an issue, since the theatre management admitted that it was unlikely that they would be able to pay damages for the lives lost. Under the ten-thousand-dollar legal limit, the 600 lives might be valued at six million dollars. Lawyers versed in personal damage law said it was doubtful that the Owens family could receive damages for death or injury sustained on property not owned by the city. One attorney, William H. Lee, said, "The city cannot be held for damages in civil suits growing out of a fire." Another attorney, Thomas Knight, added that "law and precedent show unmistakably that a municipality cannot be held in damages for failure to enforce its ordinances."

Lawyers representing various clients were allowed to attend the proceedings, but were barred from questioning witnesses. A state's attorney and his assistant were present to gather evidence for a grand jury probe after the coroner had completed his investigation.

The fireman William Sallers testified that the theatre opened before it was completed, a fact corroborated by others who said that city building inspectors had ignored fire codes and allowed the theatre to open because they had received "complimentary tickets" to *Mr. Bluebeard* from the theatre's management. When he was asked about fire protection, Sallers replied, "There were no buckets filled with water, no casks of water, no pumps of any description or portable fire extinguishers or pike poles."

"Did you tell the theatre owners that these things would be needed?"

"No, sir, I did not," Sallers replied. "I presumed they would know what was needed in the way of fire extinguishers." He said he had informed the business manager and that Noonan told him "the theatre management would attend [to those issues] when the house was completed, the plumbing all connected up and so forth."

On January 15, the *InterOcean* reported that the fire department was given "a terrific shaking up," because of "amazing revelations [at the inquest] of incompetence and lack of a system in seeing to it that buildings are thoroughly equipped with fire appliances according to [city] ordinances, which may result in the severing of a number of official heads . . . Fire Marshal Musham, Assistant Fire Marshal Campion, John "Jack" Hannon, chief of the First Battalion, and other members of the department, showed astonishing ignorance of the requirements and their duties under city ordinances.

"They seemed to be under the impression that they were required only 'to fight flames' and appeared surprised that their department was expected by the public to take every precaution to prevent fire from starting and even commanded to do so by city ordinances. Every effort was made by these witnesses to shift the responsibility for fire appliances to the building department."

Musham, in particular, was pilloried.

Deputy Coroner Major Lawrence Buckley bore in on the fire marshal, who sat in the witness chair, one arm casually slung over the brass rail of the speaker's table in the city council chamber. Musham's testimony was startling. Asked, "Did you ever confer with the building department or with the board of underwriters with reference to anything pertaining to theatres or the enforcement of the ordinances as they stood on the books?", his answer was "No."

When the coroner asked him whether he knew that it was necessary for the fire marshal to confer on those things, Musham said, "I don't think it is." At that point Coroner Traeger read aloud Section 165 of the Building Ordinance which mandated that sprinklers and other devices be approved by the board of underwriters, the building commissioner, and the fire marshal, and asked Musham if he had ever read that section. When Musham said that he had, the coroner asked him, "Did you comply with it in reference to the Iroquois Theatre?" Musham answered, "I didn't consider I had anything to do with the Iroquois Theatre. . . ."

"Do you consider it would be your duty when, in the wisdom of the city council, they approve of an ordinance insisting on having sprinklers and appliances of that kind in the theatre building, to see they are enforced?"

"I have no authority under the ordinance," Musham said. "That would be encroaching on another department . . . ."

"Do you consider you were doing your duty . . . in not knowing that any theatres did not have these sprinklers, hose or appliances for putting out fire?"

Musham was defiant. "I consider I did my duty in this particular case, because I was never notified. I have nothing to say about it other than when I have been officially notified to approve of the appliances."

He said he was aware that a fireman or firemen whose appointment to the theatres he had to approve was required to report to him at least once a week. But when he was asked the inevitable follow-up question, "Did the firemen appointed or selected by the Iroquois Theatre report to you weekly?", he answered, "No, he didn't report to me at any time."

"Why didn't you insist on his doing it?"

"Well, I don't know if I can answer that." Pressed, he was forced to admit that he was "not at all familiar with these different ordinances. . . . I am not, no sir. . . ."

"You know," he was asked, "you had the power to close that theatre if the ordinances were not complied with?"

"No," he said. "I didn't think I had that power."

Battalion Chief Hannon fared no better. He testified that he had visited the theatre in late December, weeks after it had opened, and had seen that "the necessary precautions had not been taken." But he had not reported that to any higher authority because he had never received an order to that effect.

A week later, Sallers submitted to the inquest jury a long memorandum he had written directly accusing Chief Musham of dereliction of duty: "He came to the theatre on October 23 and inspected it. I did not think it my duty to report to the chief what he had seen. Knowing that he and [Building Inspector] Loughlin knew the law and the conditions in the theatre, I did not report or ask for fire appliances. I knew I would receive the same reply from Musham that I did when I reported from McVicker's [Theatre] that he had nothing to do with the theatre and to report to the management. I was afraid to report to the management for fear that I would be discharged for being too active."

More damning evidence came to light when Dusenberry, the auditorium superintendent, testified that two securely pad-locked iron gates blocking the main stairways at the Randolph Street entrance were responsible for the deaths of scores of people, most of them women and children. The gates, he said, had remained locked against the frantic crowds through all the terrible rush to escape, but had been "quietly removed" after the fire. Dusenberry said it was the custom of management to open the gates after the intermission at the close of the second act, to give people an unobstructed passageway to leave the house when the show ended. The reason they were locked in the first place, he said, was to keep people in the cheaper seats from moving down into the more expensive orchestra section.

Dusenberry's revelations were astonishing. He had never, he said, received instructions from the owners or managers of the theatre about what to do in case of fire. Powers had told him "in a general way," to instruct the ushers on their duties and familiarize them with the house. There had been no fire drills.

Eddie Foy, corroborating others' experiences, said that he had never seen any fire equipment or hoses in the building. Coroner Traeger asked, "Did you consider it a dangerous lot of scenery to travel with, lights and scenery combined?"

"I don't know," Foy said. "I consider all scenery dangerous."

❧

The inquest had been scheduled to last for six days, but it went on through the month of January as court stenographers took hundreds of pages of testimony containing one revelation after another. Witness after witness told of trying, and often failing, to force exits open from both inside and outside the theatre, and of remarkable escapes. James Strong of Chicago explained in graphic detail how he, with his wife, mother and niece, tried to get out of an upper gallery exit toward the foyer. "The narrow stairway was crowded, and we kept on straight ahead down the wide stairs and along the promenade toward the door ahead of us. The door was locked and the crowd pressed against it. I got through the transom but I found that I could not force the door from the other side. My wife, mother, niece and many others perished because they could not get out through the door. After I found that it was useless [to try to pry the door open] . . . I followed the stairway down to the street entrance."

A. W. Menard, who lived on the near north side, testified that he went to the lower fire escape exit in the first balcony. "It was hidden by a drape and many people passed it not knowing it was an exit," he said. "When I attempted to open it I could not, and then I went to a second exit. That, too, was covered with drapery, but I got it opened and took my family out that way."

On January 20, Edwin H. Price, the *Mr. Bluebeard* manager, put the onus squarely on the Chicago building department, saying that he had frequently seen city inspectors examining exits in other theatres during performances, but never at the Iroquois.

But the star witness that day was David Jones, a Fuller Construction Company foreman who removed some fixed wooden scantlings from the skylights on the Iroquois roof the day after the fire. Asked why he had done that, Jones replied that he was afraid glass would fall and hurt one or more of the many inspectors and city officials who were visiting the ruined theatre.

"What business is it of yours to tear down any portion of that building, even if it was dangerous?" the coroner asked. "Don't you know that work belongs to the police and fire department? Isn't it a fact that you were sent there to destroy evidence?"

"No, sir," said Jones. "I was not sent there by anybody. I went of my own accord." The assistant state attorney pointedly asked him if he had talked to any official of the Fuller Company between the time he removed the scantlings and when he visited the company's lawyer. At first Jones denied that he had, but eventually admitted, "I think now that I did see [Fuller] Superintendent Lynch."

As dramatic testimony went on in the council chamber, the usual business of politics continued elsewhere in City Hall. From the beginning of January, theatre owners and managers, angry and fearful because of Mayor Harrison's crackdown on various violations, had begun lobbying city aldermen to give them some slack. At first, the managers agreed among themselves to make all improvements and repairs—to comply in every respect with the mayor's wishes. But as days passed and well over one hundred dance halls, public assembly rooms and even churches were ordered closed by the city building department, the spirit of cooperation started to fade. Theatre managers began meeting with a special committee of aldermen appointed to examine the new ordinances, which would not only be costly to execute but would keep the playhouses closed while thousands of theatre people were out of work indefinitely.

By January 20, newspapers were reporting that the city council was probably going to reconsider and revise the new theatre ordinances because of a general feeling among the aldermen "that the essentials demanded of the theatres were too stringent."

The climactic day of the coroner's inquest came on January 22 when the Iroquois co-owners and resident managers, Harry Powers and Will J. Davis, appeared separately before the panel. Neither was allowed to be present during the other's testimony.

Powers was a portly, balding man who sported a large mustache with twisted ends and favored wide cravats. He placed responsibility for the management of the theatre squarely upon Davis, who was the "active manager" while he, Powers, was only the passive official in the conduct of Iroquois affairs. The theatre had no fire apparatus because it had not been ordered by Sallers, the house fireman, whose responsibility it was. It was Deputy Fire Marshal Campion who had recommended Sallers for the job and it was Davis who had hired him, and as a result, "I said nothing to Sallers as to what should be provided for fire protection, nor did I do anything else about procuring or seeing about fire protection appliances. I understood that those orders were given by Mr. Davis."

As a stockholder, director and treasurer of the Iroquois Theatre Company, Powers said he was associated in a "general way" with preparation of the plans for the theatre, and approved of them as a layman and interested party. Klaw and Erlanger were also interested stockholders and also approved the plans. He said he knew the law required signs over the exits but although the theatre had been open for over five weeks, he had really had no idea that those signs were not in place.

"While I acted as assistant manager,' said Powers, "it was more in an advisory capacity or in consultation. All orders were given through Mr. Davis for Mr. Noonan, [the business manager]." It was Cummings, the carpenter, he said, whom he considered the man in charge of the stage. Asked, "And what was the limit placed on Mr. Cummings' expenditures?", Powers replied that there was no limit on them. He admitted that he knew the theatre had not been accepted from the Fuller Company as complete. It would have been necessary, he said, to have a final statement from the company and an architect's certificate before final acceptance. He added that some changes had been made in the seating arrangements of the house, which he believed was done with the knowledge of the city building department.

It was then Will Davis' turn to take the stand. A slender, soft-spoken man with thinning gray hair and an aristocratic bearing, Davis refused to place blame, saying he had had confidence in the employees of the theatre and had believed that the Fuller Company would erect the building in compliance with local ordinances. It was true that he had been managing theatres in Chicago for twenty years, but he had only a general knowledge of what was required.

In response to the question, "When the theatre was opened November 23, was it completed?", he responded vaguely, "For the purposes of giving a presentation, I should say 'yes.'" And when asked whether there were any signs over the exits, his answer was, "I don't know that there were." He, like Powers, did not know whether there was fire protection in the theatre. When asked whose duty it was to see to these things, he replied, "Well, I don't know that I could say. We had a fireman there sent by the city fire department." Davis said he considered it the fireman's duty to issue requisitions for all things needed, and when none were made, he took it for granted that none were required.

"Do you want to give us the idea," asked Coroner Traeger, "that you placed all the responsibility as to the fire apparatus upon the fireman, Mr. Sallers?"

"I do not want to place the responsibility on anybody," Davis replied.

The coroner would not let him off the hook. "As president of the company, do you want to assume the responsibility yourself?"

"I do not."

"Do you not think that as general manager it was your duty to see that those fire appliances were there to protect the public?"

"I had employees there in whom I had every confidence."

"You say you left the matter of fire protection to your employees. To which ones did you leave it?"

"I couldn't say to anyone in particular."

In an inquest studded with startling revelations that kept thousands of Chicago newspaper readers enthralled, Charles Collins believed that the big bombshell was dropped just before the conclusion of the hearing. The courtly Davis said that a few days before the Iroquois opened in November, he had talked with Building Commissioner Williams after Williams had made an inspection of the theatre. And what was the result of that inspection? Williams, according to Davis, had declared the Iroquois to be "the safest and most complete theatre he had ever seen."

Williams had testified that he had accepted Inspector Loughlin's okay because he "supposed that it meant the whole building was completed . . . I did not know that the theatre was violating any ordinances until after the fire. I was not familiar with these ordinances. I have been head of the department only a few months and have not had the time to get things in shape. . . . the department is so poorly supplied with money that we have not more than half as many inspectors as we need."

Loughlin told the coroner's jury that his okay covered the structure only. "I don't believe the ordinance required me to report on anything else. The inspection of the fire appliances is the duty of the fire department; the inspection of the fire escapes is the duty of the fire escape inspector; the wiring is the duty of the electrical department. I was not instructed in my duties by Commissioner Williams and never read the building ordinances myself until after the fire."

It turned out that the day before the theatre opened, when Loughlin gave his official okay, he had been accompanied on his tour by a second building inspector, Julius A. Lense. "I went with him out of curiosity," said Lense, "and because he invited me. The building was not complete, and had I been there in an official capacity I should have reported it not ready for the public. As I was not there officially I made no report."

The testimony of all these people was bizarre. Certainly public interest was aroused across the country, and some of that interest was also bizarre. Eleven days after the fire, on Saturday, January 9, a short item on new toys for children appeared on page 6 in the *New York Times*: "If the interest in fires has reached the children's world there is just the kind of a toy for them, and there is no doubt they will enjoy it, anyway, whether the parents do or not. It is a two-story tin house with the flames bursting out of the lower story. On the second floor is the lady of the house, with her hands raised . . . in supplication and terror, and a fireman . . . at the top of a ladder . . . is reaching out to the fire victim. There is some kind of mechanical work with this ladder, and the fireman can go up and down on it. Another little fireman stands upon the roof of the house with a real rubber hose in his hands. It is a most realistic toy."

On that Saturday, Chicago newspaper editors were not interested in toys in poor taste. What concerned them were city ordinances, graft and duplicity. Said the *Tribune*, "An inert city administration, subordinates looking for 'graft,' and aldermen eager to do favors for [theatre owners] will connive in the work of evasion [of new safety ordinances]. Conditions will become as bad as they were three weeks ago."

{17}

THE GRAND JURY

"Lives were snuffed out as the flame of a candle."
—*Chicago Fire Marshal's Report for 1903*

THE DELIBERATIONS OF THE coroner's jury did not take long.

On January 25, certainly sooner than Collins and most of the press expected, verdicts were returned naming Mayor Harrison, Fire Marshal Musham, theatre owner Davis, Building Commissioner Williams, Building Inspector Loughlin, house fireman Sallers, stage carpenter Cummings and light operator McMullen, to be held for action by the grand jury. City ordinances were found to have been violated: on fire alarm and firefighting equipment, on regulation of dampers and flues on and above the stage, on the fireproofing of scenery and woodwork. Aisles were enclosed on both sides of the lower boxes and there was no fire apparatus on the orchestra floor, the balcony or the gallery

The asbestos curtain was found to be inadequate.

Davis was held responsible for observances of the laws: as president and general manager, it was his obligation to see that his employees were properly instructed on their duties in case of fire.

Mayor Harrison was held responsible, having "shown lamentable lack of force, and for his efforts to escape responsibility, evidenced by the testimony of Musham and Williams; and as heads of department under the mayor, following this weak course has given Chicago inefficient service which makes such calamity as the Iroquois Theatre horror a menace until the public service is purged of incompetents."

Building Commissioner Williams was guilty of "gross neglect of his duty in allowing the theatre to open when the theatre was incomplete and did not comply with building ordinances."

Fire Marshal Musham was held responsible for "gross neglect of duty in not enforcing the city ordinances and failure to have his subordinate, William Sallers, report to him the lack of fire apparatus in the theatre."

Sallers was accused of neglecting to report the lack of apparatus, McMullen of carelessness in handling the light, and Cummings of failure to provide the stage with proper lighting protection.

Each man posted bail and was released. The humiliated Musham and Davis flatly refused to speak to reporters. Mayor Harrison was said to be "furious" and Commissioner Williams was described as downcast. Williams had good reason to be depressed: eleven days later some of his inspectors would be charged with taking bribes from building contractors, one of whom, it was alleged, had regularly set aside for payoffs $1000 a year on the company expense account. Williams' angry response to these charges was that they were not only "false" but "demoralizing to the department."

The mayor, who was later cleared, said that the jury's findings were political and based on "flimsy charges," and that the jury had been handpicked by a political enemy, Deputy Coroner Lawrence Buckley, so as to "insure a certain amount of odium attaching to me . . . the jury based its decision on ostensible charges that politics and favoritism had influenced the appointments of Musham and Williams."

The press speculated that Harrison really owed his freedom to City Hall department heads who testified that, prior to the theatre's opening, the mayor had issued a blanket order to the License Department that no theatre licenses should be issued except on the report of Building Commissioner Williams. That testimony, while clearing the mayor, had the effect of making unavoidable the indictment of Williams for malfeasance.

"I have been compelled to make bricks out of straw," said Williams. "I am tired of it. I didn't have time to get my hands on the run of things in the office and I did not have men enough to do anything with. I am getting soaked for the faults of others. Say, if I had enough men to make even a cursory inspection I could have closed up this town in three days."

Though officially off the hook, the bellicose Harrison must have been deeply wounded by newspaper editorials, both in Chicago and elsewhere, condemning him for being at first too lax in enforcing city ordinances and then, in the wake of the disaster, going on a belated and inappropriate offensive, declaring he would "give the city all the laws on the books" by enforcing them. One of his harshest critics was the *New York Times*, which said prior to his exoneration, "Chicago boasts of many remarkable things, but we venture to say she has nothing more remarkable . . . than her Chief Magistrate, Mayor Carter Harrison.

"If he has a right to enforce the ordinances which he has previously disregarded, he confesses previous neglect of duty, fully justifying the condemnation of the coroner's jury for official nonfeasance. If he has no right to do this, he will invite indictment for official misfeasance. One would have expected that after escaping from the position in which he was placed by the stinging verdict of the jury, he would be eager not to show he could have performed, had he chosen to, the duties he so persistently and continuously neglected."

The *Chicago Tribune* went further. It called the mayor one third of "an evil trinity": "The responsibility rests upon the city administration, and especially the mayor. Many of the [city ordinances] were not complied with because the building department carelessly or corruptly decided that some of them might, for a consideration, be disregarded. The installation of automatic sprinkler systems is obligatory, but the building department, for reasons known only to itself, did not require them to be put in at the Iroquois. The head of the department [Williams] says, with unconscious humor, 'the sprinkler ordinance never has been enforced.' The building department, in this instance, incriminates itself."

The theatre's owners, "willing, eager even, to evade specific requirements . . . in order to save a certain amount of money in construction were quite ready to 'trust to luck.' . . . Responsibility also rests upon the builders . . . who were willing to connive with the owners at the violation of ordinances of which they were thoroughly familiar . . . A city government unfit to perform its plain duty and owners and builders anxious to save money by disregarding the law compose an evil trinity that have brought upon Chicago the worst of its misfortunes."

Editorial fury was not limited to America's two most populous cities.

"There may be a modicum of satisfaction in the refusal of the coroner's jury to be swayed by Mayor Harrison's inspiring show of indignation or misled by his tremendous zeal to place the blame on somebody—anybody but himself," wrote the *Detroit Journal*, "but the joy of ripping off this official's mask cannot be made to compensate for the damage done [by him] and other terror-stricken officials in their frantic efforts to find shelter from the storm of public wrath."

In Iowa, the *Marshalltown Republican* commented, "The jury did right when it laid a share of the responsibility . . . at the door of a careless and venal city administration. It is not enough that the skirts of the Chicago administration are clear of actual and active criminality. There is passive crime in carelessness."

"There is fortunately every prospect that both criminal punishment and pecuniary loss will be visited upon all concerned," thundered the *Philadelphia Press*.

"If [mayors] can be convinced that the public will exact rightful penalties for maladministration resulting from 'playing politics,'" said the *Kansas City Star*, "there will be less liability to such sickening affairs as that at the Iroquois Theatre."

And in Michigan, from the *Marquette Journal*: "Mayor Harrison declines to discuss the action of the coroner's jury in holding him in a degree responsible . . . but he impassionedly defends Building Inspector Williams and Fire Chief Musham and thus, in effect, defends himself. Everything the mayor can say, everything that Mr. Davis can say, everything that any one can say pales into insignificance in the light of the one overwhelming fact that the Iroquois was a hopeless death trap. . . ."

Harrison was ridiculed by many Chicago newspapers, in particular in a series of *Tribune* front-page cartoons by John T. McCutcheon, who would much later become the paper's first Pulitzer Prize winner. The cartoons ranged from one of a burly Chicago Bluecoat boarding up the theatre's entrance after the fire, to another of a group of three frightened male figures—the responsible trinity—trying without success to open a locked exit door from the inside while a black cloud labeled "Punishment" closes in on them.

But what undoubtedly moved Chicagoans most was a McCutcheon drawing captioned "His Sunday Dinner." It showed a hollow-eyed, grief-stricken man sitting before an untouched meal, an infant son his only companion at a bare table surrounded by three empty chairs and a high stool. In the window is a Christmas wreath and behind him, on the wall, a framed plaque bearing the inscription, "Blessed Are the Poor in Spirit."

In another page one cartoon, *Record-Herald* artist Ralph Wilder also captured the anguish, if not the anger. In a schoolroom filled with downcast pupils looking into their *McGuffie's Reader*, one sad child, chin cupped in hand, stares not at the book but across the aisle at an empty desk and chair. The caption is "The Vacant Seat."

If those poignant reminders were not enough for Harrison in the first month of the New Year, his "in" basket was stacked with fresh reports of the Iroquois tragedy, including a private report he had ordered himself, and both the Chicago Fire Marshal's official report for the year 1903, and a Chicago Fire Underwriters Association preliminary report. The Marshal's report, coming as it did from Musham's department, consisted, not surprisingly, of understatement and obfuscation, especially when it sidestepped the issue of why the theatre had no significant firefighting equipment: "The Kilfyre was used, but with little or no effect, its operation being upon the principal of suffocation of the fire by surrounding it with a heavy and uninflammable gas, thus excluding oxygen. Had the fire been upon the floor, above which the gas would have accumulated, it is possible that the Kilfyre might have proven effective.

"The theatre had been but lately opened, and was not yet provided with other means of fire fighting. . . . the [fire] was now quite beyond the reach of any means at hand for suppressing it. When the doors upon the stage were thrown open . . . the flames, heat, smoke and generated gasses were forced under the suspended curtain and upwards to the open ventilators above the auditorium, in the natural line of draft. Numbers perished instantly by suffocation [and] many others, hindered in their egress . . . were burned, suffocated or trampled to death. The fire department was on the scene within probably two minutes from the receipt of the alarm, [but] lives were [already] snuffed out as the flame of a candle. Within thirty minutes from its inception the fire was extinguished . . . and the department rescued 104 people from the theatre." The report concluded that the damage to the building was slight, that as a structure it was practically unharmed and it could probably be entirely refitted for fifty thousand dollars.

In its summary, the Underwriters' report said, "Although the general character of the building construction was superior for this occupancy, its unfinished condition, together with highly inflammable scenery . . . combined a remarkable set of very unfortunate circumstances, most of which seem to have contributed liberally to augment the disaster.

"The superior characteristics of the building construction apparently created overconfidence, which caused the absolute necessity for proper fire protection and ordinary precautions to be overlooked. The inflammable contents of the fireproof building, without proper supervision, are scarcely any safer than if they were contained in a building of ordinary construction."

The operative word seemed to be "overconfidence."

Even before the special grand jury convened, there were those who were hustling to cash in on the tragedy. One songwriter composed something called "The Burning of the Iroquois Theatre" that "droned on for four pages and two verses." Another tune, "The Iroquois on Fire," appeared and just as quickly, mercifully disappeared. A writer, Wesley A. Stranger, turned out a potboiler entitled *Rescued from a Fiery Death.* It did not sell well. Within hours of the disaster a Hartford insurance company inserted a large ad in a Chicago paper which ran next to a long list of the fire victims:

9 MILLION DEAD OR INJURED IN THE
U.S. LAST YEAR BY ACCIDENTS.
PROTECT YOURSELF BY INSURING WITH THE
TRAVELERS INSURANCE COMPANY.

The Orr & Lockwood hardware store, which had rushed over hundreds of lanterns the day of the fire, began running a series of local ads for dry powder extinguishers, ("$2 apiece; $20 a dozen"), with the thoughtful suggestion, "Get it Today — You May Need it Tonight." In early January, the Klein Optical Company of Chicago bought space in the *New York Clipper* advising readers "We are receiving many inquiries concerning lantern slides and films of the Iroquois fire. . . . there were no moving pictures or lantern slide photographs made of the fire. Our offices were almost adjacent to the theatre but commercialism gave way before the sight of bodies piled on the sidewalks and the horror of the catastrophe. We should have ready six lantern slides. One will show the exterior, almost undamaged. The other five will be taken from drawings by artist Charles Lederer, who was present at the fire. They will show characteristic scenes but ghastly sensationalism will be absent."

On the same note, but with less credibility, in the January 16 *Clipper,* the S. Lubin Company of Philadelphia advertised that it had available "Film of the Chicago Theatre Fire" and urged readers to "See the Thrilling Fire Rescues." The following week the *Clipper* carried an ad for "Asbestos Curtains from the Tiffin Scenery Company of Tiffin, Ohio."

On the day that seventeen-year-old Edna Hunter was undergoing a skin grafting operation in a Chicago hospital, the January 30 issue of *Billboard Magazine*, an entertainment weekly, ran the following advertisement:

WANTED

A HUSTLING MANAGER TO PUT BIG LIFE

MOTION PICTURE SHOW ON THE ROAD,

FEATURING

MR. BLUEBEARD

(900 FEET)

REPRODUCTION OF CHICAGO FIRE PLAY

Billboard also ran an ad in which the Boswell Electric &
Optical Company of Chicago, manufacturers of the twenty-
dollar Boswell Jr. Stereopticon, announced a package of twenty
colored slides of the fire, complete with a "lecture" for $7.50.

Edna Hunter was the last person to escape from the top
gallery of the Iroquois. At the end of January she was undergoing surgery to replace burnt areas on the top of her scalp, the
right side of her neck and beneath her chin, with seven square
inches of grafts taken from the arms of volunteers, one of whom
was her brother. The treatment, preparation and consultation
among those from whom the skin was grafted had taken one
month.

That was less time than the grand jury took to report to the
Chicago Criminal Court. Indictments were returned on February 23.

"The jury believes the direct duty of protecting lives of those
in the theatre lay upon the persons responsible for furnishing
apparatus necessary to extinguish fire."

This duty, the grand jury found, was the responsibility of
Will Davis, the manager; Thomas Noonan, the theatre's busi-
ness manager who had been cleared by the coroner's panel, and
James Cummings, the stage carpenter. All three were indicted
for manslaughter. Charges against Musham, Sallers and Mc-
Mullen were dismissed for lack of evidence.

The jury found it fully evident that city ordinances regulating the inspection of theatres for the purpose of determining their safety had not been complied with, and issued indictments against the two men primarily responsible, Building Commissioner Williams and Building Inspector Edward Loughlin, for "palpable omission of duty."

Finally, the panel exonerated Mayor Harrison but said there should be "a more intelligent administration of City Hall departments."

Harrison brushed the matter aside. "The grand jury might have indicted me," he said, "but State's Attorney Charles Dineen took the same position as had City Judge Richard Tuthill, who declared the findings of the coroner's jury were 'unwarranted in law' . . . that ended the matter as far as I was concerned."

Charles Dineen had in fact warned from the start of the inquest that it would be hard to prove guilt because the coroner did not have sufficient evidence for a criminal prosecution showing that "[a] locked door was responsible for [certain deaths], even if the responsibility for the locked door [was established]."

Days after the fire, standing at the end of a blind gallery passage where, because of a locked exit, thirty people had perished, Dineen had cautioned Coroner Traeger to "make every possible effort to [establish] the identity of some persons who died in this corner." Dineen's directive raised one of the most vexing problems that the grand jury would have to confront: fixing of criminal responsibility. In order to sustain a prosecution for manslaughter, Dineen said, it would be necessary for the coroner to determine the identity of one or more of those whose deaths were caused specifically by the locked door.

"The grand jury cannot indict a person for causing deaths . . . of persons unknown to the jury," explained another criminal attorney. Because of the frantic efforts of police, fire and volunteers to remove dead and injured at the time of the fire, no records were kept of where individual victims were found. Without such evidence, the attorney said, it would be next to impossible for any jury to determine exactly who was responsible for what specific deaths. "If the closing of the skylights and ventilators on the stage roof was responsible for all the deaths, then the man responsible for the closed [sky] lights might be held. But that would [excuse] the persons responsible for the locked exits. The moral responsibility of the coroner might be easily fixed and the fixing of civil responsibility might also be easy, but the grand jury will not have an easy task."

In the matter of the manslaughter indictments of Davis, Noonan and Cummings, the stage was now set for a long and dramatic legal battle in which responsibility for the defense would fall for the most part on a tough, tenacious Chicago attorney, the son of Bavarian immigrants. His name was Levy Mayer.

"NOT GUILTY"

*"Deficiency in the law in no way releases Mr. Davis
from . . . moral responsibility."*
—Maude Jackson, Fire Victim's Mother

LEVY MAYER COULD HAVE been a model for Horatio Alger, the
author of more than one hundred boys' books in which the
heroes rise from rags to riches through virtue, hard work and
pluck. Like Eddie Foy, Mayer was a first-generation American,
the sixth of thirteen children. He was born in Richmond, Vir-
ginia, the son of Bavarian Jews who had immigrated to the
United States in 1855 from Germany. By the time Levy was
eight, his parents had been caught up in the turmoil of the Civil
War, and finding security in the South to be illusory, had moved
to the more stable Midwest, first to Milwaukee and then to
Chicago.

Levy's father went into business selling tobacco, furnishings and other merchandise, but the family was poor because
although Henry D. Mayer was an educated, cultured man, he
simply had no head for business. Young Levy, a brilliant student, decided on a law career before receiving his high school
diploma. With financial aid provided by an older brother, at

the age of sixteen he entered Yale Law School, where the minimum age rule of eighteen was waived for him. It was then a two-year course, and he graduated in 1876, second in his class. Back in Chicago, being too young to be admitted to the bar, he took a job at the Chicago Law Institute library, where he supplemented his four-dollar-a-week salary by writing for legal periodicals, editing books and helping attorneys with legal research. This early experience paid off handsomely when Mayer was admitted to the bar in 1877. Early in his career, he was described as having "a remarkable knowledge of case law."

He and an early law partner prospered in America's new industrial era, with its rapidly changing business and industrial conditions. Though he began a criminal and civil law practice, Mayer soon gained a reputation for expertise in corporate, business and antitrust law, working with some important clients including the Chicago Telephone Company, Corn Products Refining Company and the Union Stock Yard & Transit Company.

At the end of 1903, Mayer, forty-five years old and the founding partner of the firm Moran, Mayer and Meyer, was considered to be one of the city's brightest and most aggressive attorneys, a "legal genius of the commercial age." His success was said to be "due not only to his intellect, his unremitting work and his loyalty to his clients, but to an almost unequalled ability to express himself simply and clearly, both orally and in his briefs." Mayer was a man who could quickly and accurately absorb facts from clients and associates and, though he remained calm in court battles, was looked upon as a combative adversary. He was physically imposing, being nearly six feet tall with a dark leonine head.

As could be expected, not everyone liked him. Mayor Harrison, who had once crossed swords with Mayer during a battle over reforming the city's hiring system to award jobs based on merit rather than on political patronage, dismissed him as "a political schemer" and one of "a bold, unscrupulous, crafty, powerful lot of machine politicians who . . . would be lined up for my undoing."

Less than twenty-four hours after the Iroquois disaster, Klaw-Erlanger, which had earlier insisted it had only a marginal financial interest in the Iroquois, at first asked Mayer to act as special counsel to represent not only their interests but Davis and the others who would be indicted by the grand jury. After an all-night session with executives of the Theatrical Trust in a Loop office building, Mayer's firm was selected to head the defense team. It would be one of the major criminal cases of his career and, according to his great-grandnephew, "It took courage and showed a willingness on [his] part to take on an exceedingly unpopular cause. . . ."

Calling that cause "unpopular" was a classic understatement. At first numbed by horror, the city became enraged as the indictments were handed down charging non-compliance with safety ordinances for theatres. It did not help his case that in the first hours following the fire, Davis had said, "If the people had remained in their seats and not been excited by the cry of fire, not a single life would have been lost."

In preparation for the trial, Mayer and his staff combed through Chicago's written building and safety ordinances, line by line. The determining question was whether or not the city ordinances were valid. Mayer, for one, believed that they were not. He took the position that the essential point was whether there was any cause and effect between the conditions in the theatre and the fire: "The question which was at the core of the matter, was whether the failure to observe the requirements of the ordinances was the proximate cause of loss of life. . . ."

Despite the immediate anger roused by the inquest testimony and the grand jury indictments, two major factors were working in Mayer's favor: time and a public distracted by other events. The *Tribune* had surmised only weeks after the tragedy that "the horrors of the Iroquois are already being dimmed. Soon they will be out of mind altogether, except with a few mourners." The paper was prescient. Incredible as it may seem, the fire story began to slip off front pages and out of many newspapers altogether.

Other things were happening. One was the death of the last of the great Confederate generals. James Longstreet, who had openly opposed Robert E. Lee's failed attack at Gettysburg, was gone and with him, a piece of American history. In Muskogee, Indian Territory, a band of Cherokees, dissatisfied with land allotments, donned war paint and threatened an uprising "leaving only birds and snakes alive." On the other side of the globe, the first scattered bulletins on the Russo-Japanese War began to appear in February, 1904, mentioning for the first time places like Port Arthur, Chempulo, Chefoo and the Yellow Sea, with maps of their locations. No one had ever heard of, or could hardly pronounce, tongue-twisters like General Kuropatkin, Admiral Viteft, or Kuroki, Nogi and Togo.

War in a distant part of the world was not the only diversion for newspaper readers. That same month brought the lingering illness and death of the powerful Republican Mark Hanna. And a fire which raged for twenty-seven hours nearly wiped out the city of Baltimore, causing $127 million in damage. March roared in with a Chicago snowstorm of huge proportions that temporarily obstructed street traffic, and in that same month President Roosevelt had a major "trust-busting" victory with the Supreme Court decision in the Northern Securities Company case.

Taking advantage of these distractions, the crowded court calendars and other legal delay tactics, Mayer and his staff probed for loopholes in the city ordinances. He also used local prejudice against his clients, arguing in late September, 1904, almost a year after the fire, that because feelings on the tragedy were still running so high in Chicago, he wanted a change of venue to Peoria, so that Noonan and Cummings could get a "fair and impartial trial." Days later he followed up with a motion to quash the manslaughter indictment against Davis. Over the strenuous objections of state prosecutors, the change of venue to Peoria County for Noonan and Cummings was granted. In early November, a Chicago and a Peoria judge heard the argument to quash the Davis indictment, and on February 9, 1905, Mayer scored a major victory when both judges quashed the indictments against Davis, Noonan and Cummings. The state's case was beginning to fall apart.

Judge Kersten in Chicago held that because the municipal building ordinances did not "specify exactly who was charged with providing adequate fire apparatus in a theatre . . . the defendants cannot be found guilty of manslaughter or of omitting to perform an act unless there was a legal duty to perform that act, or unless they voluntarily had assumed the duty of its performance, and nowhere is it alleged in [the] indictment that they ever took upon themselves the duties imposed by the ordinance on the owner or lessee of the building."

Judge Green in Peoria delivered an even stronger opinion, denying that the tragedy had been caused by the failure of the three defendants to provide adequate fire apparatus: "This terrible fire is not attributable to the fact that such apparatus was not in the theatre, but that there was a certain electric light close to the stage and that set fire to the curtain. Inasmuch as there is no evidence that any of the defendants caused the light to be put there, and the inference being that someone else placed it there, I take it that this fact alone is a fatal objection to the indictments."

Mayer announced that "any future indictments would not be worth the paper they were written on."

Davis now talked to reporters for the first time since the fire, spilling out his bottled-up emotions in a long, rambling statement of what he called his "true position" on the case: "I can't help saying that at least a part of the public has been unfair and unjust to me. It would be just as fair to hold the president of a railroad company for manslaughter because there was an explosion in one of the . . . trains, and fire ensued and passengers were burned to death. . . . No human agency could have prevented the theatre catastrophe. Everything known to architecture, science, and art was used to make the theatre the safest in the world . . . no money was stinted in any possible direction. No human agency could have dreamed that on account of some inherent defect . . . a carbon [lamp] would spit out a spark which would ignite the scenery and produce the fire. The building had been thoroughly examined and approved in writing by city authorities before the theatre opened. We could do no more. Why should we be charged with murder because the audience stampeded and the ushers lost their reason? I am asking no sympathy, but God knows I have suffered enough and should be let alone."

This argument failed to evoke any sympathy from the press, the public or the state prosecutors, who had no intention of withdrawing the indictments. Less than a month later, on March 7, 1905, on evidence submitted by witnesses to the fire, a second Chicago grand jury re-indicted Davis on manslaughter charges, along with the deputy building inspector Edward Loughlin and George Williams, the city building commissioner. The jury refused on grounds of insufficient evidence to indict Klaw and Erlanger, Powers, Cummings, Noonan and Sallers.

Once more Mayer argued for a motion to quash the indictment and once more time worked in his favor. Because of overloaded dockets and other delays within the Illinois court system, it was not until January 13, 1906, more than two years after the tragedy, that the Davis indictment was sustained and preparations for a new trial were begun. But by February, newspaper readers were devouring every detail of a romance that for months had entertained two continents and which culminated in the fairy tale wedding of Alice Roosevelt to Nicholas Longworth in the White House. One thousand guests looked on as the president escorted his daughter into the softly lit East Room to the strains of the grand march from *Tannhauser*.

Once again Mayer delayed the proceedings by demanding a change of venue from Chicago's Cook County, and outmaneuvered state prosecutors by producing a mountain of over 12,000 affidavits attesting to prejudice, as against the state's 4000 counter-affidavits. He did not fail to impress the bench by noting the number of names of respected judges and other eminent citizens among those who had signed the affidavits. His motion for change of venue was heard and granted in June, 1906.

But two events so dominated the newspapers that once again public attention was diverted from the Iroquois tragedy. On April 18 the city of San Francisco lay in ruins from the mightiest temblor to shake the North American continent since the series of quakes in New Madrid, Missouri, ninety-one years earlier. Hundreds were crushed in the rubble, martial law was declared, landmarks and homes were destroyed in the resulting fire and residents fled to the hills. Then two months later, screaming headlines described the murder of architect Stanford White by the millionaire Harry K. Thaw over the affections of a beautiful young actress, Evelyn Nesbit Thaw, a shooting that occurred in front of startled spectators on the roof of New York's Madison Square Garden. By the time the Davis trial was moved to Danville, a little farming community in Vermilion County 134 miles south of Chicago, the Iroquois fire was a distant memory drowned by other events. Public interest had faded so noticeably that the *Tribune* ran the story of the new trial, "after a delay of more than three years," on page nine.

Still, there were indications that the case might finally be coming to an end and that the State of Illinois was about to present an overwhelming argument against Davis and the others. Reporters noted that Assistant State's Attorney James J. Barbour and a team of stenographers, accompanied by no fewer than twenty-two witnesses, many of them relatives of fire victims, boarded the train to Danville the night before the trial. Mayer's group took the same train. In less than a week, by the time a jury of farmers, a blacksmith and a fire insurance agent had been sworn in, the Iroquois case was back on the *Tribune's* front page.

On March 7, 1907, the Vermilion County courtroom was packed in anticipation of a drawn-out, highly charged battle, particularly after it was leaked that the State of Illinois was prepared to summon not twenty-two but two hundred witnesses, some of them horribly disfigured in the fire. The first witness was to be a Chicago housewife, Maude Jackson, whose pretty sixteen-year-old daughter, Viva, was one of the victims. Before the presiding judge, E. R. E. Kimbrough, Vermilion County State's Attorney John W. Keeslar presented an opening statement. Mayer's team countered that the defense would reserve its statement until after the close of the state's evidence.

A hush descended over the courtroom when Mrs. Jackson, wearing mourning, was called to the stand. She had answered only four questions, however, when Mayer interrupted to introduce a motion to compel the state immediately to introduce the Chicago city ordinances on which the manslaughter indictment was based. The motion was granted and it soon became apparent to those in the stuffy chamber that Mayer was going to mount his well-researched objections to those ordinances.

He did not disappoint, but with a dramatic flourish, produced a 231-page brief, which he delivered to the panel over the next two days. But that was not all. In a theatrical gesture, the doors to the courtroom were flung open and a procession of bellboys and porters entered loaded down with piles of law books that they heaped on the defense counsel's table. While his associates were arranging the books into neat stacks, Mayer continued with his presentation as if nothing unusual had happened.

Against a backdrop of Chicago city maps, which he had pinned to the courtroom walls, defining fire limits and the location of various theatres, Mayer argued that Chicago safety ordinances were not valid because they were legally "beyond the power of the City under the Illinois constitution and state [statutes]." He explained that Chicago had only such power as was delegated to it by the state legislature and that no such powers had been delegated to the Chicago city council. He maintained that there had been an unlawful delegation of power when the city gave to a separate entity, the Chicago Board of Fire Underwriters, control of sprinkler systems in buildings, and that "the Common Law count of negligence could not rest as it did on [Davis'] failure to supply the equipment provided for in the ordinances" because "a reasonable man is not required to take all possible precautions but merely those which would be taken by an ordinary prudent man under the circumstances."

On March 9 the case ended. Mayer concluded his thirteen-hour marathon with the dramatic declaration, "It was the hand of God that brought about the loss of lives in the fire and Will J. Davis was no more responsible for their deaths than if a hurricane had lifted off the roof of the theatre." Judge Kimbrough ruled that the Chicago ordinances were in fact invalid and inadmissible as evidence. When Prosecutor John W. Keeslar in a desperate eleventh-hour move asked permission to drop the indictment against Davis but not to formally acquit him, Mayer jumped to his feet to object and demand that Davis receive "the verdict he is entitled to." He urged that the judge reject the motion and the jury be immediately convened to bring in a verdict. Because the state had insufficient proof of manslaughter without the ordinances, Judge Kimbrough, after delivering a moving summation, directed the jury to return a not-guilty verdict. In his summation, the judge said, "If it were in my power to bring back to life and put the bloom of youth into the cheeks of these young girls, two of whom I personally knew, by incarcerating the defendant in this case in the penitentiary for the term of his natural life, I believe I would do it; but I can not."

"The judge's decision was delivered orally," reported the *Tribune*, ". . . and he left no doubt . . . that he considered Davis morally guilty . . . but he said his duty was to hold strictly to the letter of the law."

Tears streaked Davis' hollow cheeks. He had said he was confident that he would be acquitted because "[t]hose who died . . . were the victims of circumstances over which I could have had no control." Three and a half years after the catastrophe, charges against the sixty-eight-year-old theatre official were formally dismissed and all attempts ended to hold anyone else connected with the theatre criminally liable for the tragedy.

The victorious Mayer was blunt. "The state discharged their duty thoroughly but the law was against them," he said. Speaking *post facto* of Judge Kimbrough's decision, the Illinois state's attorney tended to agree. "Under the indictment drawn as this one it was a close question whether the ordinance was valid," he said. "Being a criminal case the reasonable doubt as to the validity of the ordinance would be in favor of the defendant. Legally the judge was right. He did his duty."

For Maude Jackson, the state's only witness to testify, it had been a long, wearying trial that had ended unfairly. "I feel that the deficiency in the law in no way releases Mr. Davis from the moral responsibility of the death of our six hundred loved ones," she told reporters. "It is time the public should be protected. If laws can be devised by which the public is protected, why are they not so framed as to hold someone responsible when six hundred of our dearest are swept out of existence in an instant's time?" It was a reasonable question.

The conduct of the case was severely criticized in the *Illinois Law Review*, which complained about the "outrageous delays caused by a lack of dispatch in the conduct of the prosecution," about Mayer's policy of "postponing motions to quash indictments and for changes of venue, and the tardiness of judges in ruling on motions." The Iroquois case, concluded the *Review*, "sows . . . the seed of contempt for law and gives notice to the world of the inefficiency of our judicial system."

While attorneys, including the city's corporation counsel, debated the ruling, some claiming that new post-fire city building ordinances contained the very same flaws, Davis, haggard, with dark rings under his eyes, returned to Chicago to be given a welcoming party by performers and theatre owners. There would be no such consolation, however, for the victims' relatives seeking monetary damages. More than 200 civil actions had been brought, some of them within days after the fire. But the reality was that most of the families of the dead and injured received not so much as a dime in compensation. And unfortunately, most of the fire victims were not covered by life insurance. Except for the very wealthy, few woman and children were ensured in the early years of the new century.

"The theatre liability," reported the *Tribune*, had been placed with the Maryland Casualty Company, "for the usual limit of $10,000 on any one accident, and $5,000 for any one life. The policy, however, provides that it does not cover loss from liability, for injuries caused by boiler explosions, the use of explosives, or by fire."

The plaintiffs were not helped by an earlier decision by U.S. Federal Judge Kenesaw Mountain Landis, who ruled on the civil liability of the Iroquois Theatre Company for one of the deaths in the fire. Landis, who would become Major League baseball's first commissioner following the Chicago White Sox scandal, held that "the ordinances did not cast on the theatre owner any duty in reference to the equipment and appliances prescribed by them; and the ordinances provided only for a fine for the specific failure to have the appliances and not for liability for consequences flowing from the failure to have them."

With the trial over, newspaper coverage ended, but some of the injured parties would not give up. In February 1905, Henry M. Shabad, the attorney who had lost both his children in the fire, reportedly went to New York to seek evidence for an indictment of Klaw and Erlanger. The following October, two women, relatives of fire victims, brought a $50,000 lawsuit against the Iroquois Theatre Company and the Fuller Construction Company. There was no report on the outcome of these actions. There were rumors that the Klaw-Erlanger organization eventually paid off relatives of the victims, but there was never any real evidence of that.

In 1909, a brief wire service story from Chicago, containing few details, reported that "after five years of hotly contested litigation, settlements had been made outside of court for thirty of the nearly six hundred deaths caused by . . . the fire . . . $750 is to be paid in each of the cases by the George A. Fuller Construction Company. Prosecution in these thirty cases has been withdrawn from court . . . Many other suits against firms and individuals [connected to] the theatre are still pending. The number of unsettled cases is estimated at more than four hundred."

It is impossible to know if, or how, those cases were settled, because many were apparently dismissed for technical reasons or because lawyers whose compensation was based on a successful outcome did not believe the effort was worth their time, especially if they had to go up against people like Levy Mayer and other powerful attorneys representing the Theatrical Trust.

{19}

A WARNING UNHEEDED

"By and by there will come another terrible accident."
— THE INDEPENDENT

TWENTY-NINE DAYS BEFORE the Iroquois was destroyed, the *New York Times* carried a story headed "Great Advances in Theatre Building," informing the public that "[t]he keynote of the new structures" seemed to be the dropping of the former emphasis on decorations in favor of "a more scientific carrying out of the mechanical lines of work . . . Cement floors, fire-proof wood, standpipes and sprinklers put a destructive fire beyond all probability."

A popular social history of the period, published almost a century later, said that life for Americans from 1900 to 1910 "was mellow and secure, full of vigor, savor and fascination. All they had to do was go out and live it." That would not have been an option for 600 or more unsuspecting people who attended the Christmas week matinee that raw December day in Chicago. For them, the promise of the new century ended suddenly and horribly in what was thought to be the safest playhouse ever constructed but which became the site of the worst disaster in American theatre history.

There was an odd parallel to the Iroquois story.

Immediately after the tragedy, not only was there public rage against the theatre management in Chicago and other cities, but there was much discussion of the danger posed by public apathy combined with the hubris that seemed to stem from the new scientific and technological wonders becoming an accepted way of everyday life in the new century.

Theater Magazine, which had raised the issue of safety on the day that the Iroquois burned, reminded its readers one month after the fire that public apathy and complacency could result in another great tragedy: "It is the usual experience that disasters of this kind are followed by great public excitement, the newspapers demand reform, the theatres suffer from lack of patronage, the authorities display great activity and the managers show themselves eager to remedy defects. But the show of zeal never lasts. The disaster is forgotten in a week, the theatres do as little as they can, gradually neglecting the most ordinary precautions, the public does not give the matter a thought, and everything goes on merrily as before unless a fresh horror occurs to teach us another lesson."

"We will shut the stable door after the steed is stolen," agreed the *Independent*. "We shall be very careful for a week, a month, and then . . . we shall slacken a bit, and then a bit more, and then we shall forget, and by and by there will come another terrible accident, all caused by pure carelessness and neglect. . . ."

A few days after the fire, the Reverend James Stone of Chicago's St. James Episcopal Church told his Sunday parishioners, "Our citizens, for the greater part, do not care how things go so long as they, individually, are not disturbed. They know the right, but they leave it to someone else to do it."

Letters to editors filled newspaper columns around the world, many of them offering suggestions on how to avoid a similar tragedy. "Panic is invariably the cause of the great mortality," said one. "Our transatlantic steamers have dealt most successfully with this problem. Their motto is, eternal vigilance is the price of safety."

☙

At nine o'clock on the night of December 30, 1903, as police and firemen probed the smoking ruins of the theatre and Charles Collins worked in the *Record-Herald*'s now quiet city room on stories for the following day's edition, the *Chicago Daily News* hit the streets with a 9 p.m. "Extra" containing the first details of the great tragedy. A *News* editor had obviously selected secondary "filler" material to close up the empty space, the "news hole" in the pages of the paper where the Iroquois coverage ended. He randomly chose pieces from the AP wire, which included financial briefs from around the U.S. and abroad. Given Chicago's extraordinary disaster story, these items probably received little or no attention from readers.

Somewhere in the middle of the paper, at the bottom of one column, appearing just above an advertisement for the Chicago & Northwestern Railroad, was one paragraph from London dated December 30, reporting that a steamship company had that day ordered a new vessel for its Atlantic fleet that would be larger than anything then afloat and that construction would begin immediately in Belfast, Ireland.

The vessel, christened the *Adriatic*, was completed in 1907 and served as the company's proud flagship until her owners, the White Star Line, announced construction of a more state-of-the-art fleet of trans-Atlantic steamers, which it called its "Olympic Class."

The *Adriatic*, whose birth announcement was made public on the day the Iroquois died, was the immediate predecessor to the company's newest, safest, most technically advanced flagship, a greater, even more luxurious vessel that would, not unlike the Iroquois Theatre, symbolize the technical superiority of the new modern century. Just as the Iroquois was called "absolutely fireproof," this floating palace was termed "unsinkable."

She was the *Titanic*.

AFTERMATH

IN RECALLING THE IROQUOIS tragedy, Charles Collins always said he believed that the Chicago Fire Department "did a very fine job under difficult circumstances."

Collins ended his sixty-year career in journalism at the *Chicago Tribune*, which he joined in 1930. After a few years of general assignment reporting at the *Record-Herald*, he realized his life's ambition by becoming drama critic first for the *Chicago Daily News*, then for the *InterOcean*, and finally for the *Tribune*, where he once had the distinction of being barred from Shubert theatres for an extended period because of negative reviews he had written. In 1938, no longer the drama critic, he became the paper's "A Line O' Type Or Two" columnist. In his free time, Collins, who never married, was a novelist and librettist.

He would sometimes be called upon to write Iroquois pieces on the anniversary of the fire, but toward the end of his life he seemed to have become bored with the subject. Two years before his death in 1964, he told me that the tragedy had had no effect on him while he was covering the story. In the same interview, however, he said he could never forget the sight of one victim—a beautiful blond young woman, lying nude on a marble-topped table in Thompson's Restaurant, "looking like a classic Greek statue carved in alabaster."

Collins died believing that it was Ben Marshall, the young, relatively inexperienced architect, who was largely to blame for the disaster; the theatre was poorly designed because of its converging stairways. But Marshall went on to design other Chicago buildings, including the Blackstone Theatre, the Drake and Edgewater Beach hotels and the Polish Consulate. In a detailed oral history he recorded many years later for an architectural resource library at the University of Texas in Austin, Marshall discussed his career at length, but did not mention the Iroquois Theatre.

By 1935 the theatre horror had been forgotten by almost everyone except the survivors and their families. That same year, in a 361-page autobiography aptly titled *Stormy Years*, Mayor Harrison, who served five consecutive terms, devoted little more than three pages to the Iroquois tragedy. Saying nothing about his civic responsibilities, Harrison placed the blame for the fire on aldermen for dragging their feet on city fire ordinances, and maintained that "public hysteria" had forced the city council to close all Chicago theatres immediately after the fire.

Harrison died in 1953 at the age of ninety-three, after completing a second autobiography, *Growing Up in Chicago*, in which he made no mention of the tragedy.

Eddie Foy returned to the New York stage in 1904 after a few months in vaudeville, and took a leading role in a Broadway musical called *Piff! Paff! Poof!!* For years he received rounds of applause from audiences who remembered his act of bravery during the fire. Foy would eventually form an act with his children, billed as "The Seven Little Foys." Particularly from New York audiences, he would always get a laugh by gazing at his children lined up on stage and remarking, "If I lived in Flatbush, it would be a city!" In the early 1950s Bob Hope played Foy in a film filled with innumerable errors in its representation of the Iroquois fire. Foy died in 1928 in the kind of environment in which he had spent most of his professional life: a hotel room while he was on a road tour. He was seventy-two.

Klaw, Erlanger and the despised Theatrical Trust ran into continuing competition from the equally aggressive Shubert Brothers. Both empires would suffer in the 1929 stock market crash, and the Trust would eventually disappear. The evening before the Davis trial finally ended in 1907, Klaw was the guest speaker at a Friar's Club dinner in New York where he told his entertainment industry audience, perhaps only half in jest, "I had formerly been a newspaperman and a press agent, and I don't know now why I ever ceased so being."

Levy Mayer's corporate law practice continued to flourish; because of his success in defending Powers, he went on to represent important theatrical figures of the day, including, among others, Klaw, Erlanger, the prominent producer Charles Frohman, the Shubert Brothers and Florenz Ziegfeld, creator of the *Ziegfeld Follies*. Mayer's entertainment industry clients were only part of his burgeoning practice, which continues today as Mayer, Brown, Rowe and Maw, employing 1300 attorneys throughout the U.S. and overseas.

The beautiful Annabelle Whitford, who played the part of Stella, queen of the fairies, eventually became one of the Ziegfeld Girls. She retired from the stage in 1910 when she married Dr. Edward Buchan, one of the physicians who had done rescue work after the fire.

Will Davis continued in theatre management until he retired in 1914 and faded into obscurity.

Fire Marshal Musham, his reputation badly tarnished by the coroner's inquest, quietly resigned his post in 1904, and died soon afterward. The six firemen facing disciplinary action who helped in the rescue operations at the theatre were reinstated. Musham's white helmet is on permanent display at the Chicago Historical Society, which owns also the spotlight which is believed to have started the fire backstage.

Battalion Chief Hannon was transferred to a command outside the Loop.

The day after the disaster, Fireman First Class Michael Corrigan of Engine 13 was promoted for heroism to acting first lieutenant. Corrigan eventually became Chicago Fire Commissioner. It was said that no Chicago firefighter was killed in the line of duty during his tenure, which lasted from 1937 to 1955.

Charlotte Plamondon, the young debutante who leaped over the box railing and successfully escaped with the rest of her party, was so shaken by the experience that she was unable to return to school for many months. Unfortunately, she suffered the effects of another major tragedy, when her parents were among those lost at sea in the sinking of the *Lusitania*, torpedoed by a German submarine in 1915. Another *Lusitania* victim was the producer Charles Frohman, who had played an important part in the Theatrical Trust. His death shocked Broadway.

As happened in most other American cities, one by one, Chicago's many morning and evening newspapers eventually disappeared. The colorful City Press Association split into two entities in 1910. The Press Association maintained control over the tube system, and the new City News Bureau handled all reporting functions. Both agencies are now defunct.*

Walter Howey, the enterprising Press Association reporter who hired a boy to disable telephones so that he could scoop the competition, eventually became city editor of the *Tribune,* quit in a row with its publisher, and became editor of the *Herald-Examiner.* There, according to legend still up to his old tricks, he once hired an actress to play a dying millionairess in an attempt to lure the rival *Tribune* into printing a bogus story. Howey was said to be the prototype for the colorful managing editor in Ben Hecht and Charles MacArthur's celebrated play *The Front Page.*

---

* The old City News Bureau is now the City News Service, owned by the *Chicago Tribune.*

An Iroquois Theatre Memorial Association was set up immediately after the fire to help the victims' families. Among its first big contributors was Sir Thomas Lipton, the English tea tycoon. The association was dissolved during the Depression.

About 1910 the Iroquois Memorial Hospital was built in downtown Chicago at what was then North Market Street. Converted into a tuberculosis sanatorium around 1935, it was closed after World War II and then demolished. In the hospital had been a six-foot-high memorial to the Iroquois victims, a bronze bas relief designed by Laredo Taft, that disappeared when the hospital was torn down and was rediscovered years later in the basement of the City-County Building. It is now mounted on the wall inside the LaSalle Street entrance to City Hall. It has no explanatory legend.

A plan to erect an imposing memorial to the victims was never realized. Instead, a triangular marker was placed in a Chicago cemetery and an even smaller plaque was affixed to the wall of the lobby of an office building that was near the theatre. That building has since been demolished and the plaque has apparently vanished.

For many decades following the tragedy, survivors would gather every December 30 at City Hall to remember the victims. Former Fire Commissioner Corrigan would often attend these memorials, bringing along the alarm box he pulled that day. The so-called "Mercy Day" remembrances ended in the early sixties as the number of survivors dwindled.

The last survivor died in 1978 at the age of 86. She was Harriet Bray Crumpacker of Michigan City, Indiana, the little girl who had crawled beneath the legs of Engine 13's horses after she escaped from the theatre by jumping into her father's arms. She commented that for years after the fire, she never went to a theatre without looking carefully at the curtains around the proscenium arch. Her relative, William P. Crumpacker of Hammond, Indiana, says that family elders always admonished the children to look first for the exits when they entered any theatre. Certainly, for years hundreds if not thousands of families behaved in the same way.

William B. Warfel of Trumbull, Connecticut, whose master's thesis for the Yale School of Drama was "Theatre Fire Prevention Laws in Building Codes," said that his mother-in-law clerked in the late 1920s and early '30s for an Illinois Supreme Court justice whose wife had survived the fire. One of Mrs. Warfel's duties was buying theatre tickets for the judge, and her instructions were to buy seats only if they were adjacent to an exit. She had to go into theatres and confirm the seat locations before paying for the tickets.

The fire ended Chicago's hopes of becoming the equal of the New York stage. *Mr. Bluebeard* was also dead; it would never again play in a U.S. theatre. Colored lobby cards of the show and production photos of the cast seem to have disappeared. Major theatrical collections in both the U.S. and England have material like that from other 1903 musical productions, but I could find no *Mr. Bluebeard* items.

It would be cold consolation to the dead and their families, but it could be said that the Iroquois victims did not die in vain. Out of the public outcry over the tragedy came stringent reforms in building and fire safety codes throughout the U.S. and in some European countries, not only in theatres but in other public structures including schools, churches and office buildings.

Floor plans clearly showing the location of exits began to be included in playbills—some theatres had begun this practice before the fire—and for years an announcement on playbill covers read: "Look around now, choose the nearest exit. In case of fire, walk, do not run. Do not try to beat your neighbor to the street."

The use of fireproof materials for scenery became mandatory, as did illuminated exit signs and exit doors that open out, rather than in. These injunctions remain in force today.

Shortly after the tragedy, citing "lessons learned," the editors of the trade journal *Fire and Water Engineering* listed twelve points: stages must be protected by automatic sprinkler systems; exits must be unobstructed and marked by clearly visible signs; exit doors must open from the inside; emergency lighting is a necessity in theatres and other places of public assembly; adequate first aid and firefighting equipment and a fire alarm system must be installed and properly maintained; there must be a fire-resistant curtain at the proscenium opening of the stage that will close automatically without applied power; fire escapes should not be exposed to flames coming from doors or windows on lower floors; electrical facilities must comply with the electrical code; theatre employees should be trained in fire exit drills; scenery, curtains and other textile materials must be flameproof, and automatic vents must be installed over a stage. In addition, the editors pointed out that selling tickets to standees overloaded exit facilities and reduced the chances of orderly evacuation of the auditorium.

Days after the Iroquois burned, a letter from Andrew Carnegie appeared in the *New York Herald* urging the prohibition of combustible material on theatre stages: "As long as that liability exists there lie the seeds of panic in the audience, and it is the panic that causes disaster." Carnegie's concerns about mob panic were repeatedly proven prescient later in the century: two horrible examples were the 1942 disaster in Boston's Coconut Grove nightclub in which 491 people died and hundreds were injured, and the 1944 Ringling Brothers' Circus fire in Hartford, Connecticut, in which 168 people, two-thirds of them children, lost their lives.

The British system of routinely lowering an asbestos curtain at least once during a performance, in addition to permitting patrons at the end of a show to leave the theatre through all exit doors into streets, was generally hailed as the standard to be followed. Some London theatre executives nevertheless expressed reservations about human nature. The legendary Beerbohm Tree, proprietor of His Majesty's Theatre, said, "When all is done, the fact remains that no one has ever invented a patent for stopping a panic."

City school systems in general improved their fire drills, putting particular emphasis on the time it took to evacuate school buildings. Unfortunately, some municipalities took too much time to implement reforms. Five years after the Iroquois disaster, 171 children and two teachers died in a fire in a Cleveland suburban school where exit doors opened in and not out. Many of the victims were trampled in the crush.

Publications were inundated with all kinds of wild ideas and suggestions from readers on how to avoid an Iroquois catastrophe. Months after the fire, *Popular Mechanics* magazine printed details of a "water curtain . . . the fire curtain of the future," the brainchild of former Boston Fire Chief John W. Regan. The chief's radical solution involved a stage floor nozzle capable of shooting three sheets of water 150 feet wide and 60 feet high, "flaring out like a great fan," separating the stage from the auditorium. The water curtain was tested on the streets of Boston but was apparently never used in a theatre.

Out of the Iroquois disaster came a device still in wide use today. Carl Prinzler, an Indianapolis hardware salesman, had tickets for the December 30 matinee but missed the performance for business reasons. Prinzler was supposedly so disturbed at the needless loss of life that he determined to solve one of the principal problems in the doomed theatre: the inability to open exit doors that were locked or bolted. Prinzler and his neighbor

Henry DuPont, an architectural engineer, came up with a simple crossbar contraption that they called the "Self Releasing Fire Exit Bolt." They marketed the bolt in 1908 through the Vonnegut Hardware Company of Indianapolis under the name VonDuprin, a contraction of Vonnegut, DuPont and Prinzler. Because theatres then were still installing mandated post-Iroquois safety improvements, the bolt, now commonly called a "panic bar," was a commercial success and VonDuprin eventually became a division of the Ingersoll-Rand Company.

The Iroquois, its interior remodeled and its building updated to meet the fire code, reopened in 1904 as a vaudeville house, eventually renamed the Colonial Theatre. A building next door caught fire, frightening its audience. Eventually the Colonial was demolished to be replaced by the Oriental Theatre, a movie palace, now the Ford Center for the Performance Arts Oriental Theatre. On the sidewalk outside its entrance, a metal stanchion carries a history of the area, with a brief description of the tragedy and a picture of the ill-fated theatre that once stood on that spot.

A handful of relics, rarely if ever made public, are gathering dust in the vaults of the Chicago Historical Society. They include a wooden music stand from the orchestra pit, a bit of fabric from one of the curtains, a photograph of firemen in "Death Alley," a splinter of wood from an escape plank, a piece of chair stuffing, a sliver from one of the exit doors and a square piece of balcony drapery. There is also a scorched dollar bill supposedly retrieved from a trouser pocket in Eddie Foy's dressing room and a pair of women's rubbers recovered from the theatre. The largest artifact of all, however, is the spotlight for the "Pale Moonlight" number, the light that caused the fire.

EPILOGUE

WELL INTO THE TWENTIETH Century, disturbing moral questions remained about the tragedy and its aftermath. In 1945, forty-two years after the disaster, Louis Guenzel, a Chicago architect, published a detailed paper that he had written a few weeks after the fire at the request of the German government, following the Kaiser's order closing Berlin's Royal Opera House until it could be properly fireproofed. With a pass from the German consul, Guenzel entered the theatre on December 31, after which he spent weeks making repeated visits, writing detailed notes and examining stairways, exits, aisle widths, the upholstery of the seats and even the bolts used on doors. These bolts, he discovered, were commonly used in Europe, but were relatively unknown in the U.S., making their operation, particularly in a panic situation, so difficult as to be almost unworkable.

Guenzel wrote a cryptic preface to his confidential report, which had not been intended for publication but had been made public in 1945 because of contemporary concerns about fire hazards. He wrote that he was "interested in the various court proceedings resulting from the fire and was greatly surprised to see that, notwithstanding the many faults and defects in the planning of the [Iroquois] and the unparalleled negligence displayed in its supervision and operation, all the suits ended in verdicts: 'Not Guilty.'

"In recent years, I have repeatedly attended memorial meetings annually [and] from observations, conversations and discussions with eye-witnesses . . . but primarily in consequence of the adverse court decisions rendered in the trials of the damage suits, I have arrived at the conclusion that knowledge of the actual conditions prevalent at the Theatre at the time of the fire has been maliciously withheld from the public by clever and successful manipulation."

There was no further substantiation or clarification of his charges, but within the body of his original report, Guenzel raised a question that must have been on many minds in the weeks and months following the disaster. "But of what avail can even the best of ordinances be," he asked, "if supervision of their observance is entrusted to incompetent and unreliable officials who, as in the case of the Iroquois fire, allow a building to be opened to the public and operated for weeks with the most outrageous violations of the fire protection law obvious to and detectable at a glance by any half-way alert building inspector, fireman or police officer; and when the courts are so demoralized, that greedy and unscrupulous Theatre owners and heedless or corrupted City employees can get away with 'murder' without being taken to account for the lawlessness?"

The tragedy was also discussed in 1993 in *Lawyers and the American Dream* by Stuart M. Speiser, a noted New York trial attorney. The *Seton Hall Law Review* commented that Speiser's details would cause one to "bristle at the paltry sums received in the settlement of cases brought on behalf of the innocent victims of well-publicized national disasters at the turn of the century." Speiser told me, "[Plaintiff's] lawyers of 1903 . . . did not have the clout or the strength to enforce the law for little people against big people. The cleverest lawyers were hired by the business owners and insurance companies and just overwhelmed the plaintiff's lawyers [who] had no strength, no respect [and] were scrambling to make a living.

"The concept of responsibility, either criminally or in a civil case—damages—did not exist at that time. We were in a 'laissez faire' period when business was allowed to do what was necessary to create jobs and to build the economy. That was the philosophy at the time, that if one were a victim of an accident, 'it was just too bad.'" In the case of the Iroquois fire, he said, justice was not done, "not by any standard, whether it was criminal law or civil law."

Speiser supported the sentiments of John Altgeld, an outspoken superior court judge, later a respected governor of Illinois, who argued before the turn of the century that the "legal practice was weighted against the poor." Speiser said, "The real problem was that at the time of the fire there was not equal access to justice. The corporate, or moneyed interests, could stay out of jail very easily on something like [the fire] for they were not criminals in the sense that they were not in the business of burning down theatres and killing people.

"It just so happened that it was a terrible accident and it was their fault, but the idea of punishing them for that—they could handle the political end of fixing a thing like that. I am sure that's what they did in the sense of stalling that long, so that public indignation would die down. That's what their attorney's philosophy [was], the strategy from the beginning. When there is a real disaster, stall it and people will forget about it. If you have to go to trial next month it would be tougher on the defendant. So the strategy is to put [the case] off, people forget about it, other disasters will take its place, and the real indignation you need will not be there."

Instead of damage suits today, where "generous financial settlements with families take the indignation out of it [from

the criminal standpoint]," said Speiser, "they didn't have to
bother to do that in the Iroquois days. All they had to do was
use their political clout to stall a criminal trial and to outma-
neuver the weak plaintiff's lawyers in the civil cases, and [it]
was not difficult for them."

Sensitivity about the disaster remains. A Connecticut woman,
distantly related to one of the theatre owners, declined to be
interviewed for this book or to allow me to look through boxes
of information gathering dust in her garage, that her late husband had collected over a period of months he spent in Chicago
poring over depositions in the case.

The Official Chicago police and fire department records on the
fire do not exist, according to the respective unofficial historians of those departments, nor does the Chicago Historical Society possess such records. Cook County Court records of the
legal proceedings cannot be found. The material was apparently thrown out decades ago to make space for new documents.

The Delaware Building still stands on the corner of Randolph and State and, except for a McDonald's restaurant where
a cigar store was once located, the structure looks much as it
did nearly one hundred years ago. Inside its tiny lobby is a small
collection of framed photos of the Sherman House hotel and
prominent theatres in the area, but there is no photograph of
the Iroquois or any notation describing what happened immediately next door. Instead, there is a photograph of the theatre
building after, refurbished and renamed in 1904, it had been
turned into a vaudeville house.

Controversy about the tragedy may have ended, but mys-
tery and confusion remain, partly because of the understand-
able haste with which the city newspapers met their deadlines
at the time. On the day following the fire, for instance, the *Tri-*

bune reported on page one the name of a woman who had been revived by doctors in Thompson's Restaurant. But in the same edition, a woman with the same name appears on the paper's death list as one of those who jumped or fell from the balcony.

The exact number of victims will always remain in doubt. The Chicago coroner's office put the official number at 571; the *Tribune* at 575; the *Chicago Daily News Almanac* at 475, the Iroquois Memorial Plaque says 576. Fire Commission Corrigan gave the number as 601; the *Encyclopedia Americana* as 539; the historian Mark Sullivan listed it as 588 in his landmark book *Our Times*, and the National Fire Protection Association and the *World Almanac* both put the number at 602. The names of many of the actual victims also reflect confusion. For instance, the question remains whether the German aerialist who plunged to the stage was a male named "Florine," or a female named "Floraline." Both names appear in contemporary accounts and the person himself or herself simply disappeared from newspaper coverage following the disaster. I chose "Floraline" because other contemporary accounts described the aerialists as an all-female troupe. Even Nellie Reed disappeared. Her body was returned to New York, but British papers, apart from mentioning that she was from London, apparently never reported whether her remains were brought home.

In some of the original accounts of the fire, at least one Chicago newspaper incorrectly called the show "Mr. Bluebeard, Jr." The *New York Tribune* actually referred to the show by both names in the same page one story. This might have happened because in 1889 Eddie Foy appeared in Chicago and New York in a "lavish" but limited-run production called *Bluebeard Junior*. In delving into morgue files on the day of the fire, journalists may have pulled some of the old clippings and, under deadline pressure, confused the two. In a further complication, years after the fire as the Davis trial drew to a close, some Chicago news organizations, legal court documents and even more recent accounts, continued to repeat the same mistake. This may have been because in 1907 a production called *Mr. Bluebeard, Jr.*, based on the plot of the ill-fated musical, briefly played in Chicago and the title was picked up in subsequent reports on the disaster.

Some accounts have also reported, incorrectly, that toward the start of Act Two, as the fire broke out, Eddie Foy was preparing for his novelty act with the baby elephant instead of for the "Old Woman in the Shoe" routine. That is where it was scheduled in New York, but not in Chicago. As Foy's biographer Armond Fields notes, it was not uncommon at the time to switch the order of acts when shows moved from city to city. So for years, the belief persisted in Chicago that Foy had been working onstage with a real baby elephant that perished in the blaze and was buried somewhere in the city. In actual fact only an elephant costume was lost in the flames. The elephant act was revived later.

If there were any lessons to be learned from the Chicago tragedy, perhaps it was that the wonders of modern technology, with all their acknowledged benefits, could lull the public into a false sense of security in the mistaken belief that modern science had the answer to virtually every problem.

Despite all the technological improvements and contemporary safety standards of the twenty-first century, the Iroquois example and the current geopolitical situation raise questions about today's modern multiplex movie houses, legitimate playhouses, giant screen theatres and nightclubs, and about what would happen in a panic situation. Are exits uniformly unlocked? Are ushers properly trained? Are ushers even present? In most movie houses today, these young employees seem to be assigned to taking tickets, working concession stands and cleaning the-

atres rather than remaining in the darkened auditoriums themselves.

In the larger multiplex theatres, are there, in fact, enough
exits for capacity crowds? In these giant-screen theatres with
their steeply-banked rows of seats, one must customarily climb
a long flight of steps to exit from the rear of the theatre. In a
panic situation these steps could cause people to trip and fall
and be trampled on. What about the handicapped? In the security conscious times in which we live, what if a smoke bomb
were to be set off or some other disturbance were to occur to
create injuries and mass panic? In Israel more than thirty years
ago, when I entered theatres, I saw bags and packages being
routinely searched by armed militiamen and other security personnel. If during the performance one got up to leave, say, to
visit a restroom, the militiaman would walk the patron back to
his seat and shine a flashlight around the floor, to make sure
nothing had been "accidentally" left behind.

In November, 2002, I did an extensive web search and conducted a series of telephone interviews with fire department
officials including former chiefs and firemen, fire safety experts,
members of the staffs of the National Fire Protection Association (NFPA), the National Emergency Training Center, the Con-
gressional Fire Services Institute (CFSI), directors of fire museums, theatre employees including actors, and the owner of a
major Broadway theatre. This was of course not a scientific
study, but a cursory gathering of hard information, impressions,
anecdotes and personal observations.

Taken as a whole, the results leave many troubling questions.

The NFPA's Fire Analysis and Research Division, in a June,
2001 report, "U.S. Fire Problem Overview," states, "Although
fatal fires in [theatres] are relatively rare, the potential life safety
hazard is high." Calling the Iroquois "[t]he deadliest single-build-

ing fire in U.S. history," the report adds, "Because of the devastating potential of a single large fire in a crowded place of assembly, careful adherence to fire prevention and fire protection practices is essential." The author of the report declined to comment on the possibility that an Iroquois panic situation could happen again.

But Dennis Compton, an Arizona fire protection consultant who was assistant chief of the Phoenix Fire Department for twenty-seven years and chief of the Mesa Fire Department for five, said: "Of course it could happen again. . . . Modern fire codes are excellent, but the variables are the local enforcement of codes, what happens internally inside the theatre when an incident occurs, and the staffing levels and response time of firemen."

Dr. Peter Molloy, director of the Hall of Flame in Phoenix, one of the nation's largest fire museums, was equally blunt. "Sure it could happen again," he said, "especially from panic. Also the danger of asphyxia is higher because of the presence of cyanide gas from materials used in theatre interiors." He especially pointed to things like the use of PVC piping for electrical conduits.

What exactly does "careful adherence to fire prevention and fire protection practices" mean and who if anyone monitors it? The answer is confusing at best because there is controversy within the profession itself. According to Andrew Bowman, an Oak Brook, Illinois, fire safety expert, there have been attempts to standardize a nationwide fire code. Historically, three basic building codes have been adopted, usually with modifications, by local jursidictions. In recent years, there has been an attempt to move toward a single standard called the International Building Code developed by the International Code Council. But, Bowman says, with strong competition from the newly developed "NFPA 5000" code and the inevitable local amendments as a prerequisite for adoption, the concept of a single code across the U.S. may be difficult to realize.

A further complication is that NFPA, an international non-profit association founded before the turn of the last century, does not enforce code requirements. Neither does any other code development organization. The NFPA, according to a legislative aide to Senator John McCain, is "a voluntary consensus standards organization." Its various committees simply make code recommendations which are voted on by its 75,000 members who represent eighty different professional organizations. The safety recommendations then go to the NFPA Standards Council for a final review to determine whether they will become code. But even after all this, NFPA codes, unlike OSHA regulations for workplace safety, are interpreted by local municipalities and jursdictions as they see fit.

The problem is not with the codes," says Dennnis Compton. "The NFPA produces excellent building and fire codes. The variable is how different cities adopt them and then what amendments are put in, especially if they don't have the necessary resources. Governments prioritize where they will spend the money. Each jurisdiction has a set of policymakers that get to decide those questions." Many of the nation's fire departments, he says, are currently understaffed and in the midst of cost-cutting—an ironic situation at a time when the nation's priority seems to be homeland security.

Another problem is that in some cities and towns, beautifully restored theatres and movie palaces have been exempted or "grandfathered" from code requirements which could necessitate prohibitively expensive renovation or even demolition, because they were built before certain codes were enacted or updated. Andrew Bowman says, "When you renovate an historic building and are required to achieve code compliance, it's often very difficult to preserve all historic aspects of the struc-

ture. There are processes in place to allow waivers from the
code to deal with this, but that tends to come down to a juris-
diction-by-jurisdiction decision. . . . We are much smarter [to-
day] about fire codes and marshals saying, 'You need these exits.' It doesn't mean that those things are in place and when you
are in these grandfathered buildings, you may not be getting
the level of protection that you expect with the new theatres.
Another incident could occur."

One of New York's most famous Broadway theatres, built
less than a decade after the Iroquois disaster, provides a prime
example of what Bowman is talking about. The owner, who
spoke only on condition of anonymity, admitted that because
of grandfathering, only certain hallways, *and not his main auditorium*, are equipped with sprinklers. The men's restroom is
located two flights of stairs below ground level and new codes
mandating accessibility for the handicapped do not apply because his theatre was grandfathered in, and there is no possible
place to build that facility at ground level. Asked about safety,
he said that both the theatre's general manager and its house
manager would know what to do in an emergency situation.
He remarked that if he were in a theatre when a fire broke out,
he would probably "run to the stage and get out through the
scenery loading doors"—just as most of the *Bluebeard* company had done.

"Modifications require money," the NFPA specialist said.
"There are a host of competing interests, many of which are
varied and compelling. It comes down to risk management,
which nobody likes to talk about. What are you willing to pay
to be safe?"

A recent example of how much money it can take is provided by Ford's Theatre, the scene of Lincoln's assassination,
located just blocks from the White House. It is administered by
the National Park Service (NPS), the subject in July 2000 of

damning testimony by the Government Accounting Office (GAO) before the House Committee on the Budget. The GAO raised serious concerns about NPS "commitment and priority to ensuring that the risks of structural fires harming visitors, employees, resources and other assets were minimized. . . .

"During a visit to Ford's Theatre, we noted that serious deficiencies concerning stairwell and stage doors had not been corrected even though they were first identified by a Park Service contractor in 1993. The contractor's report also raised concerns about the theatre's sprinkler system and noted that 'If the sprinkler system fails or does not operate as designed, a fire in the stage area, particularly during a production, has the potential to kill several hundred people. . . . Fires in other theatres show that a severe fire can develop in a few minutes.'"

The GAO report quoted a 1998 Park Service study : "'Sooner or later the NPS stands to be seriously embarrassed (at a minimum) by the catastrophic loss, either of an irreplaceable historic structure or collection, or of human life, from a structural fire.'"

After a six-month shutdown and an infusion of $4.3 million, Ford's was expected to reopen before the end of 2002, according to Michael Maione, Park Service site historian, who said that the safety improvements included a new electrical system and correction of the problems cited almost a decade earlier. That is taking the Park Service at its word, especially since the GAO told me it had no plans to reinspect the theatre. One wonders why.

One Chicago fire chief dismissed the possibility of an Iroquois catastrophe, saying that the city has some of the most stringent fire and building codes on record. But he had no answer when he was asked about crowd control in any panic situation.

Are theatre employees properly trained?

A former usher at a Chicago legitimate theatre told me that while she worked there, there was no fire training or fire drills and, while a house manager could survey the theatre over a closed circuit television system, there was only one usher in the house during a performance. Other ushers remained in the lobby area. Once, she said, when patrons left the auditorium because of a disturbance, ushers had to ask them what was happening.

Other former ushers and theatre employees also complained about a lack of training. A college student who worked at a movie theatre in a major Southwestern city said he could recall no drill or training in what to do in case of an emergency. Another, who had worked off and on for seven years in one of the most historic legitimate theatres in the West, said that he was never given any training in emergency evacuation, but he noted an escape route on his own. A third person, who had worked in a multiplex cinema with a screening room large enough to accommodate 300 people, also could not recall receiving any emergency training.

What about emergency egress from such large auditoriums?

The former Chicago usher commented that in one of Chicago's older multiplex cinemas on North Michigan Avenue, screening rooms are located many stories above street level. There are internal fire stairs, but on one occasion when the theatre was completely sold out, she remembers that it took at least fifteen minutes to travel down three levels to the lobby on the one available escalator which was so narrow that it could accommodate only one person on each step. One cannot help wondering what would happen if patrons decided, for any reason, not to use the fire stairs but to go out the way they had come in. Or if the stairs were blocked in some way and the audience had to attempt to escape using the escalators?

I inspected some theatres in Santa Fe where I live. In one multiplex cinema, the largest auditorium had one exit next to the screen and another in the rear of the house. From the center of the darkened theatre the exit next to the screen looked large, but this was deceptive because on close inspection it was quite small, and it was dark: two short flights of narrow, poorly defined steps led up to an outer exit door. The steps were no more than three feet wide. It takes little imagination to visualize the possible congestion if a disturbance in the rear of the house blocked the theatre's only other exit. On the day I was there, only one young man was on duty, doubly occupied in taking tickets and manning the concession stand.

In this same theatre not long ago an acquaintance found herself trapped alone in the pitch dark in a restroom after the final evening showing when the lights suddenly went out. The employees were evidently closing down the theatre without checking the lavatories. She screamed, but no one came and she spent many frightening minutes groping her way from stall to stall until she was able to find the door and get out.

Andrew Bowman, the safety engineer, told of being in a theatre when a small fire broke out in a popcorn cooker in a kitchen off the lobby. Alarms sounded and at first the audience did not know what to do. No usher or other employee appeared. Luckily no one panicked and there were no injuries, but instead of leaving the theatre through exits opening onto the street, all the patrons chose to go back the way they had entered, a decision which led them directly into the lobby where the fire was—the last place they should have been. Bowman said that people are conditioned to go out the way they came in and "they don't know how to adequately judge what a real emergency is because they don't perceive a threat."

Apparently neither do many theatre professionals. I interviewed actors and directors, some of whom had performed for more than forty years on and off Broadway and in hundreds of cities. None could recall ever being given instructions about what

to do in case of a fire, and none had ever taken part in a fire
drill or had ever seen ushers or any theatre employees partici-
pating in a drill.

Would older, perhaps more experienced, ushers be capable
of handling a mob of panicked people all trying to get out at the
same time? Peter Molloy said it wasn't likely: "In a modern
disaster they'd all be flattened. We live in a social culture in
which it's 'every man for himself.'"

One hundred years after the Iroquois catastrophe, one must
conclude that there is still a pressing need for work in three
major areas:

    1) The code that dictates so-called "built environments."

    2) The issue of human behavior and public education.

    3) The resources of local fire departments.

Some of the same problems exist that existed in 1903: public complacency and indifference; a callous disregard of safety
regulations and commonsense by some theatre owners and
managers who, as one official said, seem to be operating under
the delusion that "it won't happen to me," and government
and industrial red tape that hobbles efforts at reform.

One of the popular songs dashed out in the aftermath of the
1903 disaster was "Never More Mention the Iroquois Theatre."
But the lessons of what happened in Chicago a century ago
must not be forgotten—or ignored.

ACKNOWLEDGEMENTS

MANY PEOPLE CONTRIBUTED TO the production of this book, not only when my initial research began in 1961, but when I resumed the project thirty-eight years later.

Many thanks to Tony Day, former editorial page editor of the *Los Angeles Times*, for his initial comments on the manuscript and his encouragement and for introducing me to Donald Lamm, the man who became my advisor, editor, agent and friend. I am indebted to Don for his unflagging support, his suggestions and, what every new writer needs, a kick-start and much encouragement. Thanks to Simm Landres, an old friend wise in the ways of the American theatre. I am most grateful too to Donald E. Meyer, David Chapnick, Stanley Cohen and Robert Warren for their help on some of the legal aspects of this story; to attorney Frank Mayer, Jr., of Chicago, for his help with information on his great-granduncle, Levy Mayer; and especially to Stuart Speiser of Scottsdale, Arizona, a partner in the New York law firm Speiser, Krause & Madole, who, through his own extensive research, provided many revealing facts about victims of disasters at the beginning of the century and whose many volumes on law have frequently been cited by the U.S. Supreme Court.

A special note of thanks must go to a most gracious and sharing individual, Armond Fields, a social historian and the biographer of Eddie Foy and other prominent turn-of-the-century American entertainers, for his encyclopedic knowledge of early American show business and for sharing some of his collection of photographs and newspaper articles related to Foy and the fire. Without his help this book could not have been written. Nor could it have been written without the help of Father John McNalis, pastor of Saint Gabriel Roman Catholic Church and assistant chaplain of the Chicago Fire Department (CFD), and Kenneth Little, senior fire alarm operator, CFD, and director of the Fire Museum of Greater Chicago, published historians of the department who shared their extensive knowledge of firemen and firefighting; to Paul Ditzel, a leading expert on fire history and firefighting, to Captain John J. O'Donnell, CFD, and to Lt. Clarence Norwood, Commander of Engine Co. 98, CFD, for allowing me to roam freely through his historic station house, built in 1903, the year of the fire.

Thanks also to Tim Samuelson, historian, Chicago Department of Cultural Affairs; Martha Goldstein of the *Los Angeles Times* for her suggestions on research sources; Gabriela Portillo Mazal, Susan McKelvey and Casey Grant, assistant vice president, Codes and Standards, the National Fire Protection Association; Norman D. Schwartz of the Chicago Jewish Historical Society; William Wleklinski, Associate Director for Public Services, the John Marshall Law School, Chicago; Dan Sharon, Senior Reference Librarian, and Rivka Schiller, the Asher Library, Spertus Institute for Jewish Studies, Chicago; Jay Satterfield, Reader Services Librarian, University of Chicago; Adam Koelsch, *Billboard Magazine*; Heywood Hoffman, Wayne Klatt, and Paul Zimbrakos, of the Chicago City News Bureau; Belle Allen; Molly McDonough, Chicago Headline Club; Cynthia Requardt, Kurrelmeyer Curator of Special Collections, the Johns Hopkins University; Melanie Wheeler, Patti Civinelli, and Jeanie Child of the Circuit Court of Cook County; Phillip

Costello, archivist, Clerk of the Circuit Court, Cook County; Professor Richard Schaefer, School of Communications and Journalism, University of New Mexico; Richard Towne, General Manager, Station KUNM-FM, Albuquerque, New Mexico; Karl Sup, president and co-founder, Eastland Memorial Society, Chicago; Mary Ellen Walsh, *Chicago Tribune*; David Lagerman, *Milwaukee Journal Sentinel* News Information Center; Richard Sklenar, Director, Theater Historical Society of America; Brett Smith; researchers Helen A. Shaw (Chicago) and Kenneth Wenzer (Washington, D.C.); Annette Marotta and Jeremy Megraw of the Billy Rose Theater Collection, New York Public Library for the Performing Arts; Kevin Winkler, Chief Librarian, Circulating Collections, New York Public Library for the Performing Arts; Karla Henry, *Smithsonian Magazine*; Mark Blackburne, Chairman, Ulster (Northern Ireland) *Titanic* Society; Joy Kingsolver, Chicago Jewish Archives; Mary Campbell, Curator, Lester S. Levy Collection, the Milton S. Eisenhower Library, (Baltimore); Jonathan Grey, Theater Museum, National Museum of the Performing Arts (London); Robert W. Karrow, Jr., Curator, Special Collections, the Newberry Library, (Chicago); Marcia Lehr, Librarian, Northwestern University Library; David R. Phillips Collection; Ken Davis; Linda Oelheim, Illinois State Historical Library; David Peter Coppen, Special Collections Librarian, Sibley Music Library, Eastman School of Music, Rochester, NY; the staff of the Chicago Historical Society; Ron White, unofficial historian of the Chicago Athletic Club; Bryan Humphry, Los Angeles Fire Department; William P. Crumpacker; the Chicago Board of Education, and Raymond Wemmlinger of Players. Thanks also to Scott Currier, chairman, the Currier & Ives Foundation, Dr. Gary Zola, Executive Director, the Jacob Rader Marcus Center of the American Jewish Archives; Russell Lewis, Director for Collections and Research, Chicago Historical Society; Dennis Bingham, historian of the Chicago Police Department. A very special note of thanks to Lyle Benedict, a most knowledgeable historian, Municipal Reference Collection, Harold Washington Library, (Chicago); Jay Satterfield, Librarian, Special Collections, University of Chicago; John Kennrick, Musicals 101.com; Danny Newman, Lyric Opera of Chicago; Linda Milano, Assistant Director, Theodore Roosevelt Association; Brett Smith 1 Direct.com; telephonymuseum.com; Marty Jacobs, Curator, Theater Collection, Museum of the City of New York; Susan Green, the Carriage Museum of America, Bird-in-Hand, Pennsylvania; Janine Henri, Head Librarian, the Architecture and Planning Library, University of Texas, Austin; Patricia Sabin, bellsouth.net; Bill Vandervoort; Patricia McFeeley, M.D., New Mexico State Medical Examiner's Office; Malissa A. White, education director, the Center for Theater, Albuquerque; John Ahouse, Curator, Special Collections, American Literature, University of Southern California (Los Angeles); journalist Sandra Blakeslee; Tim Samuelson, cultural historian, Chicago Department of Cultural Affairs and the staff of the Chicago Historical Society, especially Rob Kent, Collections Manager. Thanks also to Betsy Lutz.

For the time they spent answering my endless questions, my thanks also to Dr. Peter Molloy, Director, Hall of Flame Fire Museum, Phoenix, Arizona and Major "Tippy" Pierce, Oklahoma Fire Museum, Oklahoma City, where I had the good fortune to discover an original tube of Kilfyre; the Old Firehouse Museum, Denver, Colorado; the Shubert Archives, New York; Don White; Deborah Gillespie, Curator, Chicago Jazz Archive, University of Chicago; Donald DiStefano, American LaFrance Corp.; Louie and Mary DeCar of Madison, Indiana for their research and background information on Charles Collins; Tyneshia Thomas, Xerox Copy Center, Chicago; Martin Aurand,

Architecture Librarian and Archivist and Matthew Marsteller, Engineering Librarian and Archivist, Carnegie Mellon University Archives, Pittsburgh; Susan Harris, Bodleian Library, Oxford University; Edward Bills, Faith Burdick of the Galesburg, Illinois, Public Library and M. Celeste Jackson, Public Relations Manager of the Denver Public Library.

Thanks also to Max Wilk, Donald J. Stubblebine, John Vittal, senior research librarian, the Albuquerque Public Library; Alice Davis, inter-loan librarian, the Santa Fe Public Library; the University of New Mexico Library in Albuquerque, the New Mexico State Archives in Santa Fe, and Dr. Beryl Lovitz. Thanks also to Jennifer Sprague for her help in transcribing and organizing this book and making my computer run when it did not want to.

I could not conclude this list without offering posthumous mention of those participants and eyewitnesses of the Iroquois fire, most particularly Charles Collins, Michael J. Corrigan, George Dunlap and Frank Moore, as well as others who participated in direct interviews and in written recollections of the tragedy which I solicited in the early sixties. I must also pay tribute to my friend, the late Santa Fe artist Isa Barnett, who urged me to "sit down and write the book," but who did not live to see it published.

I must also offer special mention and thanks to Anita and Jordan Miller, my editors and publishers at Academy Chicago, who worked long and hard at shaping this book and dealing with the sometimes conflicting details inherent in a one-hundred-year-old story, and to Sarah Olson who worked on the notes, photographs and design of the book.

Finally, my thanks to Owen Laster, whom I first approached with the idea for this story but who, more importantly, introduced me, almost forty years ago, to a college chum. That friend,

Lenore Goldstein, became not only my wife but my unofficial editor, proofreader, advisor, critic and Number One Cheerleader who made the long, (and often trying), journey with me on this project and who through it all still remains the dearest thing in this world.

On the dedication page, besides the names of my wife and those of my parents, are those of two friends, mentors and colleagues, Gerald Miller and George Syvertsen, who were influential at the start of my career at the *Middletown* (NY) *Times Herald*, then at the Associated Press and whose lives ended with terrible suddenness while on assignment for CBS News in Cambodia in 1970. I have no doubt they would have provided a better report on the Iroquois disaster than I have attempted.

Nor can one forget the heroic New York City fire, police and emergency rescue workers, living and dead, who courageously responded to the savage attack on the World Trade Center Towers in Manhattan. The selflessness, bravery and devotion to duty they showed on September 11, 2001, was not unlike that exhibited nearly one hundred years earlier, on December 30, 1903 by Chicago fire, police and rescue workers and medical aid personnel. Then as now, these men and women represent the indomitable spirit of America.

NOTES

FOREWORD

ix. *Chgo Times* prediction: D.B. McCurdy, ed., *Lest We Forget*, 317–324. In 1861, editor of the *Times*, Wilbur F. Storey, stated, "It is a newspaper's duty to print the news, and raise hell." Quoted in George Seldes, *The Great Thoughts*, 401.

CHAPTER 1. OPENING NIGHT

1. "Never seen anything like it": Author's interview with Charles Collins. "Event of Chicago's century": *Chgo Tribune*, Sunday, Nov. 22, 1903, p 4. Vehicles used at time: Author's interview with Susan Green, Librarian, Carriage Museum of America. "It was a fairly lush time": Tony Weitzel, "Christmas Week, 1903: Horror at the Iroquois Theater," p 25. "Splendidly attired": Drawn from accounts and newspaper sketches of Iroquois opening in Chicago newspapers, Nov. 24, 1903.

2. "On the make": Lisa Fine, *The Souls of the Skyscrapers*, 5. "No resident of Chicago": *Chgo Tribune*, Nov. 16, 1903, p 4. John Shedd: *Chgo Tribune*, Nov. 24, 1903; Author's interview with Faith LaSure, Shedd Aquarium Public Affairs Dep't.

3. Alexander Revell cottage: *Chgo Tribune*, Nov., 1903. Plamondon's business address: Chicago Telephone Directory, 1903, Municipal Reference Collection (MRC). R. Hall McCormick and Mrs. Edward Leicht: *Chgo Record-Herald*, Nov. 24, 1903, p 3. Auction of seats: *Chgo Tribune*, Nov. 17, 1903, p 3. Collins's salary, substitution for Bennett: Author's interview with Collins. "A strong, silent man": William C. Boyden, Jr., "Chicagoans"; additional information from a phone interview about Collins with publicist Danny Newman. Collins's undergraduate jobs: Author's interview with Collins.

4. "Charlie knows his theatre": *Chicagoan Magazine* profile.

5. Description of Loop: contemporary photos, 1903–04, Chicago Historical Society, and the *NY Times*, January 26, 1904, p 28. "Rialto of the Midwest": Edgar Lee Masters, *Levy Mayer and the New Industrial Era*, 69. *Tribune* headline, Amy Leslie review: *Chgo Tribune*, Nov. 24, 1903, p 5. "The marvels had been wrought": *Chgo Journal*, Nov. 24, 1903.

CHAPTER 2. ABSOLUTELY FIREPROOF

7. "Buildings in Dearborn": *NY Times*, May 2, 1903, p 1. "Chicago to Have a Palatial Theatre": *San Francisco Chronicle*, July 29, 1903, p 3.

8. Theatre location: photograph, probably spring/summer, 1904, showing intersection of Dearborn and Randolph, the Iroquois Theatre, renamed as a vaudeville house, in relation to the Delaware Building on the corner and Northwestern University in the rear on "Death Alley" (Couch Place). Courtesy Chicago Historical Society. Iroquois construction description: *NY Times*, Nov. 24, 1903, p 5; F. J. T. Stewart, Chicago Underwriters' Association (preliminary report), issued as Bulletin #54 to the National Fire Protection Association, Jan. 9, 1904. The bulletin contains two drawings of the theatre at variance with one another, apparently rendered by two different sources. "Ground Plan" drawing indicates no scenery stage doors on the Couch Place side, but the second drawing, "Rear Elevation, Showing Emergency Exits," does, the latter plan conforming to a news photo taken on scene, late afternoon, Dec. 30, or more likely the morning following the fire, showing a fire engine, open scenery doors, smoke still issuing from the theatre, and the rescue ladder and board "bridge" in the background still in place between the theatre and the Northwestern building. Photo courtesy Chicago Historical Society. More accurate renderings of the theatre are contained in Louis Guenzel, *Retrospects: The Iroquois Theater Fire*, 6–10. Cost of theatre: *NY Times*, Nov. 24, 1903, p 5.

9–10. Theatre interior details: Charles E. Nixon, *Iroquois Theatre Opening Night Commemorative Brochure*, 16–33. Marshall lauded by Davis: *Chgo Tribune*, Nov. 24, 1903, p 6; *Chgo Chronicle*, Nov. 24, 1903, p 1.

11. Gold-embossed, red brochure: Theodore Remer, "Terror at the Iroquois," Panorama, *Chgo Daily News*, Dec. 30, 1967, p 1.

12. "Marshall studied every disaster": McCurdy, p 120. William Clendenin, *Fireproof Magazine* (Aug., 1903), quoted in McCurdy, 248. After the fire, Clendenin called the theatre a "firetrap."

12–13. Personnel of Chicago Building Dept., Chicago Fire Department Bureau of Explosives: Payroll Records, City of Chicago, 1903, MRC. Building Commissioner's report to Harrison: Nov. 2, 1903, MRC. Aldermen's response to report: *Chgo Tribune*, Jan. 1, 1904, p 6. Patrick Jennings, testimony transcript: Ibid., Jan. 26, 1904, p 6.

14. Kilfyre: Author's examination of Kilfyre tube and label, Oklahoma City Fire Museum, 2000. Kilfyre was owned and manufactured by the Monarch Fire Appliance Co., 247–9 Pearl Street, New York City, established in 1895. The product had received awards at expositions in 1889, 1901 and 1902. The company called it "The Original Fire Extinguisher." Price: $3 per tube. "They will lynch you": Jennings testimony, *Chgo Tribune*, Jan.

26, 1904, p 6. Chief Hannon's response: Ibid. Collins saw no danger: Author's interview with Collins.

15. "A sinister omen": *Chgo Sunday Tribune*, Dec 28, 1952, p 6.

CHAPTER 3. A NEW YEAR'S SURPRISE

17. Opening night reception: *Chgo Journal*, Nov. 24, 1903, p 3.

18. "Theatre is the talk of the town": *NY Clipper*, Dec. 5, 1903, p 974. Plamondon and Revell daughters attend: McCurdy, 210, 214.

CHAPTER 4. STRIKES, SNOW AND SHOW BUSINESS

21–22. *Record-Herald* circulation: *Chgo Record-Herald*, Nov. 25, 1903, p 6. Competition with *Tribune*: Author's interview with Collins. "A curtain": *Chgo Tribune*, Nov. 24, 1903, p 6.

22. "A dazzling collection": *Chgo Record-Herald*, Nov. 24, 1903, p 6. "Fuller Company second to none": Nixon, p 18.

22–23. Fuller Construction labor problems: *NY Times*, 1903, Nov. 12, p 5; ibid, Nov. 18, p 16; ibid, editorial, Nov. 20, p 10; ibid, Nov. 24, p 2.

23. Fuller strike: *NY Times*, Nov. 14, 1903, p 9; ibid, editorial, Nov. 20, 1903, p 10; ibid, Nov. 24, 1903, p 2; *Chgo Tribune*, Nov. 16, 1903, p 1.

23–24. Klaw and Erlanger: Arthur Hornblow, *A History of Theater in America*, 319; Joseph and J. B. Csida, *American Entertainment*, 131; Armond and L. Mark Fields, *From the Bowery to Broadway: Lew Fields and the Roots of American Popular Theater*, 175. In addition, an extensive review of the business of the Theatrical Trust can be found in: Jack Poggi, *Theater in America: The Impact of Economic Forces, 1870–1967*, Chapter 1, "Theater Becomes Decentralized."

24. "From freewheeling competition": Ron Chernow, *Titan*, 227.

24–26. Theatrical Trust: Fields and Fields, *From the Bowery*, 112, 116, 123, 138. New Amsterdam Theatre: Ibid, 200. Klaw and Erlanger: J. Anthony Lukas, *Big Trouble*, 577. "Corruption of Christian morals": *Chgo Tribune*, Nov. 23, 1903, p 1.

26–27. Harrison Grey Fisk and anti Semitism: Fields and Fields, *From the Bowery*, 175. *Life* magazine: John Tebbel and Mary Ellen Zuckerman, *The Magazine in America, 1741–1990*, 151, 219; Pamphlet, John Ames Mitchell: Sinclair Lewis, Thomas L. Masson, John Ames Mitchell and James S. Metcalfe. *John Ames Mitchell: The Man Who is Responsible for Life*; Edward S. Martin, "Life after Fifty Years," 22. James S. Metcalfe joined the magazine early and stayed with it for most of his career. Most famous of *Life's* contributors was the artist Charles Dana Gibson, creator of "The Gibson Girl," who became the magazine's owner after Mitchell's death. Cartoon, "The Drama": *Life* cover, Mar. 29, 1900, p 1. Cartoon, "Of the Jews": *Life* centerfold, Sept. 12, 1901, pp 210–211. "The Jewish Mind in These States": *Life,* June 20, 1917, p 983. The author of this piece and the subsequent response to an objecting letter, "More About the Jewish Mind," was Edward Sandford Martin, who briefly headed the magazine following Mitchell's death. Born in Willowbrook, NY, he was a cofounder of the *Harvard Lampoon,* graduated Harvard, Class of 1877, admitted to the Rochester, NY, bar in 1884, helped found *Life* and wrote for *Life* and *Harper's Weekly.* He and Metcalf were not the only anti-Semites among *Life's* early contributors. In an April, 1900, piece, Joseph Smith wrote: "The American theatre is a building devoted to exhibitions of filth, folly, froth and frippery, under the direction of Hebrew foxes for the education of Gentile geese. . . . Only the success of Zionism, with the return of the chosen people to Palestine, will render possible the restoration of the American theatre and drama to a condition when it will be possible to visit the one without disinfectants and view the other without blushing." "They are not Jews of the better class": Lukas, p 578. Klaw-Erlanger troubles with Shubert Brothers, et al.: Lawrence Bergreen, *As Thousands Cheer,* 50; Fields and Fields, *From the Bowery,* 178, 181, 192.

27–28. *Oz,* undisputed hit: Bruce Watson, "The Amazing Author of Oz," pp 112–113.

28. Eddie Foy hired: Armond Fields, *Eddie Foy: A Biography of a Great American Entertainer,* 142. Klaw-Erlanger investment: *NY Times,* Nov. 24, 1903, p 1. Seamstresses and English women: *NY Times,* Jan. 8, 1903, p 26.

29. "Theatre will not be opened": Ad, *Chgo Tribune,* Nov. 11, 1903, p 7. Chicago railway strike: *NY Times,* Nov. 8, 1903, p 2; ibid, Nov. 11, p 1; ibid, Nov. 13, p 2. "Delayed by labor": Fields, *Eddie Foy,* 144. "Trouble with marble finishers": *NY Clipper,* Jan. 9, 1904, p 11.

30–32. "Turn Car Barn" *Chgo Tribune,* Nov. 15, 1903, p 1. "Free tickets": *Chgo Tribune,* Jan. 3, 1904, p 6. "Davis' summer": *NY Clipper,* Oct 17, 1903, p 802. "Goddam mess": Author's interview with Collins. "Labor War" in Chicago: *NY Times,* Nov. 1, 1903, p 6; ibid, Nov. 8, p 2. "Industrial armament": *McClure's* magazine, quoted in *NY Times,* Nov. 1, 1903, p 6. Walkout begins: *NY Times,* Nov. 13, 1903, p 2. Strike spreads: ibid, Nov. 14, 1903, p 9. No crowds allowed: ibid, Nov. 15, 1903, p 5. Mob rioting, aldermen demand police: Ibid, Nov. 16, 1903, p 1. Additional police assigned, police to board mail wagons: Ibid, Nov. 17, 1903, p 1. Police fire over heads: Ibid, Nov. 22, 1903, p 3. Mobs in streets: Ibid, Nov. 25, 1903, p 7. Strike settled: Ibid, Nov. 26, 1903, p 2. "Living in a powder magazine": Ibid, Nov. 26, 1903, p 2.

32. "Business not on capacity": *NY Clipper*, Dec. 5, 1903, p 974. "Business not up": Ibid, Dec. 12, 1903, p 999. Chicago's coldest day: *Chgo Tribune*, Dec. 14, 1903, p 1. Weather headlines: Ibid, Dec. 13–17, 1903, p 1; *Record-Herald*, Dec. 14, p 1. Small attendance at theatres: *The Billboard*, Dec. 12, 1903, p 5.

33. "Plunder to police": *Chgo Tribune*, Nov. 2, 1903, p 1. Chicago crimes: *Chgo Tribune*, Dec. 6, 1903, p 1; ibid, Nov. 25, p 7; *Record-Herald*, Nov. 24, p 1; *NY Times*, Nov. 28, p 1; ibid, Nov. 29, p 9; ibid, Dec. 29, p 9; ibid, December 1, pp 1, 6. Alderman Mavor on lawlessness: *Chgo Tribune*, Dec. 13, 1903, p 2. "Teddy bears": *News of the Nation*, no. 30 (1901–1906), p 2. Christmas advertisements: *Chgo Tribune*, Nov. 3, p 14.

34. "Haute monde preps": *Chgo Tribune*, Dec. 12, 1903, p 2. "Building OK": *InterOcean*, Jan. 1, 1904, p 2; *Chgo Daily News*, Jan. 14, 1904, p 1.

CHAPTER 5. THE SONG AND DANCE MAN

35–38. Foy's family reunion: Eddie Foy and Alvin Harlow, *Clowning Through Life*, 274. Foy's early life: Fields, *Eddie Foy*, 3. Foy and the Chicago fire: Ibid, pp 31–44. "I savored the joy": Ibid, p 231.

38. "Everyone in Chicago": London *Daily Mirror*, Jan. 5, 1905, p 4.

CHAPTER 6. MIXED REVIEWS

39. Technological Improvements: Irving Fang and Kristina Ross, The Media History Timeline/1900s: The First Decade (via internet). New lexicon: Ads, *NY Clipper*, week of Nov. 20, 1903; *Billboard Magazine*, Mar. 19, 1904. Coon shouters and race records: Kohn Edward Hasse and Ted Lathrop, *Jazz: The First Century*, 13. Phonograph records: Peter Copeland, *Sound Recordings*, 5–15. Caruso and Sousa: Sanford Mirkin, *When Did It Happen?*, 86, 229. Scott Joplin: Hasse and Lathrop, 13; Advertisement, *NY Clipper*, Oct. 3, 1903, p 791.

40. "Alice in Wonderland": Lewis Beale, "When the Camera Goes Behind the Looking Glass," p 15. Indian stagecoach attack: Museum of the American West, Cody, Wyoming. The yellow stagecoach is on display at the "Buffalo Bill" section there. "Twenty-five percent": Daniel Blum, *A Pictorial History of the American Theater, 1860–1960*, 73. "Chicago came closest": Donald J. Stubblebine, *Early Broadway Sheet Music*, 2. "The modern American musical": Lehman Engle, *The Musical Theater: A Consideration*, 5; Gilbert Chase, *America's Music*, 628, 629.

40–41. English pantomime: Barbara Cohen-Stratyner, *Popular Music 1900–1919*, 1.

41. Cost of Act Two: Fields, *Eddie Foy*, 142. Drury Lane Theater: John Russell Brown, *Oxford Illustrated History of Theater*, 337. Pony Ballet: Gerald Bordman, *American Musical Theater: A Chronicle*, 190.

41–42. Nellie Reed: Fields, *Eddie Foy*, 143.

42. *Babes in Toyland*: Clifton Daniel and John Kirshon, *America's Century*, 19. Harry Von Tilzer: Bergreen, 18.

43. *Bluebeard* characters: *Bluebeard* playbill, Iroquois Theatre, 1903, Chicago Historical Society; Fields, *Eddie Foy*, 142, 143. Foy in "drag": Ibid, 55. Foy's bustle: Bordman, 190.

44. *Bluebeard* tableau effects: Fields, *Eddie Foy*, 143.

44–46. Newspaper reviews listed (with the exception of the *Chgo Tribune*), collection of Armond Fields; Jan. 31, 1903: *NY Post, Herald, Telegraph, Telegram*; *Pittsburgh Dispatch*, Sept. 29, 1903; *Indianapolis News*, Oct. 29, 1903; *Chgo Evening Post, Chgo American, Chgo Tribune, Chgo Journal*, Nov. 24, 1903.

CHAPTER 7. THE DAY: DECEMBER 30

47. "Clear and cold": Ruth Thompson McGibney Ms., p 1, CHS. Weather Report: *Chgo Tribune*, Dec. 30, 1903, p 1. Dorsha Hayes: Dorsha B. Hayes, *Chicago, Crossroads of American Enterprise*, 244–246.

48. Ludwig family: *Chgo Tribune*, Dec. 31, 1903, p 3. Caroline Ludwig's wardrobe: *Chgo Tribune*, Jan. 5, 1904, p 4. Arthur Hull: McCurdy, 198. John Thompson identification as "grocer": Chicago Telephone Directory, 1903, MRC. Thompson's restaurants were at 75–77 Randolph, 81 Madison, 175–177 Madison, 151 Dearborn, 165 Adams, 118–120 Jackson, 107 Van Buren and 254 State.

49. Thompson family story: McGibney Ms. Charlotte Plamondon: McCurdy, 129–130, 214; *NY Tribune*, Dec. 31, 1903, p 1. The young woman's story was picked up by virtually every Chicago paper and reprinted in New York and London papers. Revell: *Chgo Tribune*, Jan. 1, 1904, p 1; McCurdy, 210.

50. Eddie Foy on the size of crowd: Foy and Harlow, 274. Collins's assignment on ticket scalping: Author's interview with Collins. Distance from Sherman House to theatre: paced off by author, 2001; also based on location maps of Loop district at turn of the century, Frank Randall, *Views of Chicago: History of the Development of Building Construction in Chicago; Bird's Eye Views and Guide of Chicago*, 167, 197, 207.

51. Seating capacity: National Fire Protection Ass'n, Stewart, 1.

52. Box office receipts: *Chgo Tribune*, Jan. 6, 1904, p 1. Audience represented thirteen states: Paul Ditzel, "Theater of Death," 52. Lula Greenwald: *Chgo Tribune*, Jan. 5, 1904, p 1.

52–53. University of Chicago students: McCurdy, 87. Clyde Blair, captain of UC track team: Ibid.

53. William McLaughlin: *Chgo Tribune*, Dec. 31, 1903, p 3; *NY Times*, January 1, 1904, p 1. "What a death trap!": McCurdy, 380 (photo caption). Myron Decker's fear of fire: Ibid, 377. Harriet Bray: *Chgo Tribune*, Dec. 31, 1973, sec. 2, p 17. Henry Van Ingen family: McCurdy, 212; *Milwaukee Journal*, Dec. 31, 1903, p 1.

54. Cooper Brothers: *Milwaukee Journal*, Dec. 31, 1903, p 1. Edith Mizen: *Chgo Tribune*, Jan. 1, 1904, p 1. D. W. Dimmick: McCurdy, 92–93.

54–55. Baseball players Dexter and Houseman: McCurdy, 260–263; personal histories, author's e-mail correspondence with Brett Smith.

55–56. Dorsha Hayes: Hayes, 244–246.

56. Bryan Foy: Fields, *Eddie Foy*, 147.

56–57: Warren Toole: McCurdy, 209–210.

57. Collins meets Powers: Author's interview with Collins; Charles Collins, "The Tragedy Chicago Will Never Forget," *Chgo Tribune*, Dec. 28, 1952, pp 6, 7, 12.

CHAPTER 8. ENGINE 13

59. "Life of an American Fireman": Charles Musser, *The Emergence of Cinema: The American Screen to 1907*, 325, 327, 329.

59–60. Currier & Ives: Author's correspondence with Scott Currier, Chairman, Currier & Ives Foundation.

60. Operations of firehouse, alarms: Paul Ditzel, *Fire Engines and Fire Fighters*, 165. Musham's background and management style: Ditzel, "Theater of Death," 52. James F. McQuade, *Synoptical History of Chicago Fire Department*, 1908.

61. Chicago Fire Department companies and staffing: 1903 CFD Annual Report, MRC. Age of the automobile: Peter Furtado, *The New Century, 1900–1914*, 160. Condition of Chicago streets: Lyle Benedict, Ellen O'Brien and Shah Tiwana, *A Milennium Bibliography, Chicago in 1900* (via internet).

62–63. Engine Company 13 Roster and Payroll: City of Chicago Payroll Records, Dec. 1903, MRC. The roster and monthly salaries: John Hannon, Chief, First Battalion, $229.17; Patrick Jennings, Captain, $137.50; Pipemen

248

TINDER BOX

Michael Corrigan, Frederick Klockting, John Millar, Christian Peterman, John Murphy (driver), $94.50; Pipeman William Schultz, $70; John Stahl, Lieutenant, $107; Mathias Blaney, (driver), $115 and William McMahon (assistant engineer), $95.83.

63–66. Fire Department operations and description of Engine 13 station house: Author's interviews with Father John McNellis, Ass't Chaplain, CFD, and historian Kenneth Little, CFD, April, 2000, and Author's tour of Engine Co. 98 (built in 1903) with Kenneth Little, May, 2001. The 1903 Engine 13 station house no longer exists. Fire engine: Author's interview with Don DeSteffano, American La France Co., 2001. Fire horses: Paul Roberts Lyons, *Fire in America*, pp 100–108. Harness and preparations: Author's interviews with Kenneth Little and Dr. Peter Molloy, Director, Hall of Flame Museum, Phoenix, AZ, August, Sept., 2000. Another key source is a book written by the chief of the New York City fire department at the beginning of the century: John Kenlon, *Fires and Firefighters*, 128, 279, 280. Engineer's duties and fire engines: Ditzel, *Fire Engines*, 113, 128, 131. Standard operating procedure: Author's interview with Little, April, 2000. Engineer and after-action reports: Kenlon, 279–280. Fire alarm boxes: Ditzel, *Fire Alarm!*, 5, 7. Timing and departure from firehouse: Kenlon, 280–281.

67. "Are All Our Theaters Safe?": *Theater Magazine*, Jan., 1904 (unsigned editorial).

CHAPTER 9. "PALE MOONLIGHT"

69. Edginess backstage: Author's interview with Foy's biographer, Armond Fields, June, 2000. Daniel Frohman's postponed honeymoon: *NY Times*, Nov. 24, 1903, p 9.

70. "Belasco Declares War": Ibid, p 6. Belasco sues Klaw-Erlanger: Ibid, Dec. 3, 1903, p 8. *Babes* cast adopts orphan: Ibid, Nov. 22, 1903, p 22.

70–71. *Bluebeard* cast may disband: *NY Clipper*, Dec. 26, 1903, p 1046.

71. Foy talks of big crowds: Foy and Harlow, 274. Usher estimates overcrowding by 500 people: *Manchester Guardian*, Jan. 2, 1904, p 5. Ushers lock doors: McCurdy, 44, 300–305. Carbon arc lamp: Ibid, 109.

71–72. Act One scenario: Nixon, 1.

73–74. Swinging electrical reflectors: Louis Guenzel, *Retrospects*, 13; McCurdy, 147.

74. *Bluebeard* double octet: Blum, 57. "Moonlight" girls' names: *NY Clipper*, January 9, 1904, p 1101. Ruth Thompson sees costumes "glisten": McGibney Ms., n.p. "Pale Moonlight" number: McCurdy, 34. Conductor Herbert Dillea sees fire: Ibid, p 102.

74–75. McMullen's account: Ibid, 105–106.

75–76. Fire begins: *Chgo Tribune*, Jan. 2, 1904, p 1; Foy and Harlow, 276, 277; Fields, *Eddie Foy*, 148–150.

76. "Pale Moonlight" double octet reacts: McCurdy, 34.

76. "William Sallers": Sallers' testimony, Iroquois Fire Investigation Report to Mayor Harrison, Jan. 8, 1904, MRC, pp 33, 34; McCurdy, 111,112.

76–77. Actor Herbert Cawthorn's account: McCurdy, 113.

77. Dancer Jack Strause sees fire: *Chgo Daily News*, Jan. 9, 1904, p 1.

77. "Walter Flentye": *NY Times*, Dec. 31, 1903, p 1.

77. "The curtain will fall, the bells have rung": McCurdy, 307. Double octet keeps dancing: Ibid, 308–311.

78. Herbert Dillea, Ernest Libonati: Author's notes, CHS, 1962. Mrs. James Pinedo account: McCurdy, 257–259.

79. "Those girls remaining": Ibid, 267. "If you don't look out": Ibid, 92. Ruth Michel account: *Chgo Daily News*, Jan. 5, 1904, p 4; McCurdy, 269. Willie Dee leaves: McCurdy, 103, 104.

80–81. Charles Sweeney account: *Chgo Daily News*, Jan. 9, 1904, p 1; McCurdy, 290, 291. "Canvas the size of bedsheets": Sallers' testimony, Stewart, 36. Grigolatis aerialists: McCurdy, 100. There is confusion about whether the member of the aerial troupe who plunged to the stage was a man or woman. In some accounts, the performer is identified as "Florine," in others, "Floraline." Evidence based on the New York performance of *Bluebeard* suggests that it was an all-female troupe. Also confusing is that this person was not counted as a member of the company who perished; only Nellie Reed is cited in official reports. One explanation may be that the Grigolatis were a performing unit working independently of the *Bluebeard* company and so were not included in the count.

81. Violet Sydney rescued: McCurdy, 81. "The women were frantic": Sallers, quoted in *Albuquerque* [NM] *Journal*, Dec. 31, 1903, p 2. Joe Dougherty confused: McCurdy, 110, 111.

81–82. Foy's reaction: Foy testimony, Iroquois Fire Investigation Report, Jan. 8, 1904, p 22, MRC; Fields, *Eddie Foy*, 149; Foy and Harlow, 274, 277.

82. Keith Pickerell: *Milwaukee Journal*, Dec. 31, 1903, p 2.

CHAPTER 10. THE INFERNO

83. "A wreath of flames": *Lloyd's Weekly News*, Jan. 3, 1904, p 2; McCurdy, 131.

84. Eddie Foy and Bryan: Foy and Harlow, 279–280. Madeline Dupont account: McCurdy, 306. Foy attempts to calm audience: Foy and Harlow, 280, 281. "I saw the men": McCurdy, 129–132.

84–85. "Would burn like cinder": Annabelle Whitford Buchan, "I Was in the Iroquois Theater Fire," 133.

85. Josephine Petry account: *Chgo Daily News*, Jan. 7, 1904, p 4. Lester Linvonston: Author's notes, Ms., Iroquois Theatre Fire, 1962, Chicago Historical Society; no source noted; unrecoverable in 2001.

86. Foy recollections: Foy and Harlow, 281.

87. Ruthie Thompson: McGibney Ms., n.p.

87–88. August Klimek : *Chgo Tribune*, Jan. 1, 1904, p 1.

88. Ella Churcher: McCurdy, 259.

89. John Massoney: Ibid, 109. Robert Murray: Ibid, 268.

90. Buchan, 133. Fuller Construction's subcontractor: *Chgo Tribune*, Jan. 4, 1904, p 4; January 7, 8, 1904, p 1. "A back draft": *Chgo Daily News*, Jan. 1, 1904, p 4. "A great sheet of circular flame": McCurdy, 109. "It felt like a cyclone": Ibid, 223

91. Mrs. Pinedo: McCurdy, 257. Scenery loft collapses: Foy and Harlow, 283. "A human whirlpool": *NY Times*, Dec. 31, 1903, p 1.

92. "Asbestos" curtain: *NY Times*, Jan 3, 1904, p 2. *Chgo Daily News*, Jan. 1, 1904, p 1; January 8, 1904, p 3. "I got out as quickly as I could": Foy and Harlow, 287. "A scream of terror I shall never forget": McCurdy, 214.

92–93. August Klimek: *Chgo Tribune*, Jan. 1, 1904, p 1.

93. Robert Smith: Foy and Harlow, 283. Archie Bernard: McCurdy, 99.

93–94. Smith rescues girls: Ibid, 99, 100.

94. Usher Willard Sayles: *Chgo Tribune*, Jan. 26, 1904, p 1. Clyde Blair escapes: McCurdy, 87.

94–95. Winnie Gallagher: *Chgo Daily News*, Dec. 30, 1903, 9 p.m. Extra, p 2.

95. "I felt my face burning": Von Plecheki interview, *Chgo Tribune* Dec. 31, 1962.

95–96. D. W. Dimmick escapes: McCurdy, 92–93.

96. Georgia Swift: *NY Times*, Jan. 2, 1904, p 3.

96–97. Forensic science: David C. Thomasma, "Somatic Death."

97–98. "Flight or fight" syndrome: author's interview with Patricia J. McFeeley, M.D., Medical Examiner and Assistant Chief Medical Investigator, State of New Mexico, Albuquerque, 2001.

98. "Delayed death": C. J. Polson, D. J. Gee and B. Knight, *The Essentials of Forensic Medicine*, 323. "Pugilistic attitude": Ibid, 327. "The right arm was stretched": *London Times*, Jan 1, 1904, p 1. "Crush asphyxia": Polson et al., 470.

CHAPTER 11 DEATH ALLEY

99–100. Peter Quinn: *Chgo Daily News*, Dec. 31, 1903, p 2

100–101. Michael Corrigan: author's interview with Corrigan, Chicago, 1961. Author's interview with Little, 2001. There is some question about who pulled what alarm and when. Because Corrigan was credited for pulling Box 26, he played a prominent role in the annual memorial services for the victims. But Chief Musham, interviewed by the *Record Herald* the day of the fire, said that two or three minutes after arriving at the scene he ordered "someone" to pull Box 26. Some minutes later, he added, he himself ran to the box to signal a "4-11" alarm, bringing more companies to the scene. The exact time he pulled the box, said Musham, was 3:41 p.m. *Record Herald*, Dec. 31, 1903, p 1.

101. "It was approximately 3:33": McCurdy, 66. Musham and O'Neill leave City Hall: *Chgo Daily News*, Dec. 30, 1903, p 2; McCurdy, 66.

101–102. Galvin account: McCurdy, 252.

102–103. Anna Woodward: *NY Times*, Jan 1, 1904, p 2. Street clothing: Thomas C. Reeves, *Twentieth-Century America,* p 15.

103. Fred Brackenbush testimony: Fire Investigation Report to Mayor, Jan. 8, 1904, pp 60–61.

104. Sallers testimony: Ibid, p 37.

104–105. William Grover: *NY Times*, Jan. 3, 1904, p 1.

105–106. George Dunlap: Letter to author, Oct. 30, 1963. "Run it out": Ibid.

106. People on fire escape, Hortense Lang: *Manchester Guardian*, Jan. 1, 1904, p 4. Sister Rachel Gorman: *InterOcean*, Dec. 31, 1903, p 1.

106–107: "We tore those people loose": Dunlap letter to author.

107. View from university windows: *InterOcean*, Dec. 31, 1903, p 1. "'Crawling things'": *Chgo Daily News*, Dec. 31, 1903, p 4.

107–108. Mrs. Baldwin: McCurdy, 217.

108. "A smoking, flaming hell": Ditzel, "Theater," n.p. Saller's testimony: Fire Investigation Report, Jan. 8, 1904, p 38. "Firemen heard pounding": Ditzel, "Theater," n.p. Nets unseen: *NY Times*, Dec. 31, 1903, p 1.

108–109. McGibney Ms.; Dunlap: Letter to author.

109. D. A. Russell: *NY Times*, Dec. 31, 1903, p 1.

110–111. Frank Houseman: McCurdy, 260–264; *Manchester Guardian*, Jan. 1, 1905, p 5; *Record-Herald*, Dec. 31, 1903, p 4.

111. Harriet Bray: *Chgo Tribune*, Dec. 31, 1973, Sec. 2, p 17.

111–112. Captain Buckley: author's interview with Little, 2000.

112. "Tell me he is safe": *InterOcean*, Dec. 31, 1903, p 2.

CHAPTER 12. INSIDE A VOLCANO

113–114. Arthur McWilliams, "smoke so thick": *Chgo Tribune*, Dec. 30, 1903, pp 2, 3; Ibid, Dec. 21, 1958, p 10; *NY Times*, Dec. 31, 1903, p 1.

114. William Corbett: McCurdy, 74.

114–115. Chief O'Neill: Ibid, 51, 52, 54, 55.

115. Public response: *Chgo Tribune*, Dec. 30, 1903, pp 2, 3; *NY Times*, Dec. 31, 1903, p 1.

115–116. J. B. Evans: *InterOcean*, Dec. 31, 1903, p 1.

116. "The estimate of those": Edgar Lee Masters, *Levy Mayer*, 71.

116–117. Dorsha Hayes: Hayes, 244–246.

117. "Corrigan worked": author's interview with Corrigan, 1961. "Have mercy on their souls": *Chgo Tribune*, Dec. 31, 1903, p 1.

118. "Don't walk on their faces": *London Daily Mirror*, Jan. 1, 1904, p 1.

118–119. Musham and weeping fireman: *Chgo Tribune*, Dec., 31, 1903, p 3.

119. Deputy Chief Campion: Ibid. "From the galleries": AP story, *Santa Fe New Mexican*, Dec. 31, 1903, p 1.

120. "Through some mischance": *Manchester Guardian*, Jan. 1, 1904, p 4. "The victims looked": *Chgo Tribune*, Dec. 31, 1903, p 3.

CHAPTER 13. THE CHARNEL HOUSE

121–124. "The bodies," Thompson's interior, father and daughter reunion: author's interview with Collins. (122. *Record-Herald* phone number: Chicago 1903 telephone directory.)

123. "Some bodies were charred beyond recognition": Arthur Sears Henning's famous description, *Chgo Tribune*, Dec. 31, 1903, p 1.

124. William McLaughlin: *Chgo Tribune*, Dec. 31, 1903, p 3. Bishop Muldoon: *Chgo Daily News*, Dec. 30, 1903, p 2.

125. Dr. H. L. Montgomery: McCurdy, n.p. "Ghouls": *NY Times*, Jan. 3, 1904, p 2. Police empty pocketbooks: Dunlap letter to author. Eddie Foy "hysterical": author's interview with Collins. "I never saw anything": *Toronto Star*, Dec. 31,1903, p 3.

126. Foy in alley: Foy and Harlow, 287, 288. Collins returns to *Record-Herald*: author's interview with Collins.

126–127: Walter Howey: A. A. Dornfeld, *"Hello Sweetheart, Get Me Rewrite,"* 78–82. Associated Press network: Oliver Gramling, *AP: The Story of News*, 146.

127–128: Frank Moore: Moore letter to author, 1962.

128. Weary telegrapher: *Manchester Guardian*, Jan. 1, 1904, p 4. "With tears in their eyes": *InterOcean*, Jan. 1, 1904, p 1.

128–129: Ruthie Thompson's family: McGibney Ms.

CHAPTER 14. THE NEW YEAR

131. "The greeting for the day": author's interview with Collins. List of dead: *Chgo Tribune*, Dec. 31, 1903, p 1.

132. Bells toll: Ibid, Jan. 1, 1904, p 4. New snowfall: Ibid, Jan. 2, 1904, p 1. "Wheeled traffic": Author's interview with Collins. "Lonely vigils": *Colliers* magazine, Jan. 9, 1904, p 10. Official mourning: McCurdy, 137, 138, 139.

132–133. Liverymen return to work: *Albuquerque Journal*, Jan. 1, 1904, p 1.

133. "Thousands of carriages": Author's interview with Collins. "This frightful thing": *Chgo Tribune*, Jan. 1, 1904, p 1. "Chicago enters": *NY Clipper*, Jan. 9, 1904, p 1101. Telegrams of condolence: *Chgo Daily News*, Jan. 1, 1904, p 1.

134. "Shrieking headlines": Gramling, 146. "Death's Rich Harvest": *Albuquerque Morning Journal*, Dec. 31, 1903, p 1. Overworked clerics: *Chgo Tribune*, Jan. 9, 1904, p 1.

134–135. Party of twelve wiped out: Ibid, Jan. 3, 1904, p 3.

135. Clinton Meeker: *NY Times*, Jan. 1, 1904, p 1. "Men showed less hope": Ibid.

136. William McMauglan: *InterOcean*, Dec. 31, 1903, p 1. "Have you heard anything": *Chgo Tribune*, Dec. 31, 1903, p 5. "Dead" man revives: *Chgo Daily News*, Dec. 30, 1903, p 2.

136–137: Rita Wild: *Chgo Tribune*, Jan. 5, 1904, p 4.

137. Little Aurora girls: *Chgo Tribune*, Dec. 31, 1903, p 3. Shabad children: *Chicago Tribune*, Jan. 2, 1904, p 5. D. W. Alexander: *Chgo Daily News*, Dec. 31, 1903, p 4. John Dryden: *Chgo Tribune*, Jan. 1, 1904, p 1. Myron Decker: McCurdy, 377. Barbara Reynolds: Ibid, 380. Clyde Blair and friends: Ibid, 87.

138. Willie Dee: Ibid, 103. Edith Mizen: *Chgo Tribune*, Jan. 1, 1904, p 6. Harry Ludwig family: *Chgo Tribune*, Dec. 31, 1903, p 3. Henry Van Ingen family, Cooper brothers: *Milwaukee Journal*, Dec. 31, 1903, p 1.

139. Alexander Revell: *InterOcean*, Dec. 30, 1903, p 4. "The first thing we did": *Manchester Guardian*, Jan. 1, 1904, p 5. Lula Greenwald plot: *NY Times*, Mar. 23, 1904, p 2.

139–140. Ethel Blackburn: *Chgo Tribune*, Jan. 3, 1904, p 3.

140. Grove Avenue trolley incident: *NY Times,* Jan. 2, 1904, p 1. People filing past dead: *Collier's* magazine, Jan. 9, 1904, p 10. Six bushel baskets, McCurdy, 43. Placer mining methods used: *Chgo Daily News*, Jan. 7, 1904, p 1.

141. "Just think! I bought the matinee tickets": *Chgo Tribune*, Dec. 31, 1903, p 3. "We had only been married a year": Ibid, p 5; McCurdy, 76. Tragedy told in telegrams: *Chgo Tribune*, Jan. 1, 1904, p 7.

141–142: Postmaster Freer's family: *Galesburg* (IL) *Republican-Register*, Dec. 31, 1903, p 1.

142. News reaches *Lucania*: Gramling, 163; *London Daily Mirror*, Jan. 2, 1904, p 4. Ralph Taylor sails: *Chgo Tribune*, Jan. 2, 1904, p 2.

142–143. Foy calls fire "miracle": Foy handwritten note, Jan. 5, 1905, Armond Fields collection; Foy testimony, Report to the Mayor, Jan. 1904, p 27.

143. Harrison closes theatres: *Chgo Tribune*, Jan. 3, 1904, p 1; *NY Clipper*, Jan. 16, 1904, p 1120. Coroner's inquest launched: *NY Times*, Dec. 31, 1903, p 1.

143–144. Max Remer: Remer, "Terror at the Iroquois," 1.

152. "I came from Apple River": McCurdy, 92.

CHAPTER 15. THE BLAME GAME

145–146. Lincoln Steffens, *The Shame of the Cities*, 192–193.

146. Everleigh Club brochure: Stevenson Swanson, *Chicago Days*, 78. Overnight clerks: Ibid. "Amusing Recreational Reading": Lloyd Wendt, *Chicago Tribune: The Rise of a Great American Newspaper*, 354. Press corps numbered 600: *InterOcean*, Dec. 28, 1903, p 6. Harrison on reporter Charles Powers: Carter H. Harrison, *Stormy Years*, 278.

147–148. Harrison and aldermen's salaries: Chicago City Payrolls, 1903. "Motley crew": *Chgo Tribune*, Jan. 1, 1904; Harrison, *Stormy Years*, 156. "A human swamp": Reeves, 12; "Nearly everything was a lie": Edgar Lee Masters, *The Tale of Chicago*, 281. "Petty grafting": *NY Times*, Oct. 1, 1903, p 1. Harrison assigns blame: Harrison, *Stormy Years*, 236–239; *Chgo Tribune*, Jan. 1, 1904, p 1.

148. The "Free List" payoffs: *Chgo Tribune*, Jan. 3, 1904, p 4.

148–149: Davis and Powers defend themselves: *Chgo Tribune*, Dec. 31, 1903, p 2.

149: Jessie Bartlett Davis: *Chgo American*, Jan. 3, 1904, p 1.

149–150. Alderman's warning on fire "apparatus": *Chgo Tribune*, Dec. 31, 1903, p 4. Johns-Manville manager: *Chgo Tribune*, Jan. 3, 1904, p 1; ibid, Jan. 5, p 8. "It was not one of ours": advertisement, *NY Clipper*, Jan. 16, 1904, p 1126. "Curtain was not asbestos at all": *Chgo Daily News*, Jan. 1, 1904, p 1. Robert McClean: McCurdy, 120;

150. Fire underwriters blame city: *Chgo Sunday Tribune*, Jan. 3, 1904, p 3.

151. Marshall defends no exit signs: *Chgo Tribune*, Jan. 1, 1904, p 1. Klaw-Erlanger blamed: Csida and Csida, 75; *Chgo Tribune*, Jan. 26, 1904, p 2. *Life* cartoon: Csida and Csida, 131. Musham's defense: *Santa Fe New Mexican*, Jan. 14, 1904, p 1.

151–152. Musham contradiction: *Chgo Record-Herald*, Dec. 31, 1903, p 1.

152. "Learning the trade": *Chgo Tribune*, Jan. 3, 1904, p 8. "Bribery and graft": McCurdy, 116. "Virtually a death trap": Ibid, 116.

152–153. Fuller Company tampers: *Chgo Tribune*, Jan. 5, 1904, p 1.

153. Merriman defends Fuller: *NY Times*, Dec. 31, 1903, p 1; *InterOcean*, Jan. 26, 1904, p 1.

153–154. "The theatre had just been built": *Chgo Tribune*, Dec. 31, 1903, p 6.

154. "Not since the burning": *NY Tribune*, Dec. 31, 1903, p 8. "From the living": *InterOcean*, Jan. 6, 1904, p 6.

154–155. "In all justice": *Chgo Tribune*, Jan. 10, 1904, p 6.

155. "Tardy zeal": *NY Times*, Jan. 3, 1904, p 8. "The more the Iroquois": *Santa Fe New Mexican*, Jan. 11, 1904, p 4. "The [Iroquois] was new": *Life*, Jan. 14, 1904, p 40.

155–156. Facilities padlocked: *InterOcean*, Feb. 5, 1904, p 1.

156. "It is stated": *London Times*, Jan. 1, 1904, p 3. *Globe, Pall Mall Gazette, Daily Mirror* quotes: *Chgo Tribune*, Jan. 1, 1904, p 1. "A government of monkeys": *Chgo Daily News*, Jan. 4, 1904, p 6. "Let no guilty man escape": *Manchester Guardian*, Jan. 1, 1904, p 2.

157. Rabbis, ministers, "man's greed": *Chgo Tribune*, Jan. 4, 1904, p 3. Performers out of work: *Billboard*, Jan. 30, 1904; *NY Times*, Feb. 4, 1904, p 1.

157–158. "Frosty reception": *NY Times*, Jan. 3,1904, p 1.

158. Davis and others arrested: *Santa Fe New Mexican*, Jan. 1, 1904, p 1. Arthur Hull: *Chgo Tribune*, Jan. 1, 1904, p 3; *NY Times*, Jan. 3, 1904, p 3.

158–159. "Trod on a lock": Ibid, Jan. 2, 1904, p 1.

159. Marshall on exit signs: Ibid. "This theatre was opened": Ibid.

159–160. Marshall on stairways: Author's interview with Collins.

160–161. "A paper in this city": *NY Times*, Jan. 5, 1904, p 8.

161. "It would appear": *Independent*, Jan. 7, 1904, p 55.

CHAPTER 16. THE INQUEST

163. "Here I am": McCurdy, 180.

163–164. Changes in theatres: *London Daily Mirror*, Jan. 2, 1904, p 2; Foy and Harlow, 292.

164. Oscar Hammerstein: Foy and Harlow, ibid. No more "extravaganzas": *Chgo Tribune*, Jan. 4, 1904, p 3. "Where it was supposed at last": *Chgo Daily News*, Dec. 31, 1903, p 4.

164–165. Bertha Palmer: Ibid.

165. Berlin, Vienna, London, "keep thousands away": *London Daily Mirror*, Jan. 4, 1904, p 2.

166. Inquest began: *Chgo Tribune*, Jan. 7, 1904, p 1. Emil Von Plechecki: photograph at inquest, Jan., 1904.

167–168: Conflicting testimony: *Chgo Daily News*, Jan. 5, 1904, p 1; Foy and Harlow, 277.

168. Death toll: *Chgo Tribune*, Jan. 7, 1904, p 3. Noonan testimony: *Chgo Tribune*, Jan. 7, 1904, p 1; *NY Times*, Jan. 7, 1904, p 2. Dusenberry testimony: Ibid, p 2.

169. "Incompetence and negligence": Ibid, p 1. "Deluge of suits": Ibid, Jan. 5, 1904, p 6; *Chgo Daily News*, Jan. 5, 1904, p 1.

170. Sallers testimony: *Chgo Daily News*, Jan. 7, 1904, p 1.

170-171. "A terrific shaking up": *InterOcean*, Jan. 16, 1904, p 1.

171–172. Musham, Hannon questioned: Ibid. "He came to the theatre": Ibid, Feb. 18, 1904, p 3.

173. Dusenberry testimony: *Chgo Tribune*, Jan. 7, 1904, p 1. "I consider all scenery": McCurdy, 222.

173–174: Strong, Menard testimony: *Chgo Tribune*, Jan. 26, 1904, p 2.

174–175. Price, Jones testimony: *NY Times*, Jan. 21, 1904, p 9.

175. Owners lobby aldermen: Ibid, Jan. 3, 1904, p 1.

175–178. Powers and Davis testimony: Ibid, Jan. 23, 1904, p 2.

178–179. Williams, Loughlin and Lense testimony: *Chgo Tribune*, Jan. 26, 1904, p 2.

179. "An inert city administration": *Chgo Tribune*, Jan. 9, 1904, p 6.

CHAPTER 17. THE GRAND JURY

181–182. Coroner's jury verdict returned: *Chgo Tribune*, Jan. 26, 1904, p 1.

182. Building Department accused of bribes: *InterOcean*, Feb. 6, 1904, p 3.

182–183. "Flimsy charges": Harrison, *Stormy Years*, 236.

183. "I have been compelled": *Chgo Tribune*, Jan. 27, 1904, p 2.

183–184. "Chicago boasts": *NY Times,* Jan. 31, 1904, p 6.

184. "An evil trinity": *Chgo Tribune*, Jan. 3,1904, p 1.

184–185. Quotes from *Detroit Journal, Marshalltown Republican, Philadelphia Press, Kansas City Star, Marquette Journal: Chgo Daily News* roundup, Jan. 4, 1904.

185–186. "His Sunday Dinner" and other McCutcheon cartoons: *Chgo Tribune*, Jan. 1, 3, 4, 1909, p 1.

186. "The Vacant Seat": *Chgo Record-Herald*, Jan. 2, 1904, p 1.

186–187. 1903 Fire Department Report: Jan., 1904.

187. National Fire Protection Association Underwriter's Preliminary Report: Jan. 9, 1904, pp 1–4, with additional Iroquois Theatre diagrams showing interior and exterior of building, as well as air currents from the rear of the stage to the balconies. Information is partially credited to Mr. F. J. T. Stewart, Superintendent of Inspections, Chicago Underwriters' Association. However, a letter dated May 25, 1924, from G. H. Parker, Superintendent of the Kentucky Inspection Bureau, to Katherine Graham, librarian, Insurance Library of Chicago, says: "You will notice the [Iroquois Theatre] report is signed by F. J. T. Stewart but it was written by an inspector named W. N. Gadsden, assisted by cub inspector G. H. Parker. We inspected the theatre while under construction and several days before the fire had made quite a few recommendations. At the time of the fire I was in a nearby fire station. ... When the alarm was received, I climbed into the back of the fire chief's buggy and arrived with the first companies. I remained until late that evening and helped to carry out the dead and injured." Letter, unnumbered, found

by author in 1962 in Chicago Historical Society archives. Wesley A. Stranger, *Rescued from a Fiery Death*. "The Burning of the Iroquois": *Marquee Magazine*, vol. 25, no. 4, p 29. "The Iroquois on Fire": Woody Gelman and Barbara Jackson, *Disaster Illustrated*, 51.

187–188. Travelers Insurance Company Ad: *Chgo Tribune*, Jan. 1, 1904, p 6.

188. Hardware store ad: *InterOcean*, Jan. 16, 1904, p 4. Klein Optical Ad: *NY Clipper*, Jan. 2, 1904, p 1105. Lubin Company "film" of fire: Ibid, Jan. 16, 1904, p 1136.

189. Boswell Electric Company Ad: *Billboard*, Mar. 19, 1904. Edna Hunter: *NY Times*, Jan. 21, 1904, p 7.

189–190. Grand jury indictments returned: *NY Times*, Feb. 24, 1904, p 1.

190. "The grand jury": Harrison, *Stormy Years*, 236. Dineen's directive: *Chgo Sunday Tribune*, Jan. 2, 1904, p 1; *NY Times*, Jan. 7, 1904, p 2.

190–191. "Grand jury cannot indict": *NY Times*, Jan. 7, 1904, p 2.

CHAPTER 18. "NOT GUILTY"

193–194. Mayer background: Frank D. Mayer, "Levy Mayer."

194. "Legal genius of the commercial age": W. J. Perlman, *Jews in America: A Biographical Encyclopedia*, 257. "Due not only to his intellect": Mayer, 53

194–195. "A political schemer": Harrison, *Stormy Years*, 273.

195. Mayer's firm selected: *Chgo Daily News*, Jan. 6, 1904, p 4. "It took courage": Mayer, 47. "At the core of the matter": *NY Times*, Feb. 21, 1904, p 1.

195. "If the people": *InterOcean*, Dec. 31, 1903, p 2.

196. "The horrors are already": *Chgo Tribune*, Jan. 14, 1904. Gen. James Longstreet dies: *NY Times*, Jan. 3, 1904, p 8. Cherokees on warpath: *Chgo Tribune*, Jan. 26, 1904, p 4. Russo-Japan War: Gramling, 147. Death of Mark Hanna: Edmund Morris, *Theodore Rex*, 311. Baltimore fire: *The New American Desk Encyclopedia*, 117. Northern Securities decision: Morris, 313–315.

196–197. Change of venue to Peoria, indictment quashed: *People vs. Davis*, Illinois Circuit Court Reports, vol. 2, p 398.

197. Judges Kersten's and Green's decisions: *Chgo Tribune*, Feb. 10, 1904, p 3, and March 10, 1904.

198. "I can't help saying": Ibid, March 10. Davis and others again indicted: Mayer, 47; *People vs. Davis*, Illinois Court Reports, p 398.

199. Roosevelt-Longworth wedding: *Washington Evening Star*, Feb. 17, 1906, p 1. Case transferred to Danville: *Chgo Tribune*, Mar. 4, 1907, p 9. San Francisco earthquake: *NY Sun*, April 19, 1906, p 1. Harry Thaw murder case: *NY Evening Journal*, June 26, 1906, p 1.

200. Danville trial: *Chgo Tribune*, Mar. 10, 1907, p 2; Illinois Court Reports, pp 398, 399.

201–202. "The hand of God," "the verdict he is entitled to": *Chgo Tribune*, Mar. 10, 1907, p 2.

202. Judge Kimbrough statement: Ibid, p 2. "Those who died": Ibid. "The state discharged their duty": Ibid.

202–203. "Deficiency in the law": Ibid.

203. "Outrageous delays": Frederic E. Woodward and Frank O. Smith, "Flagrant Instance of the Law's Delays," 429–436. A response written by George Follansbee of the Chicago Bar Association appears in the same review, 437–439. Follansbee blames the plaintiffs, whom he divides into "two classes, one financially responsible, the other financially irresponsible. Possibly the first class is not legally liable and the second class not worth the time and trouble of pursuing. As evidence of this theory a very large number of plaintiffs have voluntarily dismissed their suits." Two hundred civil action suits filed: Ibid, p 432.

204. Judge Landis ruling: *Chgo Tribune*, Mar. 10, 1907, p 2. Henry Shabad; Lawsuit against Iroquois Theatre Company; Klaw-Erlanger rumors: Author's notes, 1962, CHS. Thirty settlements announced: *NY Times*, Jan. 18, 1909, p 1.

CHAPTER 19. A WARNING UNHEEDED

207. "Great Advances": *NY Times*, Nov. 1, 1903, part 3, p 27. "Was mellow and quite secure": *This Fabulous Century*, vol. 1, 1900–1910, p 34.

208. "It is the usual experience": "The Lesson of the Iroquois Fire," *Theater Magazine*, Feb. 1904, n.p. "We will shut the stable": *The Independent*, Jan. 7, 1904, p 48. "Our citizens": *Chgo Tribune*, Jan. 4, 1904, p 3.

208–209. "Panic is invariably": *NY Times*, Jan. 4, 1904, p 6.

209. Adriatic announcement: *Chgo Daily News*, Dec. 30, 1903, p 8. The announcement appeared in other U.S. and British papers the same day.

209–210. Predecessor to the *Titanic*: Author's correspondence with Mark Blackburne, President Ulster *Titanic* Society, Belfast, Northern Ireland, July, 2000.

AFTERMATH

211. Collins information: Author's interview with Collins; Collins obituary, *Chgo Tribune*, 1964.

212. Benjamin Marshall information: Author's e-mail correspondence with Janine Henri, Head Librarian, The Architecture and Planning Library, Alexander Architectural Archive, University of Texas at Austin.

212–213. Eddie Foy film: *The Seven Little Foys*, Paramount Pictures.

213. Klaw-Erlanger: Csida and Csida, 74–75. "I had formerly": *NY Times*, Mar. 9, 1907, p 9. Levy Mayer: Author's phone interview with Frank D. Mayer, Jr., at Mayer law firm. Mayer died in 1922. Annabelle Whitford: Buchan, 133. Will Davis: Chgo City Directory, MRC.

213–214. Chief Musham, Chief Hannon: Author's interview with Little, 2001.

214. Corrigan promoted: Author's interviews with Corrigan and with Little. Plamondon parents: *Albquerque Journal*, May 8, 1915, p 5. Walter Howey: Author's interview with Wayne Klatt, Chicago City News Bureau, 2001.

215. Iroquois Theatre Memorial Ass'n: *Chgo Tribune*, Mar. 11, 1907, p 2. Lipton: *NY Times*, Jan. 1, 1904. Iroquois Memorial Hospital: Author's interview with Fr. John McNellis, 2001; *Chgo Sun Times*, Aug. 13, 1967. Cemetery Memorial: Montrose Cemetery web page, www.graveyards.com/montrose/iroquois.html. "Mercy Day": *Chgo Sun Times*, Dec. 31, 1973.

215–216. Mrs. Crumpacker: *Chgo Tribune*, Dec. 31, 1973.

216. *Bluebeard* and Theatre reforms: Foy and Harlow, 293. Fire safety instruction: Theatre Program Collection of Edward Bills, Woodridge, IL.

217. *Fire and Water Engineering*, 1904. Andrew Carnegie letter: *NY Herald*, Jan. 2, 1904. Coconut Grove, Ringling Bros. fires: Stuart and Doris Flexner, *The Pessimist's Guide to History*, 254.

218. Sir Beerbohm Tree: *Chgo Tribune*, Jan. 1, 1904, p 3. Ohio school fire: Flexner and Flexner, 188–189. Water curtain: *Popular Mechanics*, May, 1904, p 508.

218–219. Panic bar, Von Duprin: Author's phone interview with Pat Olmstead, Ingersoll-Rand public realtions.

219. Iroquois conversion: *Chgo Daily News Almanac and Reference Yearbook*, 1905, 246. The theatre became Hyde and Behman's Music Hall in 1904.

SELECTED BIBLIOGRAPHY &
SOURCE MATERIAL

BOOKS

Bergreen, Lawrence. *As Thousands Cheer*. New York: Viking, 1990.

Bird's Eye Views and Guide of Chicago. Chicago: Rand McNally, 1898.

Blum, Daniel. *A Pictorial History of the American Theater 1860–1960*. Philadelphia: Chilton Company Book Division, 1960.

Boardman, Gerald. *American Musical Theater, A Chronicle*. New York: Oxford University Press, 1992.

Brown, John Russell. "Drury Lane Theater." *Oxford Illustrated History of Theater*. 2nd Ed. New York: Oxford University Press, 1995.

— — —. *Theater Architecture*. New York: Oxford University Press, 1995.

Chase, Gilbert. *America's Music*. 2nd Ed. New York: McGraw Hill, 1966.

Chernow, Ron. *Titan*. New York: Vintage Books, Random House, 1998.

Chicago Daily News Almanac and Reference Yearbook, 1905. Chicago: Chicago Daily News Company, 1905.

Cohen-Stratyner, Barbara. *Popular Music 1900–1919*. Detroit: Gale Research, 1988.

Copeland, Peter. *Sound Recordings*. London: The British Library Board, 1991.

Csida, Joseph, and J. B. Csida. *American Entertainment*. New York: Watson-Guptil Publishers, 1978.

Daniel, Clifton, and John Kirshon. *America's Century*. New York: Dorling Kindersley, 2000.

Ditzel, Paul. *Fire Alarm!* New Albany, Ind.: Buffhouse Division, Squire Book Village, 1994.

— — —. *Fire Engines and Fire Fighters*. New York: Bonanza Books, 1984.

Dornfeld, A. A. *"Hello Sweetheart, Get Me Rewrite!"* Chicago: Academy Chicago Publishers, 1983.

Engle, Lehman. *The Musical Theater: A Consideration*. New York: CBS Legacy Books, CBS Records, 1967.

Fields, Armond. *Eddie Foy: A Biography of a Great American Entertainer*. Jefferson, NC: McFarland and Company, 1999.

— — —, and L. Mark Fields. *From the Bowery to Broadway: Lew Fields and the Roots of American Popular Theater*. New York: Oxford University Press, 1993.

Fine, Lisa. *The Souls of the Skyscrapers*. Philadelphia: Temple University Press, 1990.

Flexner, Stuart and Doris. *The Pessimist's Guide to History*. New York: Quill, 2000.

Foy, Eddie, and Alvin Harlow. *Clowning Through Life*. New York: E. P. Dutton & Co., 1928.

Furtado, Peter. *The New Century, 1900–1914*. London: Chancellor Press, 1993.

Fusell, Professor Paul. *The Great War and Modern Memory*. Quoted in *The New York Times*, September 23, 2000

Gelman, Woody, and Barbara Jackson. *Disaster Illustrated*. New York: Harmony Books, 1976.

Gramling, Oliver. *AP: The Story of News*. New York: Kennicat Press, 1940.

Guenzel, Louis. *Retrospects: The Iroquois Theater Fire*. Elmhurst, Ill.: Theater Historical Society of America, 1993.

Harrison, Carter H. *Growing Up With Chicago*. Chicago: Ralph Fletcher Seymour Publisher, 1944.

– – –. *Stormy Years*. New York: Bobbs-Merril, 1935.

Hasse, Kohn Edward, and Ted Lathrop. *Jazz: The First Century*. New York: William Morrow, 2000.

Hayes, Dorsha B., *Chicago: Crossroads of American Enterprise*. New York: Julian Messner, Inc., 1944.

Hoffman, R. *News of the Nation*. Engelwood Cliffs, NJ: Prentice Hall, 1975.

Hornblow, Arthur. *A History of Theater in America*. Vol. 2. New York: Benjamin Bloom Publishers, 1965.

Kenlon, John. *Fires and Fire-fighters*. New York: George H. Doran Company, 1913.

Lukas, J. Anthony. *Big Trouble*. New York: Simon and Shuster, 1997.

Lyons, Paul Roberts. *Fire in America*. Boston: National Fire Protection Association, 1976.

Masters, Edgar Lee. *Levy Mayer and the New Industrial Era*. New Haven, Conn.: Yale University Press, 1927.

– – –. *The Tale of Chicago*. New York: G. P. Putnam's Sons, 1933.

McCurdy, D. B., ed. *Lest We Forget: Chicago's Awful Theater Horror*. Chicago: Memorial Publishing Company, 1904.

Mirkin, Sanford. *When Did It Happen?* New York: Ives Washburn, 1957.

Morris, Edmund. *Theodore Rex*. New York: Random House, 2001.

Musser, Charles. *The Emergence of Cinema: The American Screen to 1907*. New York: Charles Scribner's Sons & Simon and Shuster, 1990.

The New American Desk Encyclopedia. New York: Signet, 1989.

Perlman, W. J. *Jews in America: A Bibliographic Encyclopedia*. Chicago: Leading Jews in America Publishing Co., 1918.

Poggi, Jack. *Theater in America: The Impact of Economic Forces, 1870–1967*. Ithaca, NY: Cornell University Press, 1968.

Polson, C. J., D. J. Gee and B. Knight. *The Essentials of Forensic Medicine*. Elmsford, NY: Pergamon Press, 1985.

Randall, Frank. *Views of Chicago: History of the Development of Building Construction in Chicago.* Urbana, Ill.: University of Illinois Press, 1949.

Reeves, Thomas C. *Twentieth-Century America.* New York: Oxford University Press, 2000.

Seldes, George. *The Great Thoughts.* New York: Ballantine, 1985.

Speiser, Stuart. *Lawyers and the American Dream.* New York: Evans Publishing, 1993.

Steffens, Lincoln. *The Shame of the Cities.* American Century Series. New York: Hill and Wang, 1957.

Stranger, Wesley A. *Rescued from a Fiery Death.* Chicago: Laid and Lee Publishers, 1904.

Stubblebine, Donald J. *Early Broadway Sheet Music (1843–1918).* Jefferson, NC: McFarland, 2002.

Swanston, Stevenson. *Chicago Days.* Chicago: Chicago Tribune, Cantigny First Division Foundation, 1977.

Tebbel, John, and Mary Ellen Zukerman. *The Magazine in America, 1741–1900.* New York: Oxford University Press, 1991.

This Fabulous Century: Vol. 1, 1900–1910. New York: Time-Life Books, 1969.

Wendt, Lloyd. *Chicago Tribune: The Rise of a Great American Newspaper.* Chicago: Rand-McNally, 1979.

ARTICLES, PAMPHLETS, PAPERS & REPORTS

Lewis Beale. "When the Camera Goes Behind the Looking Glass." *NY Times,* Dec. 9, 2001.

Boyden, William C., Jr. "Chicagoans." *Chicagoan Magazine,* May 28, 1929, pp 20, 29. (Reprinted in *University of Chicago Alumni Magazine,* vol. XXI, no. 8, June 8, 1929).

Buchan, Annabelle Whitford. "I Was in the Iroquois Theater Fire." *Readers Digest,* Nov., 1957, p 133.

Collins, Charles. "The Tragedy Chicago Will Never Forget." *Chicago Tribune,* December 28, 1952.

Ditzel, Paul. "Theater of Death." *Firehouse Magazine,* December 1982.

Illinois Circuit Court Reports. Vol. 2. Chicago: T. H. Flood and Company, 1908.

Lewis, Sinclair, Thomas L. Masson, John Ames Mitchell, and James S. Metcalfe. *John Ames Mitchell: The Man Who is Responsible for Life.* Pamphlet. New York: F. A. Stokes, 1912.

Low, David J. "Following the Crowd." *Nature.* Vol. 407. September 28, 2000.

Martin, Edward S. "Life After Fifty Years." *Life* magazine. Vol. 100, No. 2574, 1943.

Mayer, Frank D. "Levy Mayer." *University of Chicago Law School Record.* Vol. 8, No. 2. Paper delivered at University of Chicago Law School, Feb 17, 1959.

McGibney, Ruth Thompson. Manuscript. Chicago Historical Society, 1962, 2001.

Nixon, Charles E. *Iroquois Theatre Opening Night Commemorative Brochure*. Nov. 23, 1903. New York Public Library Theatre Collection.

Remer, Theodore. "Terror at the Iroquois." *Chicago Daily News*, Panorama, Dec. 30, 1967, p 1.

Stewart, F. J. T. "Iroquois Fire." Chicago Underwriters' Association. Issued as Bulletin #54 to the National Fire Protection Association, January 9, 1904. Chicago Historical Society.

Thomasma, David C. "Somatic Death." *World Book Encyclopedia On Line*, Americas Edition. http://www.worldbookonline.com.

Watson, Bruce. "The Amazing Author of Oz." *Smithsonian Magazine*, June 2000, p 112–113.

Weitzel, Tony. "Christmas Week, 1903: Horror at the Iroquois Theater," *Chgo Daily News*, Dec. 28, 1963.

Woodward, Frederic E., and Frank O. Smith. "Flagrant Instance of the Law's Delays." *Illinois Law Review*, Vol. 1, No. 7. February: 1907.

INTERVIEWS & LETTERS

Benedict, Lyle. Interview with author. Chicago, IL. May, 2001.

Collins, Charles. Interview with author. Chicago, IL, 1962.

Corrigan, Michael J. Interview with author. Chicago, IL, 1961.

Crumpacker, William P. Phone interview with author. Hammond, IN. Feb. 2001.

Currier, Scott. E-mail correspondence with author. New York, NY. Feb. 22 & 23, 2000.

DeSteffano, Donald. Phone interview with author. Cleveland, NC. April 2001.

Dunlap, George. Letter to author, October 30, 1963.

Fields, Armond. Interview with author. Culver City, CA. June 2000 & June 2001.

Green, Susan. Phone interview with author. Bird-in-Hand, PA. April, 2001.

Henri, Janine. E-mail cooorespondence with author. Austin, TX. May 9, 2001.

Klatt, Wayne. Phone interview with author. Chicago, IL. June 2001.

LaSure, Faith. Interview with author. Chicago, IL. Aug. 2000.

Little, Kenneth. Interviews with author. Chicago, IL. April 2000 and May 2001.

Mayer, Frank D., Jr. Phone interview with author. Chicago, IL. July 2000.

McFeeley, Patricia J., M.D. Interview with author. Albuquerque, NM. 2001.

McNellis, Father John. Phone interviews with author. Chicago, IL. Aug & Sept 2000, 2001.

Molloy, Dr. Peter. Interviews with author. Pheonix, AZ. August & September 2000, 2001.

Moore, Frank. Letter to author. 1962.

Newman, Danny. Phone interview with author. Chicago, IL. October 24, 2001.

Olmstead, Pat. Phone interview and e-mail correspondence with author. April 23, 2000.

Samuelson, Tim. Interview with author. Chicago, IL. 2002.

Smith, Brett. E-mail correspondence with author. 2000.

Speiser, Stuart. Phone interview with author. Scottsdale, AZ. Sept. 1, 2001.

Stubblebine, Donald J. Phone interviews with author. September & October 2002.

Warfel, William B. Phone interview with author. Trumbull, CT. Oct. 2001.

ARCHIVES, COLLECTIONS, LIBRARIES

Albuquerque Public Library

Alexander Architectural and Planning Library, University of Texas, Austin

Asher Library, Spertus Institute for Jewish Studies, Chicago

Billy Rose Collection, New York Public Library at Lincoln Center

Bliss, Edward, Collection of Theater Programs

British Museum of the Performing Arts (London)

Buffalo Bill Museum, Museum of the American West, Cody, WY

Carnegie Mellon University Archives, Pittsburgh, PA

Carriage Museum of America, Bird-in-Hand, PA

Chicago Department of Cultural Affairs

Chicago Historical Society (CHS)

Chicago Jazz Archive, University of Chicago Library

Chicago Jewish Archives, Jacob Rader Marcus Center of Hebrew Union College/Jewish Institute of Religion, Cincinnati, OH

Chicago Police Department

Circuit Court of Cook County Library

Currier & Ives Foundation, Longmont, CO

David R. Philips Collection

Denver Old Firehouse Museum

Denver Public Library

Eastland Memorial Society, Chicago, IL

Hall of Flame, Phoenix, AZ

Harry Ransom Center, University of Texas, Austin

Illinois State Historical Library, Springfield

Jacob Rader Marcus Center of the American Jewish Archives, Cincinnati, OH

John Marshall Law School

Johns Hopkins University, Baltimore

Lester Levy Collection, The Milton S. Eisenhower Library, Baltimore

Library of Congress

Municipal Reference Collection, Harold Washington Library, Chicago (MRC)

New Mexico State Archives, Santa Fe, NM

New York Public Library at Lincoln Center, Billy Rose Theater Collection

The Newberry Library

Northwestern University Library

Oklahoma City Fire Museum

Santa Fe Public Library

The Shubert Collection, New York, NY

Sibley Music Collection, Eastman School of Music, Rochester, NY

Theater Collection, The Museum of the City of New York

Theater Historical Society of America, Elmhusrt, IL

Theodore Roosevelt Association, Oyster Bay, Long Island, NY

Ulster (N. Ireland) Titanic Society

University of Chicago Law School

University of Southern California (Los Angeles) Special Collections Library

SELECTED PERIODICALS

Chicago Record-Herald, 1903, 1904

Chicago Tribune, 1903, 1904, 1905, 1906, 1907

Chicago Daily News, 1903, 1904

Chicago Post, 1903

Chicago Journal, 1903

Chicago InterOcean, 1903, 1904

Chicago American, 1903

San Francisco Chronicle, 1903

The New York Times, 1903, 1904, 1905, 1906, 1907, 1908, 1909

New York Herald, 1903, 1904

New York World, 1904

New York Sun, 1903, 1904

New York Post, 1903

New York Evening Journal, 1903

New York Telegram, 1903

The Washington Evening Star, 1906

Milwaukee Journal, 1903, 1904

Albuquerque Morning Journal, 1903

Santa Fe New Mexican, 1903, 1904

Indianapolis News, 1903

Norfolk Virginia-Pilot, 1903

Toronto Star, 1903

New York Clipper, 1903, 1904

McClure's, 1903

Life, 1896–1904

Collier's, 1904

Billboard, 1903, 1904

Manchester Guardian, 1903, 1904

London Times, 1903, 1904

Fire and Engineering Magazine, Chicago, 1904.

London Mirror, 1903, 1904

London Globe, 1904

Pall Mall Gazette, 1904

Lloyd's Weekly News, 1904

Reader's Digest, 1957

Theater Magazine, 1904

Marshalltown (Iowa) Republican, 1904

Philadelphia Press, 1904

Kansas City Star, 1904

Marquette Journal, 1904

Popular Mechanics, 1904

Seton Hall Law Review, NY: 1993

Smithsonian Magazine

INTERNET SOURCES

Benedict, Lyle, Ellen O'Brien and Shah Tiwana. *A Milennium Bibliography, Chicago in 1900*. (http://cpl.lib.uic.edu/004chicago/1900/intro.html). Municipal Reference Collection, Chicago Public Library.

Fang, Irving, and Kristina Ross. The Media History Timeline/1900s: The First Decade. (http://www.mediahistory.umn.edu/index2.html).

Montrose Cemetery web page: www.graveyards.com/montrose/iroquois.html

INDEX